Contents

Foreword:

Jane Bennett-Rees, lecturer in Mathematics at King's College, London
and former schoolteacher fellow at Magdalene College, Cambridge

Foreword

Welcome to the latest publication from Oxbridge Applications.

Think You Can Think? aims to give you the confidence to show what you are capable of, not only in applying to university but within any field you venture into now or in the future. The TSA (Thinking Skills Assessment, required for certain courses at Oxford and Cambridge) is not subject specific. In fact, the skills tested are really those required in very many walks of life and are truly transferable. The TSA exam includes questions which focus on reasoning: verbal and numerical, as well as spatial. With the right preparation, the test may be embraced and welcomed as a challenge to how you think and how you solve problems.

As a university lecturer, I see students facing the demands of working at university level for the first time. They no longer have the structured questions and guidelines of A level and they have to produce arguments which will be rigorously tested. Those who can already face such challenges are off to a head start and the kind of thinking required for the TSA provides just the grounding they need.

The ability to think logically is a requirement in every area of life and, furthermore, analytical skills are essential in most professions. Slick, efficient modes of thought keep one ahead of the game, homing in quickly on the essentials and discarding irrelevancies. This applies, for example, to lawyers reading contracts, but also to anyone who agrees to 'Terms and Conditions', a feature of our everyday life. Failure to pay due attention to these may mean that your insurance policy is not valid when you need it most, as many travellers found to their cost when caught out by flight cancellations because of a volcanic ash cloud or unrest in the Middle East. In coming to grips with the TSA, you will acquire techniques which can be employed in many spheres of life.

You will learn to understand an argument, the role of a premise and how to draw logical and valid conclusions, without making unwarranted assumptions. Such techniques are not only required by barristers and philosophers; they are the basis of, for example, scientific argument, where conclusions can be based only on the evidence actually presented and not on supposition. (Politicians would do well to realise this!) University students in many subjects, from Maths and Science to History and Literature, are required to present an argument which is based on first principles and which will stand up to cross examination.

Accuracy and attention to detail is essential in these tests and is something most employers look for. Post graduation, students applying for jobs make careless mistakes on their forms which can take them out of the running for their chosen career. The TSA also provides good training for psychometric tests.

Familiarity and confidence with numbers is a pre-requisite for a supermarket visit as well as in high level physics, medicine and every profession or business from journalism and marketing to accountancy. Our news reports are littered with figures and an understanding of percentages and probabilities is certainly necessary if one is to look at these with perception and, often, some scepticism!

None of the arithmetic required is beyond GCSE level. If you do not consider yourself to be good with numbers, just make sure that you can use basic calculation techniques, do mental arithmetic and work with fractions. You do need to be slick because of the time pressure but these skills can be honed with practice. Make sure that you understand percentages – if you take a 20% pay cut, what percentage increase is required to restore your pay to its original level?

Don't be afraid of numbers, they are your friends and should be used to help you. Like many worthwhile friends, it pays to make the effort to get to know them properly and, in so doing, you will gain the confidence to question what you are told. You will not be 'blinded by science' in the many decisions and choices you will have to make throughout your life.

As a well known darts player says, 'People who can do arithmetic will always beat those who can't', a truism which applies in many fields beyond that of the pub! A tax form fills many with alarm but completing it is simply a matter of accuracy and attention to detail. If you live to 100, as many of your generation may, you will need to make arrangements for your financial security. If you delay this for 10 years, you will have to invest about 30% more to accumulate the same pension – a simple application of compound interest, which everyone, not just economists, needs to understand. In studying for the TSA you will truly acquire skills for life!

It has been said that you cannot be helped to prepare for the TSA. However, the questions are very similar to those set in the GMAT, the test set by those applying to do an MBA at universities both here and abroad. For this test, practice is considered to be essential and every would-be MBA student works through books of these questions before attempting to sit the test 'for real'.

Oxbridge Applications has the insight and familiarity with the type of approach required to answer these questions and can certainly support you in your efforts to improve your performance. This book will help you to understand what makes one answer undisputedly the right one and another, which may at first sight seem correct, actually wrong. As in so many fields of life, practice makes, if not perfect, then at least many times better.

We wish you the best of luck and hope you enjoy working your way through this book.

Jane Bennett-Rees
MA (Oxon)
Lecturer in Mathematics
King's College London
Former School Teacher Fellow at Magdalene College, Cambridge
Member of the Oxford Applications' Advisory Board
August 2011

Background to the TSA (Thinking Skills Assessment)

The TSA has been used since 2001 for entry to certain courses and colleges at Oxford and Cambridge and its use has expanded since then. It is not designed to test an applicant's suitability for any specific subject; instead it tests a wide range of skills that applicants for a variety of subjects can be expected to demonstrate. The Oxford TSA has an additional section, a writing task, in which candidates are asked to write one essay from a selection of titles. This section, again, is testing a particular skill and does not require any previous knowledge of the essay subject, although some knowledge may help in formulating a persuasive argument.

Cambridge Assessment, the organisation responsible for researching and developing the test, states on its website that the Cambridge TSA and section 1 of the Oxford TSA examine problem solving skills and critical thinking skills. Incidentally, it is worth noting at this point that there does not seem to be any difference in terms of the questions and skills required for the Cambridge TSA and the Oxford TSA, aside from the additional section in the latter test. Therefore, the guidance in this book should be taken to apply equally to both of these tests. The essay section, section 2 of the Oxford TSA, tests how well an applicant can formulate arguments and communicate these in a clear, concise and structured manner in the form of an essay.

One of the main purposes of this book is to elucidate what is meant exactly by problem solving and critical thinking skills and to understand the type of questions that test them. Problem solving skills, in the context of the TSA, are tested through questions requiring simple or complex arithmetic, visual reasoning, spatial awareness, extraction and interpretation of data, and lateral thinking. Evidently, problem solving skills are tested through different types of question.

Critical thinking skills, on the other hand, can be classified slightly more neatly since these pertain to arguments, notably understanding and responding to the reasoning presented to you in the form of an argument. Specifically, you are tested on your ability to identify conclusions, assumptions and flaws in the reasoning, draw your own conclusions, understand the structure of an argument and recognise how to strengthen or weaken an argument. The question analysis chapter goes into more detail about these skills and the types of questions in which they are tested.

Practical information on taking the TSA

It is probably a fair assumption that if you are reading this book then you are already aware that you may have to sit the TSA and that you may well have found out, or will find out, all the practical information relevant to the test. Therefore, this chapter is intentionally brief and readers are referred to the Cambridge Assessment websites (links below) to find out more detailed, up-to-date information concerning the TSA, for example, relating to dates, costs, where to sit the test, results and special arrangements.

http://www.admissionstests.cambridgeassessment.org.uk/adt/tsacambridge
http://www.admissionstests.cambridgeassessment.org.uk/adt/tsaoxford

- **Who is asked to sit the TSA?**

Cambridge

At the time of publishing, whether or not you are required to sit the Cambridge TSA depends on which college you are applying to and you should check with the individual college when applying whether or not you are required to sit the TSA. If you are applying for any of the following subjects, then you may need to sit the Cambridge TSA:

Computer Science

Economics

Engineering

Land Economy

Natural Sciences (Biological)

Natural Sciences (Physical)

Philosophy

Politics, Psychology & Sociology (PPS)

Oxford

At the time of publishing, students applying to the University of Oxford to study the following subjects at undergraduate level will be required to sit the Oxford TSA:

Economics & Management (E&M)

Experimental Psychology (EP)

Philosophy, Politics and Economics (PPE)

Psychology and Philosophy (PP)

- **Format of the test**

The Cambridge TSA and Section 1 of the Oxford TSA consist of 50 multiple choice questions for which candidates have 90 minutes to complete. Each question consists of a certain amount of information provided to the candidate, a question and then five possible answers, only one of which is correct.

Section 2 of the Oxford TSA consists of four essay titles of which candidates must choose one. There are 30 minutes available to complete this section.

Candidates have, in total, 90 minutes to complete the Cambridge TSA and two hours to complete the Oxford TSA.

- **Calculators and dictionaries**

Calculators are not allowed in either the Cambridge TSA or the Oxford TSA. Dictionaries are allowed in the Cambridge TSA but not in the Oxford TSA.

- **When?**

The Oxford TSA generally takes place just over a month before interviews at designated centres and is usually a written test. The Cambridge TSA generally takes place during the period at which the applicant is in Cambridge for interview(s) and it may be a written or on-screen test depending on the college to which the applicant has applied.

- **Scoring**

There is one mark per question on the Cambridge TSA and section 1 of the Oxford TSA. Scores are then calibrated onto a scale using the Rasch method to give a score out of 100. The raw mark (out of 50) is not simply converted into a percentage to give a score out of 100; rather the method takes into account the difficulty of each question and the overall test so that these marks can be used more accurately to compare candidates across years. There is no negative marking therefore candidates will not lose marks for an incorrect answer and should attempt every question, even if it means guessing at some!

There is very little information available on the Rasch method which may, in fact, be a blessing in disguise. It is recommended that you do not worry too much about the weighting of certain questions (since it may lead you to waste valuable time during the test, trying to second-guess whether it is worth spending more time on a question depending on its weighting). Instead, simply aim for the best raw numerical mark you can.

Section 2 of the Oxford TSA, the essay, is not formally marked and, instead, is sent to the admissions tutors at the college to which the candidate has applied.

Examination technique

It is worth providing some general advice about the TSA before the detailed analysis of each type of question in the next chapter. This general advice applies mainly to the Cambridge TSA and section 1 of the Oxford TSA. More specific advice for section 2 of the Oxford TSA can be found later in the book.

You don't necessarily have to read all of the following advice and follow our recommendations, since everyone will have their own methods of approaching tests and dealing with aspects such as timing and preparation. Indeed, the fact that you are in a position of applying or thinking of applying to Oxbridge indicates that you have done well in various tests and exams so far in your life and so, to a certain extent, you should have confidence in your methods. However, the TSA is probably quite different to the tests that you have encountered before and so it is worth reading the following general advice, if only to see what sort of issues you may have to grapple with.

- **Timing**

Timing may well be one of the most difficult aspects of the TSA although, naturally, it is the difficulty of the questions coupled with the time pressure that makes the test challenging.

- **Time per question**

Since you have 90 minutes in which to complete the 50 multiple choice questions, this amounts, on average, to just under two minutes per question (one minute and 48 seconds to be precise). This is certainly not an easy feat to accomplish and you will have to work efficiently and effectively in order to complete all 50 questions. It is not recommended that you time yourself for each question since some questions you may be able to answer in less than two minutes whereas others may take longer, so you may not be doing justice to each question if you limit yourself to only two minutes. In addition, the practice of timing yourself constantly may take up valuable seconds in itself. Instead, simply check your timing every 10 minutes or so to make sure that you are on track with the test and adjust the speed at which you work through the next set of questions accordingly.

As for leaving yourself with time at the end to go back and check through the questions, if you find after completing all 50 questions that you do have some spare time, then, naturally, go back and verify the answers for the questions about which you may have been unsure. In terms of intentionally planning to leave yourself time at the end of the 50 questions to verify your answers, be careful that this does not lead to you rushing through questions on the premise that you can come back to them later. It is probably better to answer more questions correctly the first time around and not have much time left, than to have to go back to many questions at the end.

- **Moving on from a question and returning to it later**

If you read through a question and can't find an answer, or even if you just have a complete mind blank, then, perhaps, move on from that question and leave enough time to return to it later. Sometimes you just need an inspirational moment to spot a method of answering the question. However, it can be a risky strategy to plan on returning to difficult questions at the end, because there may be a fair amount of information in the question. If you process this information but then decide to move on, when you return to the question, you will need to process this information again. It may be worth, therefore, trying various methods or thinking about the question in different ways before you abandon it and return later.

- **Chronological order?**

The questions in the multiple choice section are in no particular order and so, if you follow a chronological order, you will often be faced with one problem solving question immediately followed by a critical thinking question. There may be a case for saying that you should complete all the problem solving questions first and then do the critical thinking questions (or vice versa) so that your mind is focused completely on the numerical (and similar) questions and then completely on the questions involving arguments. This may lead to certain timing issues if you do choose this tactic since, if on a particular paper the critical thinking questions take longer than the problem solving questions and you complete the problem solving questions first in 45 minutes, then you may not have left yourself enough time to complete the critical thinking questions.

Whereas, if you stick with the order of the test, at least you will be answering the questions in a more balanced manner and this may help with the timing. However, perhaps trying one approach and then another on two mock tests will allow you to decide which approach suits you best. One approach which isn't recommended is to pick out sub-divisions of questions, for example, visual reasoning questions, and to answer these first. This is because you may end up flicking through the paper and trying to discern which the visual reasoning questions are, thereby losing valuable time.

- **Reading quickly but effectively**

Have you ever noticed whilst reading that you sometimes lose concentration but carry on reading? It is usually the case, then, that you cannot remember what you have read after you lost concentration. With the time pressure of the TSA, ensure that you are always focused when reading and that you digest all the information in each question. If you feel you need a quick pause to gather your thoughts, then do this before you begin a new question and not during it. Concentrating when reading the question will ensure that you do not miss any information and, crucially, for the critical thinking questions, it will enable you to understand the argument and any problems with it. This should lead to you identifying the answer more quickly.

- **Reading the question first?**

In relation to the critical thinking questions, candidates often ask whether it is advisable to read the question before reading the argument. Sometimes looking for something specific in the argument makes you gloss over the parts that you think are not relevant and only focus on the parts you think are. This may be dangerous if you have not correctly identified which parts are relevant and which parts are not and may lead you to waste time by needing to read the argument more than once. On the other hand, knowing, for example, that you are looking for an assumption may help you to identify it more easily when reading the argument and, as long as you digest the information properly and don't dismiss any of it as irrelevant, then perhaps this technique may assist you. As with various techniques on a test such as the TSA, sometimes trial and error may help you to decide your best approach.

- **Verifying your answer**

In general, there seem to be two methods of finding the correct answer for any given question. The first method is to eliminate all the incorrect answers so that you are left, by necessary implication, with the one remaining correct answer. The second method is to find the correct answer without dismissing the other answers as incorrect. It seems that problem solving questions are generally solved using the second method since certain calculations or reasoning need to be performed which should lead you to the correct answer. However, both methods can be used in most questions.

In order to verify your answer, which it is recommended that you try to do, naturally try and think about the answer you have chosen and ensure that there are no other interpretations or factors that you have missed which may make you change your mind. In addition, if you have selected the answer using the more positive approach, then why not try and eliminate the other answers to make doubly sure of your choice. This depends on time pressures and so, if you are pushed for time, then it may be worthwhile trusting your initial answer and moving on to the next question. Perhaps return if you have time to spare at the end of the 50 questions, to verify your answer using a different method.

- **Guessing!**

This may seem silly or indeed obvious to you but it is worth stating. If you find that you are really stumped on a particular question and there is no way that you can work out the answer or if there are seconds remaining in the test and you still have some blank spaces on your answer page, then just guess an answer. Since the test is not negatively marked you lose nothing by getting an answer wrong, but you could gain a mark or two by guessing an answer instead of leaving the space blank. Since we're in the business of numerical reasoning in this test, you should realise that if you are forced to guess five answers, then the probability is that you'll get one of them correct [N.B. it may not be one extra mark if difficulty weighted].

Preparation

One of the advantages of the TSA, from a candidate's point of view and in assisting the admissions process, is that no knowledge is required in order to sit or do well in the test. This is one reason the TSA is so versatile and can be used to assess applicants in a wide variety of subjects.

- **Some basic knowledge required**

Naturally, everything, from knowing how to count to knowing the meanings of basic words is technically all 'knowledge' and so, clearly *some* knowledge is required. However, this is minimal and it is expected that nobody sitting the TSA should struggle with any questions due to unfamiliar word meanings or numerical or everyday concepts. Cambridge Assessment has, helpfully, provided candidates with an outline of the minimum knowledge that they are expected to know, although, as you should find, you will (or should!) know most of this already:

Number concepts
- Simple fractions
- Place value (for example, knowing that the "5" in "7654" indicates "50")
- Ideas about percentages (for example, knowing that if 20% of a group of adults are men, 80% must be women)

Numerical operations

Addition, subtraction, multiplication, division, percentage operations (for example, if something was sold at £10 and is now advertised at "20% off", how much would the customer pay?) and calculations in everyday contexts.

Quantities

- Time and the calendar
- Money
- Measures (as below)

LENGTH	WEIGHT	AREA	VOLUME
kilometre (km)	kilogram (kg)	square metre (m^2)	litre (l)
metre (m)	gram (g)	square centimetre (cm^2)	cubic centimetre (cm^3)
centimetre (cm)			
millimetre (mm)			

Knowledge of the following relationships is also required:

1 km = 1000 m; 1 m = 100 cm; 1 cm = 10 mm; 1 kg = 1000 g; 1 m^2 = 10,000 cm; 1l = 1000 cm^3

Also required is knowledge of the terms for measurements which are used commonly in daily life (e.g. feet and miles) but numerical relationships for these measures (e.g. 12 inches = 1 foot) are not required.

Space and spatial reasoning

- Area (including the calculation of the area of a rectangle)
- Perimeter (including calculation)
- Volume (including the calculation of the volume of a box)
- Reflections (in mirrors) and rotations of simple shapes
- Two-dimensional (2D) representations of three-dimensional (3D) shapes

Tables and graphs

- Extracting information from graphs
- Extracting information from tables

- **Practice makes perfect**

Since there is little knowledge required for the TSA, you can devote your preparation time to practising for the test. This will help in a number of ways. It will ensure that you are not caught out by the time pressures of the test and, instead, that you practise working efficiently. It will allow you to familiarise yourself with the type of questions and the difficulty of the test. Finally, it will enable you to discover any weaknesses you have. If you find a particular type of question difficult, you can practise this more than others.

- **Mentally prepared on the day**

Following on from the fact that the TSA is not a memory test and that it simply tests how you can problem solve and think critically at the time you sit it, it is paramount that you are mentally focused on the day. Tiredness makes reading and thinking a lot more difficult and will almost certainly lead to a poorer performance. Get plenty of sleep the night before, keep well hydrated and nourished and go into the test feeling confident that you can answer every question.

Format of *Think You Can Think?*

Before taking the practice papers, do have a look at the question analysis chapter below, in which a detailed breakdown is provided of each type of question referred to above and explanations and examples of how to go about answering them. It is worth reading and understanding this section before attempting any mock tests so that you are fully prepared to face every question.

Finally, to assess your performance and see where (or if!) you have made any mistakes, the answers and commentaries for each test should assist you in evaluating your strengths and weaknesses and explaining the methods of answering each question. These commentaries vary in detail, depending on the difficulty of the question, and some contain more than one approach as to how to go about answering the question. You may find that you answered it using a different approach altogether which, as long as you reached the correct answer, should be perfectly fine.

To help you fully understand the types of questions and succeed in answering them, for some questions on the practice papers we include two distinct approaches (where possible) in answering a particular question. It is particularly useful, where the question allows it, to identify various methods of answering the question. This should allow you to have a back-up should one method fail, choose the most efficient method of approaching the question and, finally, verify your answer, time permitting, using a different approach.

A short disclaimer

A brief note should be made to clarify a few aspects about this book. Firstly, much of the factual information about the TSA test has been obtained from the Cambridge Assessment website, which it is recommended you frequently check for any updates or important information regarding the test. The rest of the book contains the author's own words.

Secondly, the advice and opinions in this book, for example, in the question analysis chapter and in the commentaries, are the author's own views which have been presented after careful research and consideration. Others may dispute some of the advice or opinions and so advice should not be taken to be factual. Information about the types of question and the structure of the TSA has been obtained from practice papers available on the Cambridge Assessment website.

Thirdly, the information in the questions in the mock tests is largely fictional. Current affairs have been used as a source of inspiration for some questions and so some of the information may be factually correct. However, as a general rule, the information should not be understood to be true.

Fourthly, there may be disagreement as to the correct answer as, occasionally, answers may depend on a subjective interpretation of information. All questions, answers and commentaries have been considered carefully and verified by a team of graduates, chaired by the author. If you have any questions about the book, or any challenges arise on working your way through the tests, please do send us an email on info@oxbridgeapplications.com.

TSA (Thinking Skills Assessment) Question analysis

Cambridge TSA and Oxford TSA section 1

Types of question: two broad categories

As you know and have already seen so far, there are two broad categories of question on the TSA that are quite distinct: critical thinking questions and problem solving questions. One of the reasons for writing this book was to explore in detail the challenges that the TSA will throw at you and how to go about successfully dealing with these challenges. For this reason, further sub-categories of question have been created in order that a more accurate and relevant analysis of the TSA can be given to you. Breaking down the test into its constituent parts should enable you to understand better what each individual question you encounter is asking you and the various techniques you can employ to complete each of these questions successfully.

Further sub-division

Sub-dividing the problem solving questions is not as easy as for the critical thinking questions. There are some natural categories that stand out but there is some overlap between the other categories. It is still worth breaking the questions down since, again, some techniques and advice can be tailored to specific types of question and, in addition, it will enable you to have a better idea of which questions you are comfortable with and which ones require more work. In this book, the problem solving questions have been divided into six categories but, due to the fact that they are not clear-cut, you may wish to create different categories for yourself in order to help you prepare for the test. The important objective is that you are prepared for all types of question that may arise on the TSA.

1	Complex calculations	Using rates, percentages, durations, costs, fractions and/or probabilities to solve sometimes complicated calculations.
2	Extracting and interpreting data	Extracting relevant data from information e.g. tables or graphs, interpreting the data and sometimes performing calculations based on the data.

3   Equation questions   Calculations which lend themselves to formulating an equation in order to solve them.

4   Visual reasoning   Reasoning or calculations with some visual appreciation of the problem.

5   Spatial awareness   A pure appreciation of space and/or shapes.

6   Lateral thinking   Solving problems with an application of logical rules that do not necessarily involve numbers.

These categories may seem to be neatly distinguished but there can sometimes be overlap between them. For example, the calculations in category 1 will involve some data. Therefore there is an overlap between these questions and those in category 2, where there is much data and some calculations which may need to be made. The difference may be in the difficulty of the calculations and the amount of data, but there is a fine line between the two. Equally, there are some questions in category 4 where candidates may not need to visualise the problem in order to solve it and, instead, may feel that these questions belong more appropriately in category 1. Category 3 is anomalous since it isn't really defined by the type of question asked; rather it is unique in that there is a specific method of answering this type of question – by forming an equation. However, forming an equation is not the only way of reaching the answer and, equally, some candidates may find it easier to form equations for questions that are not in this category.

For the critical thinking questions, natural categories are formed of the four different types of questions. Despite the fact that the wording is not exact for each type, it is sufficiently similar that you can easily discern which of the four types of question you are being asked. In addition, there is very little overlap between the different types so that the techniques and advice provided in the book for each type of question are sufficiently unique that you can quickly isolate them in your mind and remember the best way of approaching that type of question. If you struggle with any particular category of question, then you can concentrate on practising examples from that category. These are the four categories with a brief explanation of what they require from you:

1	Identifying and drawing conclusions	Identifying the best summary of the conclusion of an argument or its main conclusion.
		Identifying a statement which can be logically concluded from information stated in an argument.
2	Identifying assumptions and spotting flaws in arguments	Identifying an assumption used in an argument.
		Spotting an error in the reasoning that weakens the logical coherence of an argument.
3	Parallel reasoning	Identifying an argument with a similar structure to another argument or extracting a principle that emerges as a result of the structure of an argument.
4	Weakening/strengthening arguments	Evaluating whether certain statements strengthen or weaken an argument.

Approach for each type of question

In the remaining part of this chapter, each type of question will be analysed in detail and, using examples, we will discuss what the question requires from you and various techniques and strategies to help you answer it. For each type of question, the following structure will be used:

- What you should know by the end of the chapter

- What the questions ask of you

- What the questions test – a description of what skills are required from you

- Identifying different wordings of this type of question and any differences between them (as evidenced by past TSA tests – the wording may vary in future) as well as how to tackle these

- How to go about answering this type of question – techniques

- Example(s) of this type of question

- Summary and checklist of what you have learned in the chapter

1. Complex calculations – are they really complex?

Using rates, percentages, durations, costs, fractions and/or probabilities to solve sometimes complicated calculations.

By the end of this chapter you should be able to:

a) **Understand the skills involved in solving complex calculations**
b) **Differentiate between the types of data used in complex calculations**

    i. Clocking times & dates

    ii. Becoming a whizz at speeds, distances and times

    iii. Pounding money

    iv. Smashing fractions

    v. Conquering probability

    vi. Pummelling percentages

    vii. Sorting spatial measurements

a) Understanding the skills involved in solving complex calculations

The skills involved include:

Recognising – the data

Understanding – what to do with the data

Manipulating – the data without a calculator

Proofing – your answer

Recognising – the data

The data in complex calculations comes in different forms, primarily:

dates	times	distances	speeds
money (pounds and pence, dollars and cents etc.)	percentages	fractions	spatial (metres, centimetres, millimetres etc.)

Make sure you understand the concepts behind these data types and how they work.

With time, for example, make sure you know how to read an analogue and digital clock; know the number of seconds in a minute, minutes in an hour, days in a year etc.

You should also be aware of how these concepts are represented in a question, including their short form symbols, e.g. 'sec', 'min', 'hr'.

Understanding – what to do with the data

The only way to do this is to practise. Take one of the practice tests in this book and mark any questions where you didn't know a numerical principle or what to do with the data, then read the commentary and learn the principles you didn't know. The more practice tests you do, the more you will get an understanding of the extent of knowledge needed for the TSA and you will be alert to the type of questions when they come up again. Revise, repeat, learn.

Manipulating – the data without a calculator

You will need to do calculations either in your head or on paper. Neither way is necessarily better, but if you are able to estimate answers in your head, you can improve your efficiency and ensure your working is correct.

Before you set about your calculation, think about what data type the correct answer will be, i.e. will it be a speed, a time or a monetary unit.

TSA tip

Practise more with mental arithmetic by playing around with the numbers you see every day. Sum all the prices on a menu, find the average and percentage of items over a certain price. Work out what 10, 15 and 35% of the number on the front of a bus is. The more comfortable you are at manipulating numbers in your head, the quicker you will be able to get to an answer in the test.

Proofing – your answer

Always check that your answer makes sense. Double-check that the methodology you use is sound and that all your units are consistent with each other.

TSA tip

Imagine what the correct answer would look like. For example, if the question asks you to calculate the percentage value of a house and the percentage is less than 100%, then you know that your answer will be less than the value of the house. Understanding the correct answer before you attempt any calculations will give you more confidence in your answer and, if you are struggling, will help you to eliminate incorrect answers.

b) Differentiating between the types of data used in complex calculations

Let's have a look at the different data types and some examples of how these are used.

i) Clocking times & dates

Questions using measurements of time will either overlap with questions involving speed and distance (see the next section), percentages and fractions, or will deal only with time. Get comfortable playing with the relationships between seconds, minutes, hours, days and years. How would you work out how many minutes there are in a year?

Handy hint

Don't forget that when you are manipulating time you need to take into account that minutes have a divisor of 60. The decimal equivalent of 2 hours and 15 minutes is therefore not 2.15 hours, it is 2.25 hours because $\frac{15}{60}$ is $\frac{1}{4}$ or 0.25.

Some questions require you to work out the time difference between two places. To answer these, convert the times to a common value. This will be the local time in one of the places – think of it as similar to finding a common denominator when dealing with fractions.

Try this example:

It is currently 10:00 in Fedistan and 14:00 in Exiland. A parcel was posted in Fedistan at 16:00 yesterday and arrived at its destination in Exiland at 07:30 today. How long did the parcel take to be delivered from the moment it was posted to the moment it arrived?

Exiland is 4 hours ahead of Fedistan. If you convert the time the parcel was delivered into Fedistan local time (4 hours prior to 07:30), you will find that it was delivered at 03:30 Fedistan time. The length of time between 16:00 and 03:30 the next day is 24 – 16 + 3.5 = 11.5 hours = 11 hours and 30 minutes.

You might want to draw a diagram to visualise the information. Have a look at the diagram below:

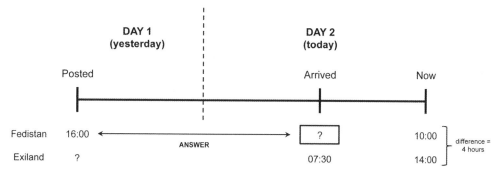

Handy hint

Remember that an analogue clock's hour hands move around the clock face twice during a day – this will be useful for any questions you get relating to the number of degrees that a clock's hands move through between two different times.

ii) Becoming a whizz at speeds, distances, and times

Do you remember the diagram below from your GCSE years? If you cover up the measurement that you want to find out, you're left with the calculation needed. All the formulae variations are listed to the right-hand side of the triangle – why not try it out?

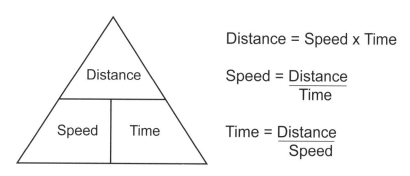

Distance = Speed x Time

Speed = $\dfrac{\text{Distance}}{\text{Time}}$

Time = $\dfrac{\text{Distance}}{\text{Speed}}$

Handy hint

Make sure you know the short forms of the measurements so that you don't confuse them (m, cm, mm, mph, m/s, sec, min, hr etc.)

Once you have the current version of the formula, make sure that you are consistent with your units throughout your calculations. Say, for example, you need to find the difference in speed between Mark, travelling at 30 mph and Sarah, travelling at 0.01 miles per second. You would need to work out either how fast Sarah was travelling in mph, or vice versa for Mark in miles per second. Think about the fraction involved:

Mark

$$\frac{30 \text{ miles}}{1 \text{ hour}} \quad \begin{array}{l} 1 \text{ hr} = 60 \text{ mins} \\ 1 \text{ min} = 60 \text{ secs} \\ 1 \text{ hr} = 60 \times 60 = 3{,}600 \text{ secs} \end{array} = \frac{30 \text{ miles}}{3{,}600 \text{ secs}}$$

Sarah

$$\frac{0.01 \text{ miles}}{1 \text{ second}} = \frac{3{,}600}{3{,}600} \times \frac{0.01}{1} = \frac{36 \text{ miles}}{3{,}600 \text{ secs}}$$

You can see then that to convert Sarah's speed to mph you have to multiply by 3,600. 0.01 x 3,600 = 36 mph. So the difference between the two is 36 mph − 30 mph = 6 mph.

iii) Pounding money

Calculations involving money will often be tested alongside percentages or fractions and the calculations will generally give answers with no more than two decimal places. If you need to make calculations with large amounts of money, make sure that you keep enough digits. This can often be a problem if you cancel zeros off the top and bottom of a fraction, or if you need to do long multiplication in your head:

$$\begin{array}{r} 2{,}300 \\ \times 120 \\ \hline \end{array}$$

230,000	first multiply by 100
46,000	then multiply by 20

276,000   add the two

iv) Smashing fractions

You may not have thought about fractions since GCSE level, but for the TSA you'll need to be able to manipulate them quickly and accurately. Think about the following when using fractions and you'll be well on your way:

- Multiplication should be done in two stages – multiply by the numerator and divide by the denominator. Note that you can do this in the inverse order (divide by the denominator first) if it is a simpler calculation.

Take a look at these two sums: $\frac{2}{3}$ x 168; and $\frac{3}{5}$ x 455.

In the first sum, it is easier to multiply by the numerator first, then divide by the denominator:

$\frac{2}{3}$ x 168 = $\frac{(2 \times 168)}{3}$ = 336 ÷ 3 = 112

whereas for the second sum, you'd be better off dividing first:

$\frac{3}{5}$ x 455 = (455 ÷ 5) x 3 = 91 x 3 = 273

- As well as simplifying the fraction itself, you can cancel down diagonally opposite numbers when you're multiplying two fractions:

$\frac{10}{28}$ x $\frac{14}{31}$ = $\frac{10}{2}$ x $\frac{1}{31}$ = $\frac{5}{1}$ x $\frac{1}{31}$ = $\frac{5}{31}$

- Sometimes it might be easier to convert fractions into percentages, especially when dealing with two or more fractions with different denominators.

$\frac{2}{5}$ x 32 = 40% x 32 = 0.4 x 32 = 4 x 3.2 = 12.8

v) Conquering probability

Fractions may also be used when calculating probabilities.

Remember that to find the number of times the event will occur, you should multiply the probability, expressed as a fraction or a percentage, by the number of trials.

E.g. if the probability of a weighted coin ending heads up when flipped is $\frac{4}{5}$, out of 100 trials the estimated number of times the coin will end heads up will be $\frac{4}{5}$ x 100 = 80 times.

The fraction that expresses the probability can never be greater than 1 and so the probability that the coin will end up in the inverse state (because there are only two ways the coin can land) is 1 − $\frac{4}{5}$ = $\frac{1}{5}$ The estimated number of times that the coin landed tails up would therefore be (1 − $\frac{4}{5}$) x 100 = $\frac{1}{5}$ x 100 = 20.

To calculate the probability of one event occurring **and** another event occurring, you should **multiply** the two probabilities.

To calculate the probability of one event occurring **or** another event occurring, you should **add** the two probabilities.

vi) Pummelling percentages

A great way of calculating percentages is to work out 1% or 10% of the number then multiply up to get the percentage required. For example, if you wanted to find 35% of 80, you could work out that 10% is 8, 5% is half of that, which is 4 and you need three lots of the 10% and one lot of the 5% = (3 x 8) + 4 = 28.

You can also attack the percentage from the other angle and take away 15% from 50% to get 35%. Sticking with 35% of 80, we know that 15% is 10% + 5% = 8 + 4 = 12, and that 50% of 80 is 40, so 35% must be 40 − 12 = 28.

Handy hint
One of the best examples of this method of calculating percentages is when VAT was calculated at 17.5%. 17.5% is made up of 10% + 5% + 2.5%, each of which is half the previous number. So to calculate the VAT that would be added to a product worth £3,080, you would find 10%, which is £308, 5% which is £308 ÷ 2 = £154 and 2.5%, which is £154 ÷ 2 = £77. Adding them all together gets you the VAT to be added, £308 + £154 + £77 = £539. Remember though that if the question asks for the price inclusive of VAT, you need to add this to the original price excluding VAT, which was £3,080 to get £3,619.

TSA tip
Be sure of which figure you are supposed to take the percentage from. Check what you are supposed to be doing with your percentage – are you finding a percentage of a figure, or are you increasing or decreasing a figure by a percentage?

Most calculations involving percentages will give an integer as the answer, but don't automatically assume that you've made a mistake if your answer includes a decimal.

Handy hint
Don't forget that a percentage less than 10 falls into the hundredths column of the decimal – 8% is therefore 0.08 and not 0.80.

vii) Sorting spatial measurements

Spatial measurements are lengths, areas and volumes – when you get a question that uses them, remember the dimensions and don't mix them. A length multiplied by a length is an area and an area multiplied by a length is a volume. Keep units consistent, so if you are given an area in cm^2 and a length in metres, convert the length to cm and multiply to get the volume.

For example, if you are asked to find the volume of a karaoke booth with a floor space of 24 m^2 and a height of 350 cm, convert the height to 3.5 m and multiply the two to get 84 m^3.

Handy hint

With all questions, if you are struggling, try using a 'trial and error' technique where you test out each answer and see if it works (this is particularly effective for speed, distance and time questions).

Try this example:

Annie and Claire, two Formula 3 drivers, decide to have a race in their new cars. They both set off from the start at the same time. The length of the race is 12 miles and Claire completes it in 6 minutes. Annie's car breaks down exactly half way between the start and finish lines. Her average speed before her car broke down was 20% higher than Claire's average speed.

How long did it take Annie to get to the point at which her car broke down?

A   2 minutes

B   3 minutes and 30 seconds

C   2 minutes and 50 seconds

D   2 minutes and 30 seconds

E   2 minutes and 20 seconds

If you are a visual person, you could draw a diagram to illustrate the problem:

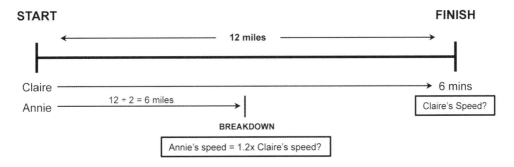

Using the RUMP approach, you recognise that you are dealing with speed, distance and time, you understand that you are being asked to find out 'how long' it took Annie to travel a certain distance, and so you need to manipulate the data to end up with a time as the answer.

You know that Annie's time will be shorter than 6 minutes because Annie travels quicker than Claire. Whilst this doesn't eliminate any answers in this question, making deductions can be a quick way of ruling out answers.

Next, you need the distance that Annie travelled to the point where she broke down. The question tells you that this is half the distance of the race. As the race is 12 miles long, she broke down after 6 miles.

You then need to work out Annie's average speed. We know that if Claire completed the race in 6 minutes and the race is 12 miles long, she must have travelled at 2 miles per minute (12 ÷ 6). Annie's average speed was 20% higher than Claire's, so you can work out that Annie's speed was therefore 2 x 1.2 = 2.4 miles per minute.

Finally, you need to work out how long it took Annie to travel 6 miles if she was travelling at 2.4 miles per minute. Using the distance, speed, time triangle, you know that time = distance ÷ speed, or 6 ÷ 2.4 = 2.5. Converting the 2.5 into minutes and seconds, it takes Annie 2 and a half minutes to travel the 6 miles until she breaks down. **D** is therefore the correct answer.

If you want to check this, you can rule out the other answers by inserting them into a speed, distance, time calculation. Or, you can say that if Annie completed the race at her average speed of 2.4 miles per minute, it would have taken her 5 minutes (12 ÷ 2.4). Since she broke down half way through, she would have reached that point in half the time it took her to complete the whole race, which is 5 ÷ 2 = 2.5 minutes.

Checklist

☐ What type of data am I dealing with in the question? (Recognise)

☐ What units will be used in the answer? Can I deduce, approximately, how large or small the figure in the answer will be? (Understand)

☐ Have I used all the data correctly and manipulated it in the right way? (Manipulate)

☐ Have I checked my answer? (Proof)

---

2. Extracting and interpreting data – charting success

Using graphs, charts, tables and other visual representations to extract and interpret data.

By the end of this chapter you should be able to:

a) **Understand the format the data is presented in and what it means**

b) **Extract the relevant information and possibly set up a calculation to answer the question**

a) **Understanding the format the data is presented in and what it means**

The line graphs, bar charts, pie charts or tables that you are presented with might not show the data in the most obvious format, so the first skill lies in understanding how information is represented in the chart.

- **Start by looking at any headings, descriptions or labels**

These should describe what the information in the chart contains. For example, if you see that the column headings in a table each contain a day of the week, and the row headings contain different types of household expenditure (as in the table below), then you can deduce that the data in the table most likely tells you the amount spent each day on various household costs.

Of course the headings or titles may be more complicated than this. They may not, for example, contain a text-based description and instead colours might represent different types of data.

		Weekdays							
		Monday	Tuesday	Wednesday	Thursday	Friday	Saturday	Sunday	Total
	Rent	55	55	55	55	55	55	55	385
	Electricity	5	5	5	5	5	9	9	43
	Water	3	3	3	3	3	4	4	23
Expenditure	Gas	4	4	4	4	4	5	5	30
	Food	8	8	16	8	8	8	12	68
	Phone	2	2	2	2	2	1	1	12
	Internet	2	2	2	2	2	2	2	14
	Total	79	79	87	79	79	84	88	575

- **Understand any units or measurements given and the implications for the data**

It might be the case that, as in the table below, the data represents the number of calories per 100 g of a certain item of food. Only by understanding any units or measurements provided can you fully understand the data.

Food Item	Calories (per 100 g)
Bacon	500
Baked beans	74
Banana	80
Beetroot	30
Blackcurrants	30
Black pudding	300
Bread (white)	235
Bread (brown)	220
Butter	750

b) Extracting the relevant information and possibly setting up a calculation in order to answer the question

- **Look at the data first**

It may only be after you have appreciated the content of the chart that you are able to understand fully what the question is asking. Look at the data first to give you an idea of what the chart shows you. This provides a context to the question and will help you visualise your next steps.

- **Look at the answers available**

Scan the answers to see whether there is a common trend. If all the answers are dates, for example, when you read the question you will be conscious of the fact that you are looking for a date.

- **Read the question**

Once you've got the context and frame of the data and what your answer should be, you will be in a much better position to understand the question.

- **Be confident in the logic you apply**

It is possible that an incorrect answer fits one of the five available, leading you to have misplaced confidence in your answer. Think through the logic that you decide to apply and check that you are happy it is correct.

- **Be efficient**

Try and focus in on the relevant data and ignore the irrelevant. The question should help you by specifying what you should be looking for.

Try this example:

In Simon the Pieman's pie-eating contest, there were 12 participants, each competing to eat as many pies as possible in 30 minutes. As a percentage, how many people ate between 21 and 40 pies?

Contestant	Pies eaten
Anthony	19
Belinda	21
Carl	35
Didier	17
Eduardo	19
Fred	22
Gail	53
Hanna	12
Iain	46
Jeremy	44
Kyle	43
Linda	45

Simon's Pie-eating Contest:
Number of Pies Eaten

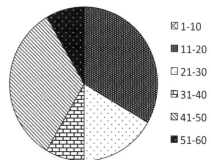

- ⊠ 1-10
- ▦ 11-20
- ☐ 21-30
- ⊞ 31-40
- ◩ 41-50
- ◼ 51-60

A   15%

B   25%

C   35%

D   45%

E   75%

You have two formats of data to look at in this question – a table and a pie chart. You can therefore work out the answer in two different ways, either by counting the number of people in the table falling into the 21-40 category and dividing by the total number of contestants (12). You might also look at the pie chart and assess how much as a proportion the two groupings (21-30 and 31-40) represent.

You know from the question that you are looking for a proportion, so the second method is by far the easier and quicker option. From the pie chart (light-spotted and brick segments), you can see that the proportion of contestants eating between 21 and 40 pies is around ¼, or 25%. As the nearest answers are sufficiently spread out from 25%, you don't need to refer back to the table and confirm. To answer the question as efficiently as possible, therefore, ignore the table and focus on the pie chart.

Handy hint
Remember that, when faced with a pie chart, there are 360° in the 'pie'.

• Do you need to do a calculation?

By this point you will either already have reached the correct answer or will need to manipulate the data you have extracted to find it. This manipulation could involve any of the concepts referred to in the advice on complex calculations. The pie-eating example above didn't require a calculation, but have a look at the example below.

Handy hint
As a general rule, any calculation required in these questions will not be as time-consuming or complicated as those in the complex calculations category of questions.

Try this example:

This graph shows the CO_2 emissions of five different cars:

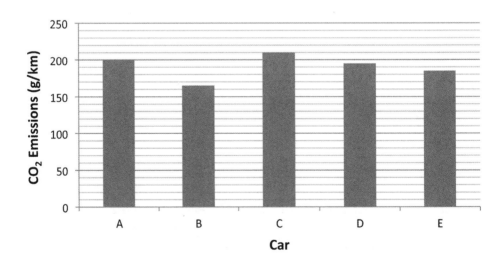

This graph shows the percentage decrease in CO_2 emissions of the same cars after each have been fitted with my new carbon-reducing device:

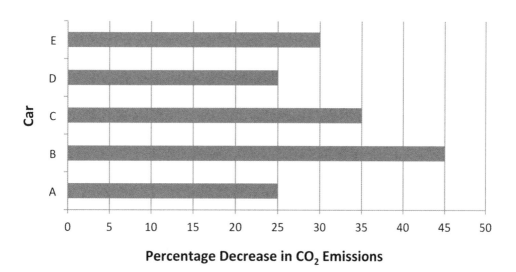

Percentage Decrease in CO$_2$ Emissions

How much CO$_2$ does Car C emit after being fitted with my new carbon-reducing device?

210×0.65

$- 1260 + 108 = 136.5$

A 73.5 g/km

B 283.5 g/km

C 21 g/km

D 136.5 g/km

E 35 g/km

This question contains two graphs and so you need to understand what each graph shows, as well as how they relate to each other:

The first graph shows the carbon emissions for five cars. As you can see, the cars are arranged along the x-axis, and the amount of carbon emitted along the y-axis. The carbon emitted is measured in g/km (grams per kilometre).

The second graph, which is slightly less straightforward, shows the percentage decrease in carbon emissions of each car after being fitted with my new carbon-reducing device. Note that the percentage decrease is the decrease to be applied to the figures in the first graph.

The question asks you to find out how much carbon Car C emits *after* being fitted with my new carbon-reducing device. You therefore know that you only need to look at the data for Car C.

To start with, find the value of carbon emissions on the first graph. Looking at the column for Car C, you can see that it emits 210 g/km. From the second graph, you can see that my carbon-reducing device reduces Car C's emissions by 35%.

To calculate the answer, you need to reduce 210 by 35%. One way of doing this is to find 35% of 210 and then subtract it from 210 (you could also multiply by 65%). Break this into stages and find 10% of 210, which is 21 and then multiply by 3.5, which comes to 73.5. Subtract this from 210 to give you 136.5. **D**, 136.5 g/km, is therefore the correct answer.

Checklist

☐ Have I understood the information contained in the chart?

☐ Do I know what the relevant information is and the most efficient way of extracting it?

☐ Is a calculation needed to get the answer?

☐ Have I extracted the relevant information and performed the calculation correctly?

---

3. Equation questions – some are more equal than others

Identifying mathematical relationships to solve an unknown value.

By the end of this chapter you should be able to:

a) **Identify the unknown quantity**
b) **Set up the equation**
c) **Solve the equation**

a) Identifying the unknown quantity

The unknown quantity will usually be what the question asks you to find. For example, if the question is, 'Frank is four times as old as Roy, and in two years' time the sum of their ages will be 64. How old is Roy?', then the unknown quantity is Roy's age. You should assign a variable to this unknown quantity such as 'x' or 'y' and then set up the equation.

$$(4x + 2) + (x + 2) = 64$$
$$5x + 4 = 64$$
$$5x = 60$$
$$x = 12$$

b) Setting up the equation

Use the unknown quantity wherever it is mentioned and insert the data around it. So, in the above example, if we know that Frank is four times as old as Roy, and we have assigned the variable 'x' to Roy's age, then Frank's age must be 4 multiplied by x, or 4x.

We know that in two years' time the sum of their ages will be 64, so take the two years and factor that into the ages. In two years' time, both Frank and Roy will be two years older than they are now so you can add 2 to both their ages, giving you Frank's age in two years as 4x + 2 and Roy's age in two years as x + 2. Next, we know that the sum of these is 64. Factoring this in gives you (4x + 2) + (x + 2) = 64. This is the equation; next you need to solve it.

	Roy	Frank
Now:	x	4x
In 2 years time:	x + 2	4x + 2
The equation:	(4x + 2) + (x + 2) = 64	

33

c) Solving the equation

Handy hint:

Solving equations requires some mathematical knowledge that you will likely have already, but if you struggle with equations, it would be useful to revisit your GCSE algebra.

Taking the equation above:

$$(4x + 2) + (x + 2) = 64$$

The first step is to simplify the equation by combining the brackets on the left hand side of the equation, giving:

$$5x + 4 = 64$$

Next, take the 4 away from both sides of the equation, leaving only 5x on the left hand side, and 60 on the right:

$$5x = 60$$

Finally, solve the equation for x by dividing both sides by 5:

$$x = 12.$$

You know, therefore, that the unknown quantity, which is represented by 'x' and equal to Roy's age, is 12. If you were asked what Frank's age was, don't forget to go back to its algebraic representation, 4x, to work out that Frank is 4 x 12 = 48.

Handy hint

The four basic rules of equations are:

   i) An equal quantity may be added to both sides of an equation.

   ii) An equal quantity may be subtracted from both sides of an equation.

   iii) An equal quantity may multiply both sides of an equation.

   iv) An equal, non-zero quantity may divide both sides of an equation.

• Checking your answer

It is quick and easy to check your answer once you have solved the equation. Go back to the wording of the question and plug in the numbers. If Roy is 12 and Frank is four times older than Roy, then Frank is 48. In two years' time, Frank will be 50 and Roy will be 14. The sum of their ages is 64 and so you can be sure that you have the correct answer.

Note that, if the correct equation is eluding you, you may also be able to find the answer using trial and error.

• Trial and error method

To find the answer using trial and error, take each of the five answers in turn (or as many as you need until you find the correct one) and assume it is true. Then plug in the numbers as in the *Checking your answer* section above. If the answer works within the context of the equation, it is correct.

Try this example:

Each day I sell tickets for two plays, Play A and Play B. At the end of a busy day of ticket sales, I find that I received £400 in total, with 10 more tickets sold for Play A than Play B. if it costs £12 for a ticket to Play A and £8 for a ticket to Play B, how many tickets to Play A did I sell?

A   10

B   14

C   38

D   24

E   16

$$12x + 8y = 400$$
$$x - y = 10.$$
$$x = 10 + y$$
$$y = x - 10$$
$$12x + 8(x - 10) = 400$$
$$12x + 8x - 80 = 400$$
$$2x = 480 \qquad x = 24$$

However you approach this question, the first task is to recognise what the unknown quantity is. In this question the unknown quantity is the number of tickets sold for Play A. Let's call this 'x' and form an equation using the information provided. You know that I sold 10 more tickets for Play A than Play B, so if the number of tickets for Play A is x, then the number of tickets for Play B is x - 10.

The amount of money I make from each play is relevant in finding the number of tickets and needs to be factored in to the equation. So, if I receive £12 for each Play A ticket, then I receive 12x (price of one ticket multiplied by the quantity of tickets). If I receive £8 for each Play B ticket then, in total, I receive 8(x   10) from these tickets. Factoring in the total amount of money I receive, the equation therefore looks like this:

$$12x + 8(x - 10) = 400$$

Simplifying the equation, you get:

$$12x + 8x - 80 = 400$$

Simplifying it further:
$$20x - 80 = 400$$

Isolating the x variable on one side and the values on the other:
$$20x = 480$$

Finally dividing both sides to find x:
$$x = 24$$

Therefore, the number of tickets that I sold to Play A was 24.

You could also form a pair of simultaneous equations to solve this problem. If you call the number of tickets for Play A, 'x' and the number for Play B, 'y', then:

1) $x = y + 10$
2) $12x + 8y = 400$

In order to find x, you can use 1) to define y, then eliminate y from 2):
$$y = x - 10$$

Substituting the $x - 10$ in for y in equation 2:
$$12x + 8(x - 10) = 400$$

Expanding this, you get:
$$12x + 8x - 80 = 400$$

Simplifying it, you get:
$$20x - 80 = 400$$

Isolating the x variable on one side and the values on the other:
$$20x = 480$$

Finally dividing both sides to find x:
$$x = 24$$

Therefore, the number of tickets that I sold to Play A was 24.

Checking the answer, then, if I sold 24 tickets to Play A, this means that I made £288 from Play A tickets (£12 x 24) and it means that I sold 14 tickets (10 less) to Play B, giving me £112 from Play B tickets (£8 x 14). In total therefore, I made £400, which is what we are told in the question and so **D** is the correct answer.

Forming an equation is probably the quickest way to tackle this question, but if you were to use the 'trial and error' method, then you would work out the total amount received by selling tickets to Play A and Play B for each different combination. In other words, you would start with the first answer, 10, work out how much I would receive by selling 10 Play A tickets at £12 (£120), then how much I would receive from selling 10 fewer Play B tickets which, in this case is none, giving me a total of £120. We know that I received £400, so this is incorrect and I could not therefore have sold 10 Play A tickets. You would do this for every answer until you find the answer that gives you £400.

Checklist

☐ What is the unknown quantity I am looking for?

☐ Can I set up an equation in order to find it?

☐ If not, will I use trial and error to try out each answer?

☐ If I have set up an equation, is it correctly formed?

☐ Have I manipulated my equation correctly to arrive at an answer?

☐ Have I checked my answer by inserting it back into the question and testing it?

4. Visual reasoning – getting your eye in

Mentally manipulating shapes or images to answer questions about a transformation.

By the end of this chapter you should be able to:

a) **Create a visual interpretation from the information in the question**
b) **Manipulate your visual interpretation**
c) **Use your visual interpretation to answer the question**

a) Creating a visual interpretation from the information in the question

The kind of data that a visual reasoning question contains includes degrees moved around a circle, distances, lengths, areas and volumes of shapes, and folds in paper. Read the question thoroughly and use it as the basis for creating your visualised image. For example, if you are told about an unconventional clock face in the question, then picture this clock face in your mind. If the question asks you about the number of degrees the hands of the clock will move between certain times, think about how the hands would move on your visualised, unconventional clock face:

b) Manipulating your visual interpretation

Once you have your visual interpretation of the shape or object, it can often help to jot it down quickly on paper. This way you can clear your mind to think about the steps needed to manipulate it in the way the question asks. Likewise, think about whether you want to draw each stage in the manipulation or whether you want to manipulate your drawn image in your head. Often it is quicker to manipulate the image in your head, but if the image is particularly complicated it may help to draw each stage.

c) Using your visual interpretation to answer the question

When you have your transformed visual representation of the original image, refer back to the question to ensure that you are picking out the relevant information to answer it correctly.

Try this example:

I have a square piece of paper with 4 cm sides. I fold it once along the vertical line of symmetry. I then fold the piece of paper along the horizontal line of symmetry. Finally, I fold the piece of paper, again, along the horizontal line of symmetry. I am now looking at a new shape. What is the area, in cm², of this shape:

A 8

B 3

C 2

D 4

E 1

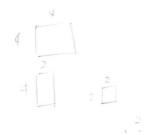

Start with the square piece of paper with 4 cm sides. If it is folded along the vertical line of symmetry then it would be folded along the dotted line:

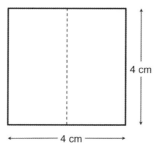

4 cm

4 cm

It would now look like the shape below. If then folded along the horizontal line of symmetry, it would be folded along the dotted line:

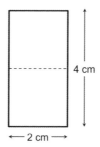

4 cm

2 cm

39

It would now look like this and have 2 cm sides. It is then folded again, along the horizontal line of symmetry, and so along this dotted line:

You are then left with this shape with sides of 1 cm and 2 cm:

The area is calculated by multiplying the width by the height, giving 2 cm² and **C** as the correct answer.

You could draw out each stage in the process as above, or you might amend or draw over your initial shape. With this question you could draw the folds in a single image in the order shown below:

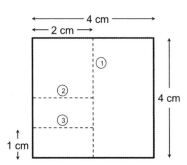

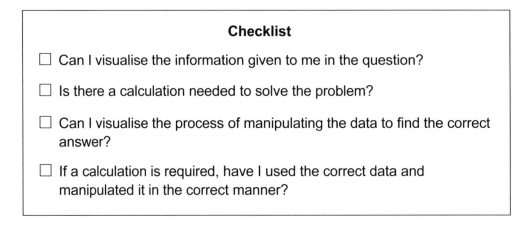

Checklist

☐ Can I visualise the information given to me in the question?

☐ Is there a calculation needed to solve the problem?

☐ Can I visualise the process of manipulating the data to find the correct answer?

☐ If a calculation is required, have I used the correct data and manipulated it in the correct manner?

5. Spatial awareness – it depends on your perspective

Manipulating a shape or object along one or multiple planes to determine a new or erroneous representation.

By the end of this chapter you should be able to:

a) **Understand what the question requires**
b) **Apply the correct process and visualise the result**

a) Understanding what the question requires

You will most likely be asked either to rotate or reflect a shape and identify which of the answers can or cannot be the original shape, or to determine which larger shape can or cannot be formed from separate, smaller shapes.

In the case of a rotation or reflection question, it will often be the case that the shape is quite complicated in its detail. Make sure you pay particular attention to how the detail of the shape changes as the whole shape is transformed.

Other questions may ask you to visualise a shape, either 2 or 3-dimensional, from a different perspective. For these questions, picture the shape and think about how it would look if you were to walk around it or rotate it.

Make sure you check the direction in which a rotation should be performed, or the line along which a reflection should be applied.

As well as manipulating the shapes that you are given in your mind, you might find (in the case of a 2-dimensional image) that you can physically manipulate the page to help you determine what a rotation looks like.

Handy hint
A reflection along a vertical line is the same as turning over the paper as you would the page of a book and looking at the image through the paper. A reflection along a horizontal line is the same as flipping the page over top to bottom and looking at the image through the paper.

b) Applying the correct process and visualising the result

You can approach the logic of the manipulation process either by applying the transformation to the object in the question and then matching it to the correct answer, or by eliminating the incorrect answers in a trial and error manner.

You might decide that you want to draw the results of the transformations. Do remember, however, that if the transformations comprise multiple stages, it might be practically difficult to draw out all the combinations.

Try this example:

The following shape can be rotated clockwise, and/or flipped about the horizontal and vertical axes shown:

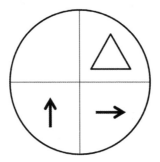

Which of the following could you NOT see after the shape is rotated, flipped, or a combination of both?

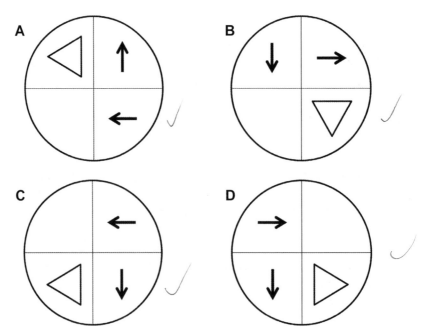

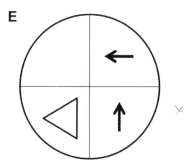

The best way of approaching this question is to take a trial and error approach and go through each of the five possible shapes, assessing whether the original shape can be rotated, flipped, or both in order to arrive at that shape.

A could be seen if the original shape was rotated 90 degrees anti-clockwise (which is the same as 270 degrees clockwise). **B** could be seen if the original shape was flipped about the horizontal axis. **C** could be seen if the original shape was flipped about the horizontal axis and then rotated 90 degrees clockwise. **D** could be seen if the original shape was rotated 90 degrees clockwise. **E** could not be seen if the original shape was rotated or flipped, or both. You can perhaps see this from the fact that the arrow that is directly below the triangle in the original shape points towards the outside edge of the circle in all of the other shapes, whereas the corresponding arrow in **E** points away from the outside edge of the circle.

Checklist

☐ What am I asked to do with the shape or object?

☐ Have I looked closely at the detail of the shape?

☐ Can I visualise the shape and manipulate it?

---

6. Lateral thinking – expand your mind

Approaching a problem and systematically applying logical rules to solve practical questions.

By the end of this chapter you should be able to:

a) **Understand the question**
b) **Decipher the rules**
c) **Apply a logical process step-by-step**

a) Understanding the question

Lateral thinking questions are made up of a situation and a series of rules. Take your time to read the question carefully and if you are unsure about any part of it, read it again until you're confident that you've understood it fully. Whilst this seems obvious, the issue is that if you misread or misunderstand a lateral thinking question and set off on a logical process in which you apply incorrect rules or apply rules incorrectly, you will find that you have wasted valuable time. This is compounded by the fact that these questions naturally take a bit longer to solve, so if you end up having to re-do the question, you will lose a lot of time.

Handy hint
Don't be put off by the fact that these questions benefit from a degree of creativity; they don't require an artistic mind and whilst creative solutions do help, finding the solution in a standard, uncreative way is still finding the solution.

b) Deciphering the rules

• Distinct or related?

Treat each rule as a separate piece of information and ask yourself whether any rules are related and whether those that are related combine to make a single, more detailed rule. For example, if you are asked to arrange the animals in a zoo and one rule says that a giraffe cannot be housed next to an elephant and another rule says that a hippopotamus cannot be housed next to a giraffe, then you can infer a wider rule that a giraffe cannot be housed next to an elephant or a hippopotamus.

- **Where do I start?**

Using the zoo example above, you could start arranging the animals from what you know about a particular animal or you could eliminate the answers in a trial and error manner based on the rules. The method you choose really depends on how the questions and answers are structured and is entirely up to you, but understanding the rules and how they relate to each other will give you an idea of where the natural starting point is. Often there will be several starting points and the best one is the one you feel most comfortable with.

c) Applying a logical process step-by-step

- **What order?**

Once you've decided where you are going to start, it is often sensible to apply the rules in the order that they are given in the question, not least because you have a logical order and will be less likely to miss out or forget a rule.

- **Step-by-step**

Taking a step-by-step approach is important – you don't want to process all of the rules at once and confuse yourself. Take your time to work through the rules one by one.

- **Write things down**

Writing down your stages is a good way to remember all the deductions you make along the way. Depending on the question, it might be worth sketching the situation before you start applying the rules. For example, if you are asked to find the frequency of a certain event during a particular month, it may be useful to sketch the month in calendar format.

Try this example: $1 + 5 + 15 \ m1. \quad 16 + 5 + 1$
$$5 + 15 \ m2.$$

> My first school term lasts from the 1st of Month 1 until the 31st of Month 3 (inclusive). I have an unusual system of truancy whereby in Months 1 and 3 I will only go to school if the date of the month contains an odd number, for example the 12th of Month 1 or the 23rd of Month 3. In Month 2, I will only go to school if the date of the month contains an even number (and I include zero as an even number).
>
> Assuming that Months 1 & 2 have 30 days, Month 3 has 31 days, and that my school requires me to go into school seven days a week, how many times will I go to school in my first term?

A   60

B   61

C   63

D   64

E   62

The question is asking you for the number of times I will go to school in Months 1, 2 and 3 based on a set of truancy rules. The important facts to take into account are that the first term lasts from the 1st of Month 1 until the 31st of Month 3 inclusive. The question therefore makes a point of saying that the 1st of Month 1 and the 31st of Month 3 are part of the data set. You are also told that Months 1 and 2 have 30 days and that Month 3 has 31 days, and that I am required to go into school seven days a week.

The first rule in the question is that I will only go to school in Months 1 and 3 if the date of the month contains an odd number. Note that this is not that the number itself is odd, but that the 1 or 2 digit number comprises an odd digit. The second rule is that in Month 2, I will only go to school if the date of the month contains an even digit. In addition, you know that you will not be discounting weekends because you are told that I am required to go into school seven days a week.

One approach would be to write out the dates for all three months and then apply the rules and note on which dates I will go to school. However, this may be quite time-consuming. Instead, you should realise that by working out the number of dates on which I will go to school in one month will help you to work out the number of dates on which I will go to school in the other months.

Start with Month 1. Again, you could write down all the dates of Month 1 and then note the dates on which I will go to school, but a quicker way of doing it is to realise that between the 1st and the 9th of Month 1 (inclusive), I will go to school five times. Then, between the 10th and the 19th of Month 1 (inclusive), I will go to school 10 times since all of these dates will include at least one odd digit in them: '1'. Between the 20th and the 29th of Month 1 (inclusive) I will go to school five times. Finally, the 30th does include an odd digit so I will go to school on this date too. So, in Month 1, I will go to school 21 times (5 + 10 + 5 + 1).

Next work out Month 3 since you are already dealing with odd numbers and it makes more sense to stick with the same rule. It should be clear that Month 3 will be exactly the same as Month 1 with the addition of one more date, the 31st, on which I will go to school because both digits are odd. I will therefore go to school 22 times in Month 3.

Finally, for Month 2, you can go through the same process as you went through with Month 1 but for even digits. So, between the 1st and the 9th of Month 2 (inclusive), I will go to school four times. Then, between the 10th and the 19th of Month 2 (inclusive), I will go to school five times. Between the 20th and the 29th of Month 2 (inclusive) I will go to school 10 times, since all of the dates will include an even digit. The 30th also contains an even digit so I will go to school on this date too. Therefore, in Month 2, I will go to school 20 times (4 + 5 + 10 + 1).

Adding up all three months, I will go to school 63 times (21 + 22 + 20). **C** is therefore the correct answer.

Checklist

☐ What is the question asking me to find?

☐ What information am I given to use?

☐ What are the rules that I must follow?

☐ What is the best approach to find the correct answer and am I applying it in a logical, step-by-step manner?

---

1. Identifying and drawing conclusions: how to spot what it's all about

In the TSA, in certain questions you are asked to identify a conclusion in a given passage. In other questions you are required to draw a particular conclusion from the text. While the two requests might sound similar, there are distinct differences:

Identifying a conclusion: This is when a conclusion has been reached in the passage and you must identify the best summary of that given conclusion.

Drawing a conclusion: This is when a particular conclusion has not been stated in the argument and you must draw a conclusion from the given information in that particular passage.

In the TSA, you will be asked questions in which you will either have to identify or draw a conclusion – you will never be asked to do both in one question. It's important that you read the passages and the questions very carefully to ensure that you choose the most sensible approach to a question.

By the end of this chapter you should be able to:

a) **Interpret a sentence in different ways**

b) **Understand that an argument contains premises and conclusions**

c) **Differentiate between a premise and a conclusion**

d) **Use certain techniques to identify conclusions**

e) **Recognise questions asking you to identify conclusions**

f) **Spot the possible wording of questions asking you to identify conclusions**

g) **Tackle identifying conclusion questions**

h) **Understand drawing conclusion questions**

i) **Understand what is being tested in drawing conclusion questions**

j) **Spot the possible wording of questions asking you to draw conclusions**

k) **Successfully understand how to crack drawing conclusion questions**

a) Interpreting a sentence in different ways

An argument is made up of words and words are often open to interpretation. The meaning of a sentence – a string of words – may be open to multiple interpretations. The good news is that if you train yourself to pick a sentence apart, you are capable of interpreting the meaning of a whole paragraph of text.

Firstly, as a test – can you find at least two interpretations of the following sentence?

I only eat fish on Friday.

Our interpretations are:
- That I don't eat fish on any other day of the week except Friday.
- That the only food I eat on Friday is fish.
- That the only person to eat fish on Friday is me (although this interpretation probably requires the word 'only' to be separated by commas).

If you struggled to pick out any of these interpretations, try emphasising different words as you say the sentence (in your head or out loud):
- *Friday*
- *fish*
- *I* and *only*

As you can see, the interpretation of one sentence alone can affect the meaning of an argument.

It's important that you can deconstruct a sentence like the one above, so that you are able to understand arguments and find the right answer to questions involving arguments in the TSA.

TSA tip

If possible, use information given in the question to ascertain the context.

Let's say the statement given was:

> *I only eat fish on Friday. Fishmongers are closed the rest of the week.*

The second sentence here strongly suggests that the most sensible interpretation of the first sentence should be:

> *I don't eat fish on any other day of the week except Friday.*

TSA tip

Remember....don't waste time interpreting sentences unnecessarily. All the information you need to discern a correct answer will be given in the question. If the information is not given, it may be that you are spending time on an unnecessary task.

b) Understanding that an argument contains premises and conclusions

Arguments are principally constructed from premises and conclusions. (A premise may also act as a conclusion and vice versa, but let's keep things simple for the moment.) The usual definition of premise is a proposition which supports the conclusion of an argument.

Premises are statements that, if understood to be true, lead to the conclusion. In other words, the conclusion should flow, logically, from the premises in an argument and the premises should support the conclusion. The conclusion is the main thrust of the argument or the main point of the argument or the result of the premises.

PREMISE 1
(a proposition which supports the conclusion of an argument)

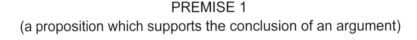

PREMISE 2

CONCLUSION
(the main thrust of the argument/the main point of the argument/the result of the premises)

c) Differentiating between a premise and a conclusion

Let's first try to separate the premises from the conclusion in an argument. In order to do this, you need to work through the sentences and identify which statement is the result of the premises. This statement will be the conclusion.

Look at the statement:

I only eat fish on Friday. Today is Friday, therefore I will eat fish.

We have three statements here but only one is the conclusion. Which is it? Only one statement is the result of the other statements.

Using the formula below should help you to understand better exactly what you are looking for, if you are finding this a little difficult:

Conclusion = Premise 1 + Premise 2

Or...

Premise 1 + Premise 2 = Conclusion

Putting our example above into the equation, gives:

I only eat fish on Friday + Today is Friday = therefore I will eat fish

The first two statements above are premises and the last is the conclusion.

d) Using certain techniques to identify conclusions

The above example is a little easier than some you may encounter because of the use of the word *therefore* which suggests that a conclusion will follow. This helps you to know where the conclusion sits in a sentence.

- **There are certain words and phrases that may indicate that a conclusion will follow.**

These include: *therefore, hence*, *thus, so*, *it follows that*

- **Remember, too, that a conclusion doesn't necessarily have to be at the end of an argument.**

It can appear anywhere in an argument, for example:

Conclusion = Premise 1 + Premise 2

Let's change the structure of our sentence to:

I will eat fish today because I only eat fish on Friday and today is Friday.

Here, the conclusion is at the beginning of the sentence – not the end – and the word 'because' acts as a signpost that a premise will follow this conclusion.

- **The purpose**

A helpful tip in identifying the conclusion is to think about the purpose of an argument.

An argument is used to persuade someone of something and, due to this, the conclusion is often worded in a normative tone. (Our definition of normative is, with the implication that something should or ought to be something - i.e. a value-judgement is expressed.)

A premise, on the other hand, is sometimes used as evidence leading to a claim, and so will often be factual or simply an observation rather than a normative statement. (Stay on your guard, as this distinction is not always present or obvious and so this tip should be used as a guide rather than a definitive method of distinguishing between premises and conclusions.)

- **The *therefore* test**

A better way, if you are uncertain about whether a statement is a conclusion or a premise, is using the *therefore* test.

Try reading out one of the statements in your mind, add *therefore* and then say the other statement. Try the test again, swapping the statements over.

This test should indicate to you which sentence follows from the other, i.e. which statement supports the other and therefore which is the premise and which is the conclusion.

Why not try applying the therefore test to the following two statements?:

It is raining outside
I will use an umbrella

When you try the two options you should find that it sounds more natural and logical to state that:

It is raining outside therefore I will use an umbrella.

rather than

I will use an umbrella therefore it is raining outside.

This test will not work perfectly every time, but it may give you a clearer idea, in the case of two statements, which seems to flow logically from the other.

e) Recognising questions asking you to identify conclusions in the TSA

These questions require you to choose an answer that paraphrases the conclusion of the argument in the question.

The arguments may not be as simple as the short examples given previously and will often consist of a few premises or statements. The arguments could be on any subject matter.

The other answers available for these questions may be incorrect for various reasons:

- They may be premises instead of conclusions – in which case the question tests whether you are able to distinguish the various components of the argument.

- They may be too general or too specific to be the exact conclusion of the argument.

- Since you are looking at the substance of the argument and what is being said, and not just at the logical structure, an incorrect answer could also be so if it simply states the substance of the conclusion incorrectly. For example, the incorrect answer could be *I will eat fish tomorrow* when, instead, the correct conclusion in the argument is *I will eat fish today*.

f) Spotting the possible wording of questions asking you to identify conclusions

The wording of these questions varies. Fortunately, the questions seem to ask the same sort of thing. Common variations are:

- Which of the following **best expresses** the main conclusion of the argument above?

- Which of the following **is a statement of** the main conclusion in the above argument?

- Which of the following **best summarises** the conclusion of the argument above?

- Which of the following **summarises** the conclusion of the argument above?

As you can see, there are some slight differences in the language of these four variations. The words 'expresses' and 'summarises' are essentially interchangeable and your approach to identifying the conclusion and choosing an answer shouldn't be affected by which of these words is used. It could be said that, when you are asked to choose a statement that best 'expresses' the conclusion as opposed to best 'summarises' it, the former may be slightly more exact whereas the latter may be more vague. However, since the best approach in answering these questions is to find the exact conclusion from the argument, your approach shouldn't be affected by whether the former or the latter is used.

The use of the word 'best', equally, shouldn't cause concern. It is sometimes the case, when looking at more than one answer, that they could both feasibly be some sort of conclusion of the argument (as opposed to one being a premise) and so the word 'best' is used to highlight the fact that there could be more than one statement which seems like a conclusion, but that one of them is better suited to the particular terms and structure of the argument than the other.

The insertion of the word 'main' in some of the questions may give you a clue to the nature of the argument in the question. It could imply that there may be more than one conclusion to be extracted from the argument, perhaps where the argument is slightly more complicated than others in the TSA. For example, there could be a premise (or premises) leading to one conclusion and then a further argument based on that conclusion (which would then act as a premise) leading to an ultimate conclusion. In this scenario, the question reminds you, using the word 'main', that you should identify the overall or ultimate conclusion and not the intermediate conclusion.

Another example may be where the argument suggests one thing but then introduces a counter-argument or makes a U-turn and finally concludes differently. In this case, the question requires you to identify which of the two directions the argument seems to focus on and to identify the main conclusion based on this.

g) Tackling identifying conclusion questions

• Read the argument carefully

This may sound obvious but it is vital. Focus and digest everything you read as you work through the argument. You will find that the premises and the conclusions will separate themselves out more naturally if you follow the argument through carefully. Ensure that you don't read only some of the argument before losing concentration. And try and refrain from going back to earlier sentences too often as this may disrupt your understanding of the flow of the argument.

A good general test to help you to prepare is to read a newspaper editorial and then write down a brief summary of what has been stated to check that you understand the argument thoroughly. One useful approach for these questions is, after you have read the argument, to try and identify the conclusion yourself without looking at any of the answers. You should be able to do this if you have understood the argument. It should ultimately speed up the process if you identify a conclusion simply by reading the argument and then spot it as one of the answers provided.

- **Understand the gist of the argument**

In many instances, when you ask yourself what the gist (the main point) of an argument is, you will respond with a statement that is the conclusion. This makes sense since an argument is persuasive and the conclusion should be a summary of *what* the author is trying to persuade you of (with the premises the reasons *why* you should be persuaded). So, by reading the argument carefully, fully understanding it and then asking yourself, 'what is the author persuading me of here?' you will find that the conclusion of the argument should become clearer.

- **Look for an explicit conclusion and do not infer**

An argument should have an explicit conclusion otherwise its persuasive effect may be weakened (since the reader may not know to what end he or she is supposed to be persuaded). However, in some cases, the conclusion may not be explicit or it may be obscure. In this case, you may have to find an expression of the conclusion from the premises or from an ambiguous expression of it.

Look for evidence of a conclusion using the words and phrases referred to previously, since a conclusion may be expressed explicitly in some of the arguments you are given in the TSA. Make sure you don't infer a conclusion from the argument.

- **Separate the premises from the conclusions**

If you find that you are having trouble separating the premises from the conclusions or that you are not sure what the *main* conclusion is, then try applying the 'therefore' test to give you a better idea. Reading the argument carefully and understanding the gist should point you in the direction of the main conclusion but, especially in arguments with many stages, finding this ultimate conclusion or gist is not always easy.

- **Verify the accuracy of your conclusion and eliminate the other answers**

If you feel that you have identified the conclusion and chosen an answer that expresses or summarises it, then, time permitting, try and verify that it is the correct answer and that the other answers are incorrect.

There are various checks that you can do to ensure that you have chosen the correct conclusion:

- **Is your conclusion too general or too specific?**

Often conclusions, even at the end of convoluted arguments, can be very specific. For example, to conclude that 'squirrels should be a protected species' is a different conclusion to stating that 'red squirrels should be a protected species'. The latter is more specific than the former. Check that the conclusion you have chosen is not more general or more specific than the conclusion of the argument in the question.

- **Does your conclusion include the correct substance of the argument?**

You need to ensure that your conclusion accurately reflects what is being said in the argument. For example, if the argument concludes that 'red squirrels should be a protected species', then a conclusion that 'red squirrels should be on the WWF endangered species list' is different in substance. There is sometimes a fine line between paraphrasing a conclusion and changing the meaning of the conclusion completely. Try to ensure that you do not choose a conclusion that changes the meaning of the argument.

- **Does your conclusion reflect the true direction or relationships in the argument?**

This is similar to the above point in that you need to ensure that the meaning of your conclusion is the same as that in the argument. Watch out for negatives or other words which may change the meaning or direction of the argument completely and which may sometimes be missed. For example, if the conclusion in the argument is that 'red squirrels should be a protected species', then ensure that you don't choose the conclusion that 'red squirrels shouldn't be looked after as a species' or that 'red squirrels shouldn't be cared for' or another variation that is completely different from the actual conclusion.

Similarly, these techniques can help you to eliminate the incorrect answers.

Try this example:

Following local conventions when in other countries can sometimes be confusing and remembering etiquette is no easy task. Fortunately, most locals, when interacting with tourists, are sympathetic to any mistakes and do not take any insensitivities to heart. This is no reason to ignore or disrespect any of these local conventions or etiquette, however, and tourists must endeavour to learn and follow them in order that they are preserved.

Which of the following best expresses the main conclusion of the argument above?

A Tourists should strive to respect local conventions and etiquette.

B Locals are generally not angry when tourists forget local conventions and etiquette.

C Locals must strive to follow their own conventions and etiquette.

D The preservation of culture is an effect of tourism.

E Tourists do not need to worry about remembering local conventions or etiquette.

This example should help to clarify some of the points discussed above.

Firstly, you need to understand what the argument is saying here.

- The first premise is that following local conventions and etiquette can be difficult.

- Next, it is stated that most locals accept mistakes made by tourists.

- The main premise is that, despite this understanding, this is not a reason to ignore or disrespect these conventions and etiquette.

- As a conclusion, it is stated that tourists must endeavour to learn and follow these conventions and etiquette. The addition of 'in order that they are preserved' is actually another premise or reason which flows to the conclusion. The fact that it is stated after the conclusion is irrelevant.

The argument can be re-stated as: *despite the fact that conventions and etiquette are difficult to remember and locals generally understand this and sympathise, in order to preserve them, tourists should strive to respect them.*

If you can re-state the argument in a slightly simpler form and separate out the various components of the argument, this should help you to find the conclusion.

You may wonder, since all the conclusion relies on is the fact that these conventions and etiquette should be preserved, whether or not the other statements are premises. This is not a crucial question in finding the conclusion and is more a question of semantics. However, the fact that the passage states that 'this is no reason to ignore or disrespect any of these local conventions or etiquette' may allow you to say that the previous statements are, indirectly, premises for the argument since they constitute what the 'this' is referring to above.

So, after separating out the various parts of this slightly convoluted argument, you should now see that you have various premises and a conclusion. It should then be easy enough to pick out one of the answers as the conclusion that you have spotted. Indeed, the conclusion is that tourists must endeavour to learn and follow etiquette and local conventions and **A** is almost an exact match of this, so **A** is the correct answer.

Even if you spotted this without eliminating the other answers, it is worth doing so in order to verify this is the correct answer. **B** is true but, as you should realise, this is, indirectly, a premise of the argument and not the conclusion of it. The conclusion relies on the fact that **B** is not a reason to ignore or disrespect any local conventions or etiquette.

C is incorrect since nowhere in the argument is a claim made about locals and how they should respond to their own conventions and etiquette. The specific conclusion here is that *tourists* must strive to learn and follow local conventions and etiquette.

D is stated as a fact but does not seem to appear in the argument. In fact, it is implied that if locals understand and sympathise with mistakes with local conventions and etiquette, then they will not be preserved. The conclusion is that tourists must endeavour to learn and follow etiquette and local conventions *so that* cultural conventions can be preserved. In other words, the argument persuades the reader of a claim which has a positive effect. It is not stated that this effect already occurs, which **D** seems to imply, and, in any case, the effect is not the conclusion of the argument; it is a premise leading to the conclusion. **E** is incorrect since the conclusion actually states the opposite of this; that tourists do need to worry about remembering local conventions or etiquette.

Checklist

☐ Look for the overall conclusion

☐ Distinguish the premises from the conclusion (the 'therefore' test and language used will help)

☐ Is your conclusion too vague or too general?

☐ Does your conclusion contain the correct substance of the argument?

And now to drawing conclusions.......

As we discussed at the beginning of this chapter, drawing conclusion questions are about working out, from the information and arguments given in a passage, what the conclusion is. Unlike identifying conclusion questions, the conclusion you are asked for is not given in the passage (even if another conclusion is reached in the passage).

h) Understanding drawing conclusion questions

Drawing conclusions requires you to assess the information in the argument provided to you and reach your own conclusion based on this argument. You are not given the conclusion in the answers and instead must create your own conclusion that follows logically from the reasoning in the argument. In some cases, you are given a conclusion in the passage but you are asked to draw another conclusion using the information given.

Let's come back to another fish example. Say that it now reads:

> *I only eat fish on Friday since the fishmonger is not open any other day. Today is Friday, therefore I will eat fish.*

We already know that one conclusion that flows logically from the two premises is that *therefore I will eat fish* and this is stated as part of the argument. However, the premises can also support other conclusions.

For example, based on the fact that I only eat fish on Friday since the fishmonger is not open any other day and on the fact that today is Friday, I could conclude that the fish I eat comes from the fishmongers. Or, perhaps I could conclude that the fishmonger must be open today. (However, the latter conclusion comes close to actually being stated in the argument and so may be construed as simply repeating a premise of the argument as opposed to drawing a further conclusion from the existing premises.)

Remember that conclusions ought to flow logically from premises but that a perfectly logical flow may not always be possible and that, in general, it is sufficient – for the argument to work – that the premises generally support the conclusion.

So, from the premises above, it is perfectly logical to conclude that today I will eat fish, but it is not easy to conclude that the fish I eat comes from the fishmongers. In other words, this new, drawn conclusion is strongly supported by the premises, but it may not *have* to be true as a matter of logic. Perhaps, for example, I am not allowed to eat fish in front of my wife and, since she works at the fishmongers and is away all day (but at home every other day), I can eat fish on Friday. Now, obviously, this is stretching the argument a little too far, which actually means that the conclusion that the fish I eat comes from the fishmongers is supported by the premises but it is not perfect.

i) Understanding what is tested in drawing conclusions questions

These questions test your ability to understand the information contained in an argument, either in the form of premises or conclusions. They also test how well you can draw a conclusion that can be supported by the terms of the argument. Answers in these questions may be incorrect for a variety of reasons:

- Perhaps there is not enough information to form a certain conclusion.

- Perhaps the information suggests a conclusion different to that contained in one of the answers, for example, if the information all seems to suggest that 'red squirrels should be a protected species' (but that this isn't stated) and one answer states that 'grey squirrels should be a protected species' then this can't be concluded from the argument.

These questions may also rely on nuances and subtleties in the language of the argument. If an argument states, for example, that:

A recent rally drew out many protesters and some demonstrated their anger at the new policy.

It would be incorrect to draw the conclusion that **all** *protesters were angry at the new policy* (emphasis added) since you have only information suggesting that *some* protesters seemed to be angry at the new policy and not that *all* of them were angry. In fact, from the wording of the argument, it is suggested that only some were angry, although perhaps all were angry and only some demonstrated this. Either way, you cannot draw a conclusion if there is insufficient information.

These questions may therefore try to catch you out by placing words such as 'all', 'none' or 'only', to qualify either the information or one of the answers.

These words can make all the difference in terms of whether a conclusion is supported or not and it is well worth looking out for these.

j) Spotting the possible wordings of questions asking you to draw conclusions

Fortunately, there is very little difference in the wording of this type of question. There are three likely variations:

- Which of the following is a conclusion that can **reliably be drawn** from the above argument?
- Which of the following is a conclusion that **can be drawn** from the above argument?
- Which of the following conclusions is **best supported by** the above argument?

The difference between the first two of these questions is the word 'reliably'. The word 'reliable' is important for these questions since it emphasises the fact that the conclusion must be supported by the premises. In other words, it must be a reliable statement to conclude based on the information you have been given.

There is little difference between what the question requires of you in all three of these variations, however, the word 'reliably' may simply denote a trickier question whereby more than one of the conclusions may seem to be drawn from the argument. In this case, you will have to be careful to choose the one that is reliable, i.e. the one for which the information provided genuinely can lead to the conclusion.

Equally, with the third variation, this is simply a different way of expressing the second variation. More than one of the conclusions may be supported by the argument, however tenuously, but there will be one conclusion which the information in the argument can support strongly, or at least more strongly than the others. This will be the correct answer.

k) Successfully understanding how to crack these types of questions

- **Absorb all the information**

These questions rely on your ability to assess whether a conclusion flows from the information in the argument. This means that it is vital that you read the argument carefully and fully understand the information in it. If there are any descriptions or definitions of words or concepts that perhaps may differ from your understanding, then be especially aware of these. A conclusion may, at first sight, seem incongruous when it may just be that it works, based on a particular description or definition provided in the argument.

- **Identify relationships of ideas**

There may also be connections made between ideas in an argument that you need to look out for. For example, arguments often rely on statistics in order to persuade the reader. A statistic may be presented to you, followed by an explanation of what that statistic means. Perhaps it could be the case that, as a result of this explanation, other conclusions may be drawn from the same statistic. Therefore, you need to ensure that you fully understand what the statistic refers to and the implications of it. If it is stated that *40% of all car drivers are male;* this is not the same as saying that *40% of all males drive cars.*

Similarly, if there is no causal relationship between certain ideas in the argument then avoid drawing a conclusion that does create a causal relationship since you would be basing this on other information and not that presented to you.

- **Use only the information in the passage/even if obvious**

This is an important point to remember. You cannot use any other information other than that presented to you in the argument, otherwise, you would be drawing it from other sources, such as your own knowledge, and not purely from the argument. It may be tempting to rely on your own knowledge either to choose a conclusion based on this knowledge or to fill gaps in the information. It's essential that you do not do this, as you would be moving beyond the remit of the information you are allowed to use and therefore would not answer the question.

The words 'reliably' and 'best supported' are sometimes found in the questions, and, should you rely on any information outside of the argument, then your drawn conclusion would no longer be reliable or best supported by the argument.

Furthermore, do not be put off by answers that may seem obvious. It could well be that the conclusion that can be drawn is obvious based on what you know. However, in the context of an argument with limited information, the fact that it is obvious does not prevent it from being supported by the argument.

- **Beware of subtle variations in language used**

We've already touched on how subtle variations of language can affect information presented to you and the possible conclusions that can be drawn. However, be aware of those words (which are often short words) that can change the meaning of ideas, sometimes drastically. Be especially careful when quantities are discussed, as these can easily be overlooked and may dramatically change the meaning of a sentence.

Try this example:

More sitcoms have been appearing on television at an alarming rate. This has led to less diversity in terms of what appears on our televisions and to comedy programmes that contain a similar type of humour as each other. Some have criticised this trend and argued that we should resist more of these programmes from being shown on television, but, at the end of the day, television companies that produce and broadcast these sitcoms know what the majority of people want to watch.

Which one of the following conclusions can reliably be drawn from the above argument?

A   The majority of people argue that we should resist more sitcoms from being shown on television.

B   What appears on television is affected by consumer demand.

C   Sitcoms will continue to appear on our televisions at the same rate.

D   Most programmes on television are now sitcoms.

E   Calls to resist more of these programmes from appearing on television will lead to fewer sitcoms appearing.

The first task when faced with a question like this is to make sure that you have taken in and digested all the information. After this, take each answer in turn and assess its reliability in terms of a conclusion that can be drawn from the above passage.

A is incorrect as it is not the *majority of people* that argue that we should resist more sitcoms from being shown on television; rather all we are told in the argument is that 'some' have argued this. The reference to the 'majority of people' refers to the television companies that produce and broadcast these sitcoms and who know what the majority of people want to watch. As you should realise, this conclusion is, essentially, the antithesis of what the argument states since the majority, we would assume, would not argue against more sitcoms from appearing on television since, it seems, they want more sitcoms.

B seems to be a conclusion that can reliably be drawn from the argument. You are told that 'more sitcoms have been appearing on television at an alarming rate' and that 'television companies that produce and broadcast these sitcoms know what the majority of people want to watch'. If you assume that it is television companies that have been producing and broadcasting these new sitcoms that have been appearing, then, since they know what the majority of people want to watch, a conclusion can be reliably drawn that they respond to this and have been producing more sitcoms. It could be argued that this is just a coincidence and that what the majority of people want to watch happens to be the same as what these companies produce and broadcast. However, it seems likely, from the information provided in the argument, that there is a connection here, especially given the use of the word 'know' which implies that the companies base their choice of programme on consumer demand. Therefore, **B** can reliably be drawn as a conclusion.

C is incorrect since, although we know that sitcoms have been appearing on our televisions at an alarming rate, we do not know whether they will continue to do so. There is insufficient information in the argument to conclude this reliably. The fact that this conclusion states that 'more sitcoms will continue to appear' makes it uncertain based on what we already know, but the fact that it adds 'at the same rate' adds even more uncertainty and makes it even more unreliable as a conclusion to be drawn from the argument.

D tests whether you interpret the fact that sitcoms have been appearing on our televisions at an alarming rate as indicative of the number on our televisions. The number cannot reliably be inferred and, moreover, the statement that 'most programmes on television are now sitcoms' is totally unsupported by the information in the argument. It could be that the number of sitcoms on television, as a proportion of total programmes, has increased in six months from 1% to 49%. This would be alarming, but does not mean that *most* of the programmes on television are sitcoms. **D** is therefore incorrect.

E is incorrect as there is no information as to what response there will be from the 'some' who have argued that we should resist more of these programmes from being shown on television. In fact, it is implied that, as long as the majority of people want to watch sitcoms, then they will continue to appear on our televisions. Further, calls by this minority, to resist more of these programmes from appearing on television, will not lead to fewer sitcoms appearing.

Checklist

☐ What conclusion, not stated in the argument, can the information support?

☐ Have you fully read and understood all the information?

☐ Are you using only the information in the argument?

☐ Do you have enough information to support your conclusion?

☐ Are there any words that change the meaning of the information or any of the answers subtly?

---

2. Identifying assumptions & spotting flaws in arguments

As part of the TSA, you will need to tackle certain questions that ask you to identify assumptions in an argument and others that ask you to spot flaws. To answer these types of questions successfully, you need first to understand what we mean by assumptions and flaws.

By the end of this chapter you should be able to:

a) **Understand what an assumption is and its role in an argument**
b) **Understand what is being tested in assumption questions**
c) **Tackle questions using different wording**
d) **Feel confident about tackling these questions successfully**
e) **Understand what a flaw is and its role in an argument**
f) **Spot a flaw in an argument**
g) **Understand what questions on flaws test**
h) **Tackle questions using different wording**
i) **Feel confident about tackling these questions successfully**

a) Understanding what an assumption is and its role in an argument

An assumption is an unwritten or unspoken piece of information in an argument which, without it, weakens the logical flow from the premises to the conclusion. In other words, in order for the conclusion to follow from the rest of the argument, an assumption is needed to bridge the gap.

In crime shows on television, we see the police using assumptions to form an argument as to who is guilty e.g: if they assume the perpetrator's car can only have left from one location, this assumption might underpin their argument that only individuals who could have left from this location could be guilty. This assumption allows the police to form an argument that leads to a conclusion.

Take this example of an argument:

Whales have bigger brains than humans, therefore, whales are more intelligent than humans.

The assumption in this example is the premise that bridges the gap from the premise that whales have bigger brains than humans, to the conclusion that whales are more intelligent than humans.

STATEMENT

whales have bigger brains than humans

ASSUMPTION

(brain size is linked to intelligence)

CONCLUSION

whales are more intelligent than humans

(The main thrust of the argument / the main point of the argument / the result of the premises)

Even though you may disagree with the argument here, this example illustrates how to identify an assumption.

Top tip

Remember that an assumption is always missing from the argument and, despite the fact that the label 'assumption' may be applied to information that is stated in everyday life, in this context, an assumption is something going on in the background or in the author's mind and is not stated explicitly in the argument itself.

You can think of an assumption as information that is taken for granted whilst the author forms the argument.

b) Understanding what is being tested in assumption questions

These questions test your ability to find the conclusion of the argument, understand the premises leading to this conclusion and spot the missing link in the chain of the argument.

Each question should have a conclusion that you are able to extract from the argument as well as premises that lead to this conclusion. You are then expected to assess the information given and decide whether the premises lead logically to the conclusion. The argument in the question is deliberately designed so that there is some information missing. In turn, this should mean that the conclusion does not flow from the premises as well as it would if the information were included. Another way of looking at the argument, as it stands, is that there may be an implicit link made between one or more premises and the conclusion and it is this link you are looking for.

The role of the assumption in the argument is the important aspect – and not what its impact seems to be when viewed in isolation. It could be that the conclusion is so specific and the premises so general that the missing information needs to be very specific in order to make the argument work. This may make it seem relatively insignificant when viewed in isolation whereas it, in fact, is a vital piece of information in the context of the flow of the argument. Equally, it could be that the missing piece of information is so significant that it seems to underlie the whole argument and, without it, the argument seems redundant.

An assumption may therefore be, when viewed in isolation, a specific piece of information that seems relatively insignificant or a general statement which seems to underpin the whole argument. In both cases, the omission of this information leads to a weakening of the logical flow of the argument. What is important to remember is the structural impact of the information that these questions test and not the nature of the information itself.

In a similar vein, the missing information could seem obvious to you, such that you too would omit it when arguing the same point. However, as long as the information is required in order to make the conclusion flow from the premises, and as long as it is omitted, then, irrespective of how obvious it is, it is still being assumed.

c) Tackling questions using different wording

There is little difference in the wording of these questions as, in essence, they are all testing the same skill. Currently, two variations tend to dominate:

1 Which of the following is **an underlying assumption** of the argument above?

2 Which of the following is **an assumption on which the argument depends**?

In addition, some of the questions in this book will ask you for the 'main' assumption. This does not vary the task required of you; it simply emphasises the fact that one or more of the other answers may also be assumptions, but that they may not be relevant (or as relevant) to the argument as the correct answer.

This is simply a more explicit method of asking you for the 'underlying' assumption or the assumption on which the argument 'depends'. The difference in wording between the questions does not change what is required of you.

d) Feeling confident about tackling these questions successfully

- **Fully understand the flow of the argument**

Make sure you understand how the various components of the argument fit together. This requires you, firstly, to identify the conclusion of the argument. Then, identify premises which seem to lead to this conclusion. It is unlikely that the premises are completely unrelated to the conclusion or that the conclusion seems random in light of the rest of the argument.

After understanding the premises and the conclusion, you should be left questioning how persuasive the conclusion is in light of the premises that supposedly lead to it. Often, an implicit link is made between one or more premises and the conclusion, in order that the argument can flow. The assumption will be the information that would make this link explicit.

- **Realising the assumption or finding it by testing out each answer**

The more you practise looking for assumptions, the more obvious they should be to you as you read through an argument. The best case scenario is if, after reading an argument, you realise immediately what information is missing in the argument and you are aware of what the argument is assuming in order to work. In the case of the TSA then, all you are left to do is match up the assumption you believe is being made with one of the answers.

However, you should be able to reach the answer even if it isn't immediately apparent, by testing out each of the answers to check whether or not these are assumptions in the argument. Equally, it may be worth eliminating the other answers, even if you have already realised what the assumption in the argument seems to be, in order to confirm your answer.

There are two questions to ask when testing out each answer; in order to help you eliminate it. Firstly, does the argument rely on this information in order to work? Secondly, is this information already stated in the argument?

- **Does the argument rely on this information in order to work?**

This is the crucial question which should help you to eliminate incorrect answers. It is also the reason why it is important to understand the premises on which the conclusion relies, in order to work out the exact meaning of the conclusion itself. For each answer, you should be asking yourself whether it makes any difference to the argument.

Essentially, does inserting this information into the argument mean that the conclusion flows more logically than before? If there is an implicit link between one or more of the premises and the conclusion and you have identified where this is made, then you can test out each answer by inserting it into the place where this link is made, re-reading the argument and then assessing whether or not the link is stronger as a result of this extra information. If you are still left questioning why the conclusion states what it does, even after inserting the answer into the argument, then it is likely that this particular answer is not relied upon by the argument.

- **Is this information already stated in the argument?**

An answer will be incorrect if it has already been stated in the argument. This is another reason as to why it is crucial that you understand all the information provided. If an answer seems to help the argument or is required in order that the conclusion flows from the premises, then this information could be either a genuine assumption or a statement made expressly and relied upon in the argument.

Avoid falling into the trap of simply choosing a premise that already exists in the argument. Also remember that the information in a possible answer may not be stated in those exact terms in the argument. It can be difficult to differentiate between information that has already been stated in the argument and information which could be said to be additional but which is relied upon by the argument and therefore assumed.

If you are faced with this situation and it is not clear whether this is new and unstated information, then hopefully eliminating the other answers will allow you to reach the correct conclusion. Alternatively, perhaps another answer seems to be more definitively unstated and is also relied upon by the argument, in which case you may be able to dismiss this answer and choose the other one instead.

Try this example:

> There has been a huge increase in the number of people playing poker over the last few years with the result that numerous professional poker tournaments are now televised and many websites have been launched on which people can play the game. However, society needs to keep a careful eye on poker since debt is becoming a huge problem and gambling is a sure-fire way for an individual to get into debt.
>
> Which one of the following is an underlying assumption of this argument?
>
> **A**   Playing poker for money may lead to an increase in debt for that player.
>
> **B**   Websites are the only means of playing poker.
>
> **C**   Televising poker leads to an increase in people playing the game.
>
> **D**   Society cannot do anything about gambling or debt.
>
> **E**   Poker involves gambling with money.

The first task when faced with a question asking for the assumption in the argument is to identify the conclusion. The conclusion in this argument is that 'society needs to keep a careful eye on poker'.

This is supported by two main premises in the argument. Firstly, you are told that 'there has been a huge increase in the number of people playing poker' and that this is supported by evidence of televised tournaments and the launch of many websites on which people can play the game. The other main premise is the fact that 'debt is becoming a huge problem and gambling is a sure-fire way for an individual to get into debt'.

So, from the fact that more people are playing poker and the fact that gambling often leads to debt, which is becoming a huge problem, the argument concludes that society needs to keep a careful eye on poker. There is an explicit link made between gambling and debt, which is that the former often leads to the latter. However, there is no link made explicitly between poker and gambling.

What if it is the case that there has been a huge increase in the number of people playing poker, but that they all play for fun without any money? Even more fundamentally, it does not state anywhere that poker even involves gambling with money. The argument relies on this, otherwise the conclusion does not follow; society would not have to keep a careful eye on poker if it did not involve gambling and so would not lead to more debt. Therefore, the argument assumes **E**, that poker involves gambling with money.

A is not an assumption since, as long as you accept that playing poker for money is equivalent to gambling, which it is since there is *some* luck involved, then the argument states this when it says 'gambling is a sure-fire way for an individual to get into debt'. If the answer read: 'playing poker may lead to an increase in debt for that player', then that would be an assumption, but if you are told that there is money involved in playing poker which may lead to debt, then that is essentially stating what is already said in the argument.

B is incorrect since the argument does not rely on the fact that websites are the *only* means of playing poker. It is simply stated that 'there has been a huge increase in the number of people playing poker' which could mean that they play anywhere – at home, in casinos or on websites. The only fact that the argument is concerned with is that poker involves gambling with money and not where or how it is played aside from this.

C is incorrect since, again, the argument does not need to rely on this in order to work. In fact, it is stated explicitly that 'there has been a huge increase in the number of people playing poker' and so the argument does not need to rely on any implicit link between televising poker and an increase in people playing the game. You are told that there has already been an increase. However, it is more the fact that many people are playing the game, (perhaps the case prior to the huge increase) and not the increase itself, which is material for the argument. It follows that, if playing poker may lead to debt and debt is a problem, then any sizeable number of people playing poker, irrespective of recent increases or not, is a problem.

D is incorrect since, if anything, the assumption is that society *can* do something about gambling or debt, otherwise the conclusion that 'society needs to keep a careful eye on poker' may not work. This holds even though society may be able to keep a 'careful eye' on it without being able to do something about it. Even if this is the case, the statement that society cannot do anything about gambling or debt is not relied upon by this argument and would more appropriately belong in a descriptive argument about how society has failed to deal with gambling and debt rather than this argument, which is a normative claim that society *needs* to be careful about gambling and debt.

Checklist

☐ What is the conclusion of the argument?

☐ What information in the premises leads to this conclusion?

☐ What is the missing piece of information that would enable the conclusion to flow from the premises?

☐ Does the argument rely on this information in order to work?

☐ Is this information stated anywhere in the argument?

...and now to spotting errors in an argument....

To recap, we've just gone over how arguments can lack a vital piece of reasoning that means that the conclusion doesn't strictly flow from the premises – and how these missing links are called assumptions.

Now we are going to look at what a flaw is and how you can tackle questions that ask you to identify flaws in an argument. You might find there is some overlap as you read on.

e) Understanding what a flaw is and its role in an argument

We could say that assumptions are flaws in an argument, since they may prevent the premises from fully supporting the conclusion of the argument, but now we are going to look at flaws in arguments rather than assumptions.

Flaws in reasoning often take the form of a missing piece of information or a missing statement.

Think about the whale example again:

> *Whales have bigger brains than humans, therefore, whales are more intelligent than humans.*

First of all, you should realise that the use of the word *therefore* in this argument indicates that the second statement, *whales are more intelligent than humans* is the conclusion of this argument.

What is wrong with this as a logical argument? The assumption in this statement can also be identified as a flaw in the reasoning.

Don't focus on whether or not you agree with what is stated in the passage. Take as correct the statement: *Whales have bigger brains than humans.*

Instead, your analysis should focus on the structure and logic of the argument rather than the trust of its premises.

When you look closely, a piece of information is missing here, which is required for the conclusion to follow from the premise.

To put it baldly, there is something odd about the structure as it stands:

> *Whales have bigger brains than humans, therefore, whales are more intelligent than humans.*

Whales have bigger brains than humans = whales are more intelligent than humans.

Specifically, you should be asking - what it is about the brain size that means that we can jump to a conclusion about intelligence?

Something is assumed in the author's mind as he or she states this argument. This can be identified in this example as an assumption or a flaw.

f) Spotting a flaw in an argument

This category of questions encompasses various different types of question within it. In general, questions that ask you to identify the flaw in the argument focus on any weaknesses in the logical flow of reasoning in the argument.

These weaknesses can manifest themselves in various ways.

The common factor in all these questions seems to be the fact that the conclusion does not flow from the premises in the argument. If this sounds familiar from the explanation and analysis of an assumption - it's no coincidence - since an assumption, based on this explanation of a flaw so far, does fit into this category. And you will find that some questions, which ask you to identify a flaw will, in fact, require you to spot an assumption.

Therefore these questions will require you to identify why the conclusion in the argument may not follow logically from the premises in the argument.

Here are some of the main instances in which this may be the case:

- **Insufficient information in the premises**

This is where the conclusion goes further than the information in the premises in terms of what it states. Essentially, you are looking for whether there is enough information in the argument that supports the conclusion. It may be the case, for example, that the conclusion is too specific, based on what has been said previously. For example, if it is stated in the premises that 'red squirrels are on the verge of extinction and that grey squirrels are rising in number' then this is not enough information to suggest, by way of a conclusion, that 'grey squirrels should therefore be culled'.

- **Generalising from too few examples or premises**

This is another common flaw that arises in an argument. It is very similar to the idea of insufficient information in the premises, in that the conclusion does not seem to be supported by what has been stated elsewhere in the argument. It is sometimes the case that the conclusion is stated as being too definitive or assertive based on the premises, whereas in fact there could be other, more likely, conclusions which better follow from the information.

- **Creating a causal link between unconnected ideas**

This is a common flaw that you may encounter in many arguments, particularly where statistical evidence is used. This is when two independent ideas or reasons are stated in the argument and the conclusion makes an implicit link between them by suggesting there is a relationship between the two. For example, if the premises in an argument are that 'funding for the health system has decreased at the same time as the waiting times for most operations have increased', then it does not necessarily follow, as a conclusion, that 'the decrease in funding has led to an increase in waiting time for most operations'. There is no evidence or explanation offered in the argument that these two premises are linked; it is only the conclusion that states or relies upon a link being made.

- **Semantic flaws**

This is similar to the idea of insufficient information, although the flaw here is that the conclusion either misinterprets the information in the rest of the argument or simply ignores it. Often, certain ideas or words will be defined or explained in the premises. It may be the case that the conclusion does not follow based on this definition or explanation or that the conclusion confuses the information. For example, if an event is described as having two twenty-minute periods of play, then the conclusion is flawed if it relies upon the event having three twenty-five-minute periods of play, for example. It may not always be the case that you are given an explicit definition or explanation of a word or phrase. Instead, you may be asked to judge whether a conclusion follows based on the everyday definition or inherent connotation of a word or phrase. For example, the word 'infinite' denotes that there is no end, so any conclusion that is based or relies on this word meaning something different, perhaps that there is an end, would be flawed.

- **Assumptions**

As stated above, if the argument makes an assumption, then this could be regarded as a flaw, both in general and for the purposes of the TSA. The explanation and advice for the 'Assumption' questions apply equally for these questions.

g) Understanding what questions on flaws test

All these questions, asking you to identify a flaw, test your understanding of the flow of reasoning from the premises to the conclusion. You are required to understand the information presented in both the premises and the conclusion, paying particular attention to the relationship between the premises and any particular definitions or explanations, either explicit or implicit, of crucial words or phrases. As a result, the language used in the argument will be important in identifying the flaw and even single words may create a flaw in the argument, particularly those that have a quantitative impact such as 'never', 'none', 'every' and 'all'.

h) Tackling questions using different wording

Unfortunately, the wording of these questions does not reveal the type of flaw that you are asked to identify and, in fact, there is little substantive difference between the variations in wording of these questions. Here are some of the possible questions you could be asked:

1   Which of the following is the **main flaw** in the above argument?

2   Which of the following is the **best statement of the flaw** in the above argument?

3   Which of the following is the **best expression of the flaw** in the above argument?

4   Which of the following **best explains a flaw** in the above argument?

5   The argument is flawed. Which of the following **identifies an error in its reasoning**?

Most of the variations capture the idea of identifying the 'main' or 'best' expression or statement of the flaw. There may possibly be more than one problem with the argument, and, if so, this is just a reminder that you are asked to choose the major flaw.

i) Feeling confident about tackling these questions successfully

• Fully understand the reasoning of the argument

It is crucial, as with most critical thinking questions, but especially here, that you fully understand what is being said in the argument. This requires you to understand the information in the premises, including any specific details, for example, statistics or short words with strong implications, and the exact meaning of the conclusion. Naturally, in order to do this, you should be able to identify the conclusion and the premises leading to this conclusion so that you can follow the flow of reasoning in the argument.

• Pay attention to the language used

Any subtleties with the language may be important and so it is vital that you do not miss any words or concepts that affect the meaning of the information or, significantly, how any of the information may link together. As stated, any words that may have quantitative implications, either in the premises or the conclusion, are worth paying attention to, since they could change significantly whether the conclusion flows from the premises. In addition, any words that signify a relationship between ideas should be identified, especially for those flawed questions that create a causal relationship between two independent and unrelated ideas.

- **Understand any definitions of words or concepts**

This is especially relevant in those flawed questions where there is some confusion or misinterpretation of semantics in the argument. Firstly, check whether a definition or explanation is relevant for the reasoning in the argument. Where an explicit definition or explanation is offered, make a note of this and ensure that if the word or phrase is used again, that the same definition or explanation is used or relied upon, particular if it is used in the conclusion. Also, since the definition or explanation does not have to be explicit, ensure that, if any particular words or concepts are used in the reasoning of the argument without a clear definition, that you understand what that word or concept means. More importantly, ensure that it is used with the same meaning if it is used again in the argument.

Try these examples:

Example 1

I encourage my children to practise their musical instruments at least three times a week for a minimum of half an hour each time. They all play their instruments well and play professionally in an orchestra. At the last concert, however, the conductor informed me that my son, who plays the clarinet, did not play well and that if he did not improve he would be asked to leave the orchestra. It must be the case, therefore, that my son did not practise enough before the concert.

Which of the following is the best statement of the flaw in this argument?

A   Practising for three times a week for a minimum of half an hour each time does not constitute 'enough practice'.

B   It assumes that the conductor is able to ask my son to leave the orchestra.

C   Just because they play their instruments well, this does not mean that my children do not ever play badly.

D   There may be another explanation as to why my son did not play well in the last concert.

E   Encouraging my children to practise does not necessarily mean that they will practise.

In this argument, the conclusion is fairly straightforward to identify, which is 'it must be the case, therefore, that my son did not practise enough before the concert'. The reasoning leading up to this conclusion is that, despite encouraging the children to practise their instruments and despite the fact that they play their instruments well and play professionally in an orchestra, at the last concert the conductor informed the author that the son did not play well and would be asked to leave if he did not improve. You should be asking yourself, 'from this reasoning, does it follow that it must be the case that the son did not practise enough before the concert?' In fact, the main premise in the reasoning is that the son did not play well which leads to the conclusion that therefore it must be the case that he did not practise enough. There is not enough information in the argument to suggest any reason as to why the son did not play well and so there is, by implication, not enough information to suggest that it is because he did not practise enough. Therefore, **D**, that 'there may be another explanation as to why the son did not play well in the last concert,' is the best statement of the flaw in this argument. The flaw here is that the conclusion has no support in the rest of the argument and so does not logically flow based on the information in the premises.

A is not a flaw and is moving into the realms of criticising the accuracy of the information in the argument as opposed to the flow of the reasoning. We cannot deduce from the passage that three times a week for a minimum of half an hour does not constitute (enough practice). In fact, if we assume that the children do what the author tells them, then this is enough to make them play well.

B is not a flaw for two main reasons. Firstly, the assumption, even if true, is not relied upon by the argument. The argument is concerned with explaining why the son did not play well and not about whether he will be asked to leave or by whom. Secondly, even if this were relevant, this assumption does not need to be made since all that is stated is that if he did not improve 'he would be asked to leave the orchestra'. It does not state by whom he would be asked, just that he would be. Irrespective of whether the conductor is able to ask the son to leave, the argument still works and so, if the issue of him being asked to leave were relevant in the argument, the argument would still work without this assumption. Since it is not needed in the argument, it can't really be a flaw in the argument.

C is not a flaw since there is no suggestion that the children do not ever play badly. In fact, the conclusion is an explanation for why the son *has* played badly.

E is incorrect and is not a flaw since, whether this is true or not, it doesn't affect the reasoning in the argument. The crux of the issue here is whether there is

2. Identifying assumptions and spotting flaws in arguments

enough information to conclude that the reason the son did not play well was because he did not get enough practice. If the children do, or do not, actually practise as much as the author encourages them to do so, this does not affect whether the conclusion follows from the premise here. There still could be other explanations as to why he played badly.

Example 2

Most people have been through the experience of leaving their freezer door open with the result that the food inside thaws out completely. The general advice is not to eat any food that is subsequently frozen again. However, some people ignore this advice and eat this food anyway. Research has found that, people that have, at some point, eaten this food again have suffered from food poisoning more than twenty times during their life. The lesson is clear – if you want to avoid food poisoning, do not eat any food that has been re-frozen after thawing out.

Which of the following is the best statement of the flaw in the argument above?

A   There is no explanation provided as to why eating food that has been re-frozen after thawing out will cause food poisoning.

B   The situation of having all of one's food thawed out is one that most people will not experience.

C   Food poisoning may not necessarily result from eating food that has been re-frozen after thawing out.

D   No source is provided for the general advice.

E   People ignore the general advice given about eating food that has been re-frozen after thawing out.

The conclusion of this argument is that 'if you want to avoid food poisoning, do not eat any food that has been re-frozen after thawing out'. This is based on the research that 'people that have, at some point, eaten this food again have suffered from food poisoning more than twenty times during their life'. You should realise that the rest of the argument is not really that relevant and the flow of reasoning that you are interested in is the link between this premise and the conclusion. Specifically, you should be asking yourself 'does that fact that people who have, at some point, eaten this food cause them to have suffered from food poisoning more than twenty times during their life?' All that you are presented with is one statistic relating to a group of people but you are not informed of any link between the behaviour of this group of people and the statistic. The flaw arises, therefore, due to the fact that the conclusion makes a causal link between the behaviour of this group of people and the statistic and implies that eating this food caused these people to have food poisoning more than twenty times in their life. This causal link is unsupported by the information in the argument and accordingly it is not possible to conclude that food poisoning necessarily results from eating food that has been re-frozen after thawing out. Therefore, **C** is the correct answer.

A is incorrect since it is not a flaw that no explanation is provided. This may make the argument less persuasive but, when assessing the logic of an argument, you should assume that the information provided is true and does not require further explanation.

B is incorrect since you are told in the first sentence that 'most people have been through the experience of leaving their freezer door open with the result that the food inside thaws out completely'. Therefore, the situation of having all of one's food thawed out is one that most people *have* experienced according to the argument.

D is incorrect since, as with **A**, this contributes only to the persuasiveness of the argument and, the fact that no source is provided, does not affect the flow of reasoning in the argument and is, therefore, not a flaw.

E is incorrect and is not a flaw since all this statement is doing is repeating what has already been stated in the argument. You are told that 'some people ignore this advice and eat this food anyway'.

Example 3

Hotstuff FC, a talented Frisbee team, is doing well this season. In their league consisting of twenty teams, the teams in the bottom half of the league at the end of the season are automatically relegated into the league below. Even though Hotstuff has already secured enough points to finish the season within the top five teams in the league, the manager of Hotstuff is worried by its recent lack of form, especially after losing its star player, Heraldo, to injury. Therefore, extra training sessions have been arranged to improve performance in order that Hotstuff do not get relegated.

Which of the following is the best statement of the flaw in the above argument?

A   There cannot be a recent lack of form if Hotstuff will finish the season within the top five teams in the league.

B   There is a possibility that Hotstuff may still be relegated.

C   Relegation is not as bad a prospect as people think.

D   There is no chance of Hotstuff being relegated.

E   A causal link is created between losing Heraldo to injury and getting relegated.

The inherent flaw in this argument should be evident on first reading but, if not, you should be persuaded by one of the answers even without eliminating the others. The argument here consists of various premises and a final conclusion. You are told initially that in the league of twenty teams, the teams in the bottom half of the league will automatically be relegated at the end of the season. It is then stated that Hotstuff has already secured enough points to finish the season in the top five teams in the league. At this point, you should realise that, therefore, there is no chance that Hotstuff can be relegated since it will be in the top half of the league at the end of the season. However, the argument continues by stating that the manager is worried about the recent lack of form and then, "*in order that Hotstuff do not get relegated*", extra training sessions have been arranged to improve performance. Here, the conclusion that extra training sessions have been arranged relies on the reasoning of preventing Hotstuff from being relegated. However, the rest of the argument tells you that there is no chance of Hotstuff being relegated and so this conclusion does not flow from the reasoning and is flawed. **D** is the correct answer.

A is incorrect since, although it may seem persuasive, you must assume that the information in the argument is true and so, even if Hotstuff will finish the season within the top five teams, if you are told that there has been a recent lack of form, which is clear in the argument, then you must assume that this is true. **A** cannot be a flaw if it is untrue.

B is incorrect since there is no information in the argument to suggest that Hotstuff may still be relegated. The only information that is stated leads logically to the conclusion that Hotstuff will not be relegated. In any case, **B** would not seem to be a flaw since it actually supports the argument as it stands since, if there is still a chance that Hotstuff may get relegated, then the conclusion that they should arrange extra training sessions in order to improve performance and avoid relegation may logically follow (on the assumption that training improves performance and better performance will avoid relegation).

C is incorrect since it is irrelevant. The argument is not persuading the reader that relegation is a terrible prospect; irrespective of how bad it is, the argument is concerned with whether or not Hotstuff will avoid relegation. Also, this answer seems more directed at the substance of the argument as opposed the flow of reasoning, the latter of which should be your concern when identifying a flaw.

E may seem more like a criticism of the logic in the argument and, indeed, creating a causal link where there is none is often evidence of a flawed argument. However, it is not correct in this question since it is not clear that a causal link has been created. All you are told is that the manager is worried by the recent lack of form, especially after losing Heraldo to injury, and that extra training sessions have been arranged in order to improve performance and avoid relegation. There is no link that losing Heraldo *will* lead to relegation. The word 'especially' may imply that the manager would still be worried even if Heraldo was not injured. In any case, even if you conclude that a causal link has been created, this is not the flaw in the argument, since, as it stands, this causal link wouldn't flow from the rest of the argument. There cannot be a causal link between one idea and another, the latter of which, relegation, is not possible. The flaw is in the possibility of relegation itself and not in any link between relegation and any other factor.

Checklist

☐ What is the reasoning in the argument?

☐ Is there sufficient information to support the conclusion?

☐ Are any causal connections made in the argument?

☐ Are any definitions or explanations relevant in the reasoning?

☐ Are any assumptions made in the argument?

---

3. Parallel reasoning: identifying an argument with a similar structure to another

Or...extracting a principle that emerges from the structure of an argument.

By the end of this chapter you should be able to:

a) **Understand what parallel reasoning is**
b) **Understand what parallel reasoning questions test**
c) **Tackle questions using different wording**
d) **Feel confident on your method of tackling these questions**

a) Understanding what parallel reasoning is

These questions can broadly be separated into two categories:

- those that require you to identify an argument which has the same structure or parallel reasoning as the argument in the question.

- those that require you to choose an argument which illustrates the same principle as that in the argument in the question.

These questions may look slightly different to other critical thinking questions since the arguments in these questions are sometimes slightly shorter and the answers slightly longer. There is one factor which may mean that these questions take slightly longer to answer than others, which is that you usually need to read each answer before deciding which is correct.

b) Understanding what parallel reasoning questions test

These questions differ slightly from the other critical thinking questions, which are concerned with the logical flow of reasoning in the argument. Here, you are not so much analysing the flow of reasoning, although this is still inherently the case, but you are looking at the structure of the argument and how the various components of the argument fit together.

With questions that involve identifying a similar structure or parallel reasoning, you are looking at aspects in the argument, such as the number of reasons (sometimes conditions), any relationships between ideas and the direction of these ideas, i.e. are they positive or negative or increases or decreases.

The skill is to break down the components of the argument and then read each answer, assessing whether or not it contains those same components.

There are, thus, two skills at work:

- The first is discerning the various components of the argument and understanding each of them individually.

- The second is looking at each of the answers provided and matching those components to each of those in the answers. This needs to be done in order to decide which of them has the same structure or reasoning as the argument in the question.

The questions requiring you to identify a principle from the argument test similar skills, notably, your ability to understand the relationships between certain ideas in the argument and how each idea relates to the next (and it is for this reason, incidentally, that they appear in the same category in this book). From this, you should be able to extract a principle, that is to say, a generic argument that does not involve specific ideas, but instead involves certain general statements that link together and lead to a conclusion. This principle should, essentially, be a summary of the argument in the question but without reference to the specific subject of that argument. From this, as you read the answers provided, you should be able to identify another argument (with its own subject) that, when summarised or expressed in terms of a principle, would be similar to the argument in the question.

Language, which comes as no surprise, is important in answering these questions. Conjunctions, especially, can be powerful in terms of recognising the structure of these questions, since they distinguish ideas and can control the relationship between two or more ideas. Take the following examples of statements:

1. *I have a pet dog and therefore I go for daily walks.*
2. *I have a pet dog and I go for daily walks.*
3. *I have a pet dog because I go for daily walks.*
4. *I go for daily walks and therefore I have a pet dog.*
5. *I go for daily walks despite having a pet dog.*

If you can recognise the difference between these statements then this will help considerably in your understanding of the relationship between certain ideas.

It can be extremely helpful to express the argument in terms of an algebraic expression. This can help to orientate you to the correct answer as algebra can identify both whether a premise or statement is positive and its relationship with the other premises or statements in order to reach the correct conclusion.

Here are the five statements above, translated into algebraic expressions:

1. *I have a pet dog and therefore I go for daily walks.*

   $A \longrightarrow B$

2. *I have a pet dog and I go for daily walks.*

   $A \ + \ B$

3. *I have a pet dog because I go for daily walks.*

   $A \longleftarrow B$

4. *I go for daily walks and therefore I have a pet dog.*

   $B \longrightarrow A$

5. *I go for daily walks despite having a pet dog.*

   $B \ / \ A$

c) Tackling questions using different wording

There are two different types of question in this category (although the skills required to answer them are fairly similar). Here are the possible questions you can be asked:

1. Which of the following **most closely parallels** the reasoning used in the argument above?

2. Which of the following arguments **has the same structure as** the argument above?

3. Which of the following **illustrates the principle** that the author argues for in the above passage?

4. Which of the following statements **is an application of the principle** underlying the argument in the passage?

5. Which of the following **best illustrates the principle** underlying the argument above?

Whether the question asks which of the answers 'most closely parallels' the reasoning or has the 'same structure' as the argument in the question, you are being asked to perform the same task. The addition of 'most closely' in the question merely implies that the reasoning may not be exactly the same, but there will certainly be one answer that is closer to the argument in the question, in terms of its structure, than the others.

As for the questions requiring you to identify the answer which illustrates or demonstrates an application of the principle from the argument in the question, there is little difference, again, between the wording of the questions. The use of the word 'best' implies, as with 'most closely', that the principle to be extracted from the correct answer may not be exactly the same as that extracted from the argument in the question. However, it will certainly be very similar and, in any case, more similar than the other answers.

d) Feeling confident on your method of tackling these questions

- **Separate out the various components of the argument**

Understanding the various components or elements of the argument is crucial in answering these questions. As with all critical thinking questions, finding the conclusion is a good start, although it is not always the best place to start with these questions. Equally, you should find the various premises that lead to the conclusion. However, you may have to go further than this initial separation since premises can sometimes be made up of more than one idea and these questions require you to break down the argument into all of its constituent parts. Therefore, if it seems that a premise can be broken down further into two different parts, then do so.

The risk of oversimplifying the argument is that you may miss a structural nuance that proves determinative. One method of separating out the various components of the argument is to identify relevant nouns and verbs in the passage. It may be the case, although not always, that each component contains just one noun and/or verb. Another method is to spot conjunctions since they are often used to separate clauses in a sentence. Different clauses will generally be different components, although there may be more than one component in the same clause. Punctuation can also be helpful in separating out different components, especially where a clause is followed by a subordinate clause or where there are lists of conditions or premises.

- **Number of components**

The number of components may be relevant in some questions, for example, where there are conditions required for an outcome but not all of them are satisfied. It is worth, therefore, keeping count of the number of components in the argument. This is especially the case where there are proper nouns or lists of ideas.

- **Relationship between components and the direction of the relationship**

The relationship between the components is a crucial aspect of understanding these questions and will often be a factor in eliminating the incorrect answers. The components will not generally be listed without any indication of how they relate to each other. You should ensure that you understand how the components are linked in order that you can find the same link in the answers provided.

The direction of these relationships is also crucial. 'Direction' refers to the specific relationship between two ideas and how they affect each other. It is especially relevant where there is some quantitative aspect involved. So, for example, if red squirrels are affected by the number of grey squirrels in the same area, then a causal relationship has already been established. If the number of red squirrels decreases as the number of grey squirrels increases, then, not only is there a causal relationship, there is also a direction to this relationship and we know *how* one affects the other and not only that it does, in fact, affect the other.

Even if there is no quantitative relationship, knowing how one factor affects another is still important. For example, two ideas can be related because both of them may be required in order for a certain outcome to occur. However, they could also be related since, despite one of them not existing, the outcome could still occur. Or, it could be that the outcome can occur only if neither of them exists. Understanding how components fit together, therefore, is vital in understanding these questions.

Often, certain words, especially conjunctions, will assist you in spotting relationships and determining the direction of the relationship. Some familiarity with the usage of words such as 'despite', 'although' and 'whereas' will help. Look for these sorts of words and assess the effect they have on the components around them.

- **Generalise each component**

This refers to the practice of turning each statement, which will often contain a certain noun or verb, into a statement that generalises the subject-specific statement. For example, I can generalise the statement 'we should prevent overspending on presents at Christmas time since most people don't receive what they want' by stating that 'we should prevent something if it does not efficiently allocate resources'. By generalising statements such as this, questions, especially those in which a principle needs to be extracted, become easier to approach and you will find that, with a generalised statement of the argument in the question, it is quicker to assess each of the possible answers.

- **Narrow down the answers**

These questions often require you to go through each possible answer provided, as opposed to knowing the correct answer immediately. Therefore it may be worth narrowing down the answers by eliminating those that clearly don't have the same structure or illustrate the same principle and then focusing on the remaining two or three in more detail.

- **How specific does the structure need to be?**

This is actually quite a difficult question and you may ask yourself this after attempting a few practice questions. For example, if increasing one component leads to an increase in another component thereby resulting in an outcome, does the answer with the same structure need only a similar outcome, or does an outcome and two components, or does it need the increase in one component leading to an increase in another component thereby resulting in an outcome? The final option is most similar in terms of structure, but not all correct answers will be exactly the same. However, in terms of your approach to identifying the structure, it is worth extracting all of the detail from the argument in the question so that you have the exact relationships and directions of the components. If the correct answer turns out to be less detailed then this, then it may mean that you eliminate this, and all the other answers, on first reading.

- **Write down the structure in simple terms**

This is definitely a recommended practical approach to these questions. If you can write down the structure in note form, perhaps using algebraic methods, then you should find it easier to match up each of the answers with your simple structure. For example, if the argument is that 'Tim is better than Tom but not better than Tanya'. You could simplify this and write down that 'X better than Y. Z better than X and Y'. If you then allocate similar letters to the components in each of the answers, then you will have a simpler and more exact method of matching up the structures of the various arguments.

Try these examples:

Example 1

If Bobby puts his tooth under his pillow, then he will find one pound under it when he wakes up. Tonight, Bobby has put his tooth under his pillow, so he will wake up tomorrow with one pound under it.

Which of the following most closely parallels the reasoning used in the argument above?

A   Tim has a decision to make regarding his offer of a job abroad. If he accepts it, then he will be in line for a significant pay rise. After much deliberation, Tim did accept the job and now earns three times what he did previously.

B   I may no longer be scared of heights if I walk up the tower. I have just reached the top of the tower so that may mean that I am no longer scared of heights.

C   If my father can persuade my mother to come to dinner, then we can talk about the holiday. We do want to talk about the holiday, so my father will persuade her to come.

D   If I had the courage to face my teacher and tell her she spelt my name incorrectly, then I would. However, I don't feel ready for any confrontation, so I will just leave things as they are.

E   If Dominic wants a football trial with the team, then he will have to train well. He has trained well, so he will get a trial with the team.

The first task is to break down the argument in the question into its constituent parts. There seems to be a natural separation in this argument as evidenced by the punctuation used. Also, the common 'if/then' sentences naturally split into two parts. So there seem to be four parts here:

1.   If Bobby puts his tooth under his pillow
2.   Then he will find one pound under it when he wakes up
3.   Tonight, Bobby has put his tooth under his pillow
4.   So he will wake up tomorrow with one pound under it

The fact that these components don't make sense as stand-alone sentences is not fatal to the exercise at all (indeed subordinate clauses necessarily depend on or relate to main clauses). The next task is to generalise these statements and simplify them, perhaps using letters to represent the various noun or verb phrases:

1. If Bobby does X
2. Then Y will happen
3. Bobby has done X
4. Therefore, Y will happen

This simplified structure should now help in eliminating the wrong answers and finding the answer that has this same structure. One thing to note is that the pronouns or proper nouns used are not relevant in the sense that the same structure will not necessarily have to be written in the first person or third person. Ensure that if the argument in the question is written using the pronoun 'I', that you don't choose an answer based only on the fact that it uses the same pronoun.

By generalising and simplifying the five answers, you should find that they have the following structures:

A
1. If Tim does X
2. Then Y will occur
3. He does X
4. Therefore, Y will occur

B
1. I may be X
2. If I do Y
3. I do Y
4. Therefore, I may be X

C
1. If my father can do X
2. Then we can do Y
3. We want Y
4. Therefore, he will do X

D
1. If I had X
2. Then I would do Y
3. I don't have X
4. Therefore, I won't do Y

E
1. If Dominic wants X
2. He must do Y
3. He has done Y
4. Therefore, he will have X

There may be slight variations in these structures depending on whether you include the pronouns or proper nouns in each argument and depending on what letters you choose to represent your ideas. But, as long as there is consistency and you are able to do this well, the answer should become a lot clearer. In this case, the answer is **A**. The key elements are the ideas that 'if X is done, then Y will occur' and then, 'X is done, therefore, Y will occur'. The structure of each argument should be enough to rule out the other answers, but here is a brief explanation as to why the other answers differ. There may also be other reasons why they differ which you have identified.

B and **C** are incorrect since the second half of the arguments are reversed when compared with the argument in the question, as can be seen by their simplified structures above.

D is incorrect since the second half of the argument is negative in the sense that something does *not* occur. In the argument in the question it *does* occur.

E is incorrect since the second half of the argument is reversed when compared to the argument in the question.

Example 2

Many long-distance runners push themselves extremely hard when they train in order to increase their stamina. However, pushing themselves too far is the most common cause of injury which prevents them from training at all, often for long periods at a time. When they return from injury, their stamina is much lower and it takes a while to return to decent levels. Therefore, in the long-run, their stamina levels would benefit from training at a lower, steadier rate.

Which of the following best illustrates the principle underlying the argument above?

A   There is more chance of something going wrong if I host a dinner party for ten people instead of six, but I want to see as many people as possible so I will invite them all.

B   It has been a difficult year for panda breeding at the zoo. We are trying new techniques, however, and, despite the fact that these techniques may cause them distress since we spend a lot of time encouraging them to breed, we believe it will lead to more breeding over time.

C   I could wait twenty minutes for the next train and, in the meantime, relax and have a hot drink. Or, I could sprint for the train in five minutes which will make me tired and annoyed. I'm going to choose the latter option because it will mean I reach my destination earlier and in more comfort.

D   I will remember more for my forthcoming exam if I begin revision now rather than waiting until a week before the exam and then panic revising.

E   If I accept the new job, then it will mean that I can save up enough money to go travelling, which is something I've always wanted to do.

The argument here is that pushing themselves too hard does not help long-distance runners in the long-run and it is better, for their stamina levels, to train at a lower, steadier rate. In order to find the principle underlying this argument, the argument should be generalised, either by going through each component step-by-step or by generalising the point of the argument. The principle seems to be that it is more beneficial in the long-run to do something at a lower, steadier level than to try too hard to do it at a higher level.

A seems to suggest that there may be a risk if I attempt something more difficult but that I will do it anyway in order to achieve the benefit that it brings about. This principle here does not seem to acknowledge the idea that it would be more beneficial overall to take the less risky option and so the principle is missing something that is evident in the principle underlying the argument in the question.

B is incorrect since it seems to be the antithesis of the principle as it suggests that it is more beneficial to do something at a higher, riskier rate in the long-run.

C, too, seems to suggest that it is more beneficial to do something at a higher level and so is incorrect.

The principle in **D** seems to be that it will be more beneficial (because I will remember more) if I do something at a steadier level (begin revision now) rather than try too hard to do it at a higher level (panic revise). Although the principle to be extracted from this answer may not be exactly the same as that from the argument in the question, it is certainly similar here and so, out of the five answers, this best illustrates the principle underlying the argument in the question.

E recognises only that there are benefits to be achieved in the long-run by doing something at a certain level and lacks the idea that this is better than trying too hard to perform at a higher level.

Checklist

☐ What are the various components of the argument in the question?

☐ What are the relationships and direction of the relationships between the components?

☐ Are there any significant words that tell you about the relationships?

☐ Do you have enough information to support your conclusion?

☐ Have you generalised the components into generic statements?

---

4. Weakening and strengthening arguments

Identifying which statement weakens or strengthens the existing argument.

By the end of this chapter you should be able to:

a) Understand what is meant by weakening and strengthening an argument

b) Understand what questions on weakening and strengthening an argument are testing

c) Tackle questions using different wording

d) Feel confident on your method of tackling these questions

a) **Understanding what is meant by weakening and strengthening an argument**

These questions ask you to identify which of the answers provided would most weaken or strengthen the argument in the question. You are asked to assume that the content of each statement is true so that the effect on the argument does not depend on whether you think any answer may or may not be true. Instead, after assuming the statement to be true, the question asks you to assess the impact on the overall argument.

Usually the answers will be facts, rather than opinions or arguments in themselves. The fact may affect an existing premise, but more likely it will add something new to the argument and you are asked to assess the impact of this new information on the argument, particularly the conclusion.

There are two types of question in this category: those where you are asked to find the answer that most weakens the argument and those where you are asked to find the answer that most strengthens the argument. In other words, for the 'weaken' questions, you are looking for the answer that makes the reasoning in the argument flow less well in the sense that, after adding the new information, the conclusion will have weaker support from the rest of the argument. Conversely, for the 'strengthen' questions, the correct answer is the one that makes the reasoning in the argument flow better so that, after adding the new information, the conclusion will have better support from the rest of the argument than previously.

The questions in this category should require you to identify the answer that *most* weakens or *most* strengthens the argument, although it may be the case that the word 'most' is omitted. If the question does ask for the answer that weakens or strengthens the argument the most, then you are required not only to find the answer that does have this impact on the argument but also to assess the extent to which each answer affects the argument comparatively. Therefore, there may be more than one answer which affects the argument in the same way (and there often is), and you are required to assess the extent to which these answers affect it.

With these questions, it is often tricky to find an answer immediately following your reading of the argument. Instead, each answer may need to be assessed in turn in order to work out its impact on the argument.

Finally, it is worth noting that there seem to be more questions on the TSA that ask you to identify which answer most weakens the argument as opposed to which answer most strengthens the argument.

b) Understanding what questions on weakening and strengthening an argument are testing

These questions test your ability to understand the argument in the question, particularly the information in the premises and the conclusion, and then to assess the impact on the argument of additional information. You need to understand the argument first of all. This requires you to digest all the information that leads to the conclusion, which will often involve discerning which information in the argument is material in support of the conclusion, and which is not.

Understanding the conclusion is crucial in these questions since the conclusion will tell you what exactly is being argued. A good way of answering these questions is to test out each answer against the conclusion in order to understand its impact on the argument as a whole.

Importantly, ensure that you identify the 'direction' of the conclusion. For example, if it is a normative claim of some sort, ensure that you know whether it is a claim to do something or a claim not to do something. In addition, the conclusion and, by implication, the effect of new information may be affected by quantifying words such as 'never', 'always', 'all' and 'none', so ensure that you notice and take into account their presence.

These questions require you to test out each answer on the conclusion in order to assess its impact on the argument. This testing process will become more natural and easier with practice but, essentially, you need to take each statement and ask yourself, 'if this is true, does the conclusion seem to follow more or less logically now that I've added it into the argument?' You may find that the statement doesn't really affect the argument at all, perhaps because it is not relevant. On this point, ensure that you understand the specific conclusion since a statement may seem to be relevant to the general subject area of the argument but may not be as relevant to the precise terms of the argument put forward in the question.

c) Tackling questions using different wording

For these questions, there is almost no difference in wording except for the obvious distinction between asking which answers most weaken and which answers most strengthen. These are the two possible variations which are likely to arise:

1   Which of the following, if true, would **most weaken** the above argument?

2   Which of the following, if true, would **most strengthen** the above argument?

The word 'most' may be excluded and so you are required only to find the statement which weakens or strengthens the argument. This seems to imply that only one answer will weaken and the others will all strengthen or have no effect on the argument, or vice versa. This would make the question easier and so it is more likely that you will be required to assess the extent, as well as the nature of the impact on the argument, of each answer.

d) Feeling confident on your method of tackling these questions

* **Understand the conclusion and the premises**

As emphasised above, understanding the conclusion is crucial for these questions. The conclusion is the backbone of the argument and tells you of what the argument is trying to persuade the reader. Therefore, go about finding the conclusion in the usual way and, if possible, try to find an explicit statement of it in the argument. By seeing the words, as opposed to just remembering some conception of the conclusion, you should find it easier to test out each answer against it.

Understanding the information in the premises will help you in various ways, although it is not as crucial a task as identifying and understanding the conclusion. Firstly, it will enable you to identify the conclusion more easily, especially if you are struggling to do so. The premises should at least tell you what the argument seems to be saying and you should find, after reading the premises, that you can make a reasoned judgment of what the conclusion may say. Importantly, you should be able to glean, from reading the premises, the direction of the conclusion.

For example, if the premises for an argument are that *my child is a brilliant gymnast* and *I want her to compete on the world stage*, a conclusion stating *therefore I will push her to get a place in the Olympic team* is far more likely than a conclusion stating *therefore I will resist pushing her to get a place in the Olympic team*.

Secondly, by reading the premises, you may be better able to assess the weight or the extent of the impact of the new information you are testing. If the argument as it stands contains some premises, which do not seem to flow that strongly to the conclusion, then an answer which provides additional reasons leading to the conclusion may have a significant impact on the argument compared to an argument where the existing premises already lead strongly to the conclusion. Thirdly, the nature of the existing premises may help you in deciding the impact of the new information. For example, if the premises of an argument currently consist of opinions and the argument would benefit considerably from some form of statistic or other type of evidence to substantiate such opinions, then an answer that contains this form of information may have a greater impact on the argument than simply another opinion. So, whilst finding the conclusion and using this to test out each answer is crucial, understanding the premises of the argument may help this task.

- **What should the correct answer do to the argument?**

Before you begin to look at each answer, ensure that you are clear what you are looking for. This requires you, firstly, to understand the question: are you being asked to find a statement that would make the argument weaker or stronger? Secondly, after understanding the question, ensure that you know what the correct answer should be doing to the argument. So, for example, if you are being asked to find a statement that most weakens the argument and the conclusion of this argument is that *I should push my child to get a place in the Olympic team*, then the correct answer will be a statement that would weaken the support for this statement to the greatest extent. In other words, it would make the argument point towards a conclusion that I shouldn't push my child to get a place in the Olympic team.

- **Think about missing information that would weaken or strengthen the conclusion**

After reading the argument, it may be worth briefly thinking of the type and the content of information that would weaken or strengthen the conclusion depending on what you are being asked to do. Make sure that you do not spend too long thinking about this!

- **Assume the information is true**

The question should state 'which of the following, if true,…' and so you should assume that the information in each of the answers is true. Do not test out each answer on the conclusion with your interpretation of whether the information is true or not – assume that it is.

- **Assessing the impact of each answer**

The main task here is to take each answer and test it on the conclusion and evaluate the extent to which it affects the argument. The first task is to decide whether the answer weakens or strengthens the conclusion before you assess the extent to which it does. This will allow you, hopefully, to eliminate one or more answers. This first task should be relatively straightforward and it should not be difficult, as long you understand the conclusion, to determine the initial impact on the direction of the conclusion

It could perhaps be the case that you cannot tell whether the answer has any impact on the conclusion. This may be because the information is irrelevant to the conclusion. In this case, it is unlikely that this information will *most* weaken or strengthen the argument and you should be able to eliminate it as long as you ensure, by comparison with the other possible answers, that this is the case.

Another possible scenario is that the information could both weaken and strengthen the argument because it is too vague and could be interpreted both ways. In this case, make sure that it can be interpreted both ways and then eliminate it. If it is not certain whether this information would weaken or strengthen the argument, then it is highly unlikely that it could *most* weaken or strengthen the argument. In both of these cases, and if you eliminate answers generally, you should verify the remaining answer before concluding that it must be the correct one. If you find that there is any doubt, you may have to re-visit those answers that you eliminated to ensure that your initial analysis was correct.

The second task is to analyse the extent to which the answers weaken or strengthen the conclusion. If there are any incorrect answers due to the fact that they weaken the argument when you are asked to find an answer that strengthens it, or vice versa, then you should have eliminated these. So, from the answers that do impact the argument in the same way, you need to assess the extent to which they do so. This process is difficult to articulate but it will essentially involve you applying each of the answers to the argument and thinking whether the conclusion follows more or less logically as a result. This process should lead you to the correct answer as long as you have understood the information in each answer and the terms of the argument in the question.

- **Is the conclusion impossible or more difficult as a result?**

One useful tip for the 'weaken' questions is to ask whether the conclusion is simply not possible, or more difficult to reach, as a result of the additional information. This may be the case and that answer is likely to be the correct one. For example, if a simple argument is that 'the shop is only open for another 10 minutes so I should go there now to buy my groceries' and the additional information is that 'it takes 20 minutes for me to reach the shop', then the argument is destroyed because it is impossible for me to buy my groceries.

Try these examples:

Example 1

Hay fever sufferers tend to experience a blocked nose, watering eyes and sneezing as symptoms. Taking an anti-histamine tablet rarely seems to alleviate all of the symptoms and sufferers generally have to turn to nasal sprays and eye drops in order to be free of all symptoms. However, all three of these medications contain a chemical that causes drowsiness and so, when all three are taken together, this side-effect increases three-fold. It is time the pharmaceutical industry produced a drug that alleviates all three of these symptoms without this combined side-effect.

Which of the following, if true, would most weaken the above argument?

A   Many people find it difficult to swallow a tablet.

B   The number of people suffering from hay fever has fallen since the year 2000.

C   A drug that would alleviate all symptoms of hay fever would contain treble the amount of the chemical that causes drowsiness as the current medication available.

D   Drowsiness has long been the main reason for car accidents in this country.

E   Some hay fever sufferers experience other symptoms such as a loss of appetite and skin problems as well as the usual symptoms.

The first task in this question is to understand the argument and, most importantly, the conclusion. The premises seem to be that hay fever sufferers have to use three different medications in order to alleviate all their symptoms but that, since they all contain a chemical that causes drowsiness, when all three are taken together this effect is trebled. Therefore, the conclusion states the pharmaceutical industry should produce a drug that alleviates all three of these symptoms without this three-fold side-effect.

You are asked to find the answer that most weakens the argument and so you are looking for an answer that, when added to the argument, would provide least support to the conclusion. For this argument, then, the correct answer will suggest that perhaps the pharmaceutical industry shouldn't produce a tablet that alleviates all three of these symptoms without this combined side-effect or that it is difficult to do so.

Firstly, go through the answers and try to eliminate those that do not weaken the argument or are irrelevant to the argument. If the conclusion is that a drug should be produced then **A** does seem relevant and may weaken the argument since some people may not be able physically to take this drug (if it is in tablet form). If the number of people suffering from these symptoms and the side-effect has fallen then perhaps this too may weaken the claim for the pharmaceutical industry to respond so **B** is relevant. **C** is relevant and may weaken the argument since it seems it may not be possible for the pharmaceutical industry to respond in any meaningful way. **D**, if true, seems to strengthen the argument since it would allow hay fever sufferers to experience less drowsiness and may help to reduce the number of car accidents, so **D** can be eliminated. **E** does not seem relevant to the argument since it concerns other symptoms of hay fever, whereas the conclusion relates to a particular side-effect of the current medication. **E** doesn't seem to weaken the argument and so can be eliminated.

Left with **A**, **B** and **C**, therefore, the extent to which they affect the argument can now be evaluated. The fact that many people cannot swallow a tablet may weaken the argument to a certain extent. However, the specific conclusion is that the pharmaceutical industry should produce a *drug* and not necessary a *tablet*. This drug could be in any form – perhaps a spray – and so the fact that many people can't swallow a tablet would weaken the argument only if the conclusion was that a tablet should be produced. Since this is not necessarily the case, **A** does not weaken the argument to a significant extent.

B, if true, may lead to the conclusion that there is no need for a drug of this sort, if the number of people suffering from hay fever has fallen. This may weaken the conclusion that the pharmaceutical industry should respond. However, the extent of the impact of this information on the argument is doubtful. What if, for example, the number had fallen from 90% of the population to 85% of the population? It would not weaken the claim much, if this were the case, that a better drug is needed. So, if more statistics were provided then a better evaluation could be made of **B** but, as it stands, it does not weaken the argument to a significant extent.

However, **C** would significantly weaken the argument. The specific conclusion is that a drug should be produced which alleviates the symptoms of hay fever *and* doesn't have the combined effect of three-fold drowsiness from three separate drugs. However, if this drug, when produced, would have treble the amount of the chemical that causes drowsiness as the current medication available, then this would seem to indicate that it is not possible to produce a drug which alleviates the symptoms *and* doesn't have this combined effect. There is an assumption here that three times the amount of the chemical leads to treble the effect but this seems to be a fair assumption, especially in light of the fact that the argument states that three different drugs with the chemical produces a three-fold increase in drowsiness. Therefore, **C** weakens the conclusion significantly and is therefore the correct answer.

Example 2

Whilst traffic management is a complicated task and those who are involved in this task should be praised, one problem still persists. Traffic light timings, for example for how long a certain traffic light stays on red, vary depending on the time of day. However, whether it is due to a lack of resources or technical inability, traffic light timings do not seem to vary when unforeseen circumstances arise, for example, an accident. In order that traffic can flow more smoothly on our roads, those involved in traffic management should be better able to control these temporary timings.

Which of the following, if true, would most strengthen the above argument?

A Those people whose job it is to manage traffic lights are unaware of any accidents.

B There is always a controller on hand to change instantly the timing of traffic lights and who works with traffic management staff.

C It would cost significantly more money to monitor constantly roads and change traffic light timings more frequently than is currently done.

D The same technology that is used to vary traffic light timings depending on the time of day can be used to vary traffic light timings in response to unforeseen circumstances.

E Traffic light technology has developed at an astounding rate over the past few years.

The argument here is that, despite traffic light timings varying depending on the time of day, they do not vary in response to unforeseen circumstances. So that traffic can flow more smoothly, those involved in traffic management, it is concluded, should be better able to control these temporary timings.

The question asks you to find the answer that most strengthens the argument. Therefore, you are looking for the answer which adds more support to the conclusion. In this case, the correct answer would mean that those involved in traffic management should be *even* better able to control these temporary timings.

Firstly, it is worth going through the answers and eliminating those that do not strengthen the argument. **A** doesn't strengthen the argument since, if those whose job it is to manage traffic lights are unaware of any accidents, then the conclusion that those involved in traffic management should be better able to control these temporary timings is not supported as strongly as without this fact. This is because it would be difficult to expect those responsible to be better able to react to a situation if they are unaware of it. **B** does strengthen the conclusion since, if there is always a controller on hand to instantly change the timing of traffic lights who works with traffic management staff, then this would appear strongly to support the idea that those involved in traffic management should be better able to control temporary timings. They seem to have sufficient means by which to do so. **C** would appear to weaken the argument since, if it costs significantly more to vary traffic light timings more frequently than currently, then we should lower our expectations that those involved will be better able to control these timings. **D** would seem to strengthen the conclusion since, if no new technology is needed in order to vary these timings on a temporary basis, then perhaps those involved in traffic management should be better able to control these temporary timings. **E** shouldn't be eliminated since it doesn't appear to weaken the argument, although the extent to which it strengthens it is not clear.

Having eliminated **A** and **C** then, the next task is to decide which of **B**, **D** and **E** *most* strengthens the argument. **E** is very vague and more information would be needed before the extent to which it strengthens the argument could be decided. This is because the rate of traffic technology may have developed at an astounding rate over the past few years, but this doesn't tell you anything about the level at which it is currently at. For example, you still don't know whether or not technology to control temporary timings exists. Also, even if the technology exists, it is not clear whether those involved in traffic management have the means to utilise it. Therefore, it is unlikely that **E** can be said to strengthen the argument most.

D seems to address one of the problems with **E** since it explicitly states that the technology to control these temporary timings does exist. Therefore, it would strengthen the argument, if true, since it is no longer a valid reason that adequate technology does not exist for not being able to control temporary traffic light timings.

However, whilst **D** strengthens the argument more than **E**, the issues of whether those involved are able to utilise the technology is not addressed. **B**, which states that 'there is always a controller on hand to instantly change the timing of traffic lights who works with traffic management staff', significantly strengthens the argument. This is because it is inherent in this statement that adequate technology exists in order to control temporary traffic light timings and also because it states that there are the means available with which to do so. This would significantly bolster the claim that those involved in traffic management should be better able to control these temporary timings, or, at least bolster it more than any of the other answers would. Therefore, **B** is the correct answer.

Checklist

☐ Are you asked to find an answer that 'weakens' or 'strengthens' the conclusion?

☐ What is the conclusion of the argument?

☐ What effect will the correct answer have on the argument?

☐ Can you eliminate any answers initially?

☐ What is the extent of the impact of the remaining answers?

Thinking Skills Assessment: Practice test 1

Cambridge TSA paper
Oxford TSA section 1

Cambridge TSA instructions

There are 50 questions in this paper. For each question there are five possible answers, only one of which is correct. No marks are deducted for wrong answers so you should attempt all 50 questions.

You have 90 minutes to complete this paper. You may NOT use a calculator but you may use a dictionary (book or electronic).

Oxford TSA instructions

Section 1 of this paper contains 50 questions. For each question there are five possible answers, only one of which is correct. No marks are deducted for wrong answers so you should attempt all 50 questions.

You have 90 minutes to complete Section 1. You may NOT use a calculator.

Section 2 of this paper contains four essay questions of which you must choose **one**.

You have 30 minutes to complete Section 2. You may NOT use a dictionary.

1 The global tiger population continues to fall as a result of poaching and a lack of conservation. These majestic creatures are now on the verge of extinction. Many governments have therefore taken measures to address poaching and the illegal trade of tigers in order to curb the steep decline in their numbers. The measures have already proven successful. However, governments need further support from charities and from the wider public in order to pursue these measures, so we should all try to help these governments more in some form or another.

Which of the following is an underlying assumption of the argument above?

A Charities and the wider public are not currently supporting governments.

B Governments are the only institutions capable of saving tigers.

C Tigers are worth saving.

D Poaching and a lack of conservation are the only reasons for decreasing tiger populations.

E Government measures have been successful in saving tigers.

2 Bharti has an unusual shopping list whereby, instead of listing the amount of each product she needs, she notes the proportion of each type of product needed (either as a fraction or percentage of the total shopping). Here is this week's list:

Shopping List

Fruit and Vegetables = $\frac{1}{4}$ 25%

Dairy Products = 15%   18%

Frozen Food = $\frac{1}{10}$ 10%

Tinned Food = 5%   5%

Toiletries = ?

Cleaning Products = $\frac{1}{8}$ 12.8%

Cereals = $\frac{1}{10}$ 10%

Drinks = 15%   18%

92.8

What fraction of this week's shopping is toiletries?

A $\frac{3}{10}$

B $\frac{1}{2}$

C $\frac{3}{40}$

D $\frac{3}{20}$

E $\frac{1}{5}$

3 Buying a brand new car has significant drawbacks. The main problem is that the value of the car falls steeply as soon as it is driven out of the forecourt and, even though the clock only has a few miles on it and the car is essentially the same, the value of the car is greatly reduced. For this reason, it is advisable to buy only second-hand cars as they are cheaper and their value does not reduce significantly from one owner to the next.

Which of the following best expresses the main conclusion of the argument above?

A Second-hand cars are essentially the same as brand new cars.

B People should be wary of the number of miles on the clock of a brand new car.

C The immediate decrease in the value of brand new cars means that we should buy second-hand cars instead.

D The value of the car is the most important factor in deciding whether to buy brand new cars or second-hand cars.

E It is better to buy second-hand cars for various reasons.

4 My team of traders completes deals on a daily basis. If it takes 120 traders to complete 40 deals in one day, how many more traders will I need to employ to complete 735 deals in seven days?

A 245

B 195

C 125

D 35

E 155

5 Children in the UK spend far too much time indoors playing computer games and watching television these days and as a result become less sociable, have less exposure to the outside world and, significantly, have less sporting talent than they perhaps should. Children in Australia and New Zealand, for example, spend a lot of time outdoors and consequently the sporting talent of youngsters in these countries vastly outstrips that of British children. Due to this, and because of the other advantages derived from being outdoors, the government in this country should discourage the use of computer games and television for youngsters.

Which of the following best summarises the conclusion of the argument above?

A Children should spend more time outdoors.

B Parents need to encourage their children to engage in more sporting activities than they do currently.

C Our government should model itself on that of Australia or New Zealand.

D Playing outdoors brings about many other positive changes than simply increasing sporting talent.

E The government needs to intervene to change the habits of youngsters.

6 Lucinda drinks wine every day and is wondering whether it would be more economical for her to buy a larger bottle of wine instead of the usual-sized bottles she buys. Lucinda drinks 200 ml of wine every day and, at the moment, she buys bottles of 200 ml, priced at £2.60.

Assuming that 25 ml of wine evaporates each night after a bottle is opened, which of the following bottles of wine would be more economical for Lucinda to buy?

A An 875 ml bottle for £12.80

B A 425 ml bottle for £5.20

C A 650 ml bottle for £9.50

D An 875 ml bottle for £10.20

E A 425 ml bottle for £6.20

7   The following graph shows the cumulative distance travelled by a skier whilst passing through various stages on a slalom ski run:

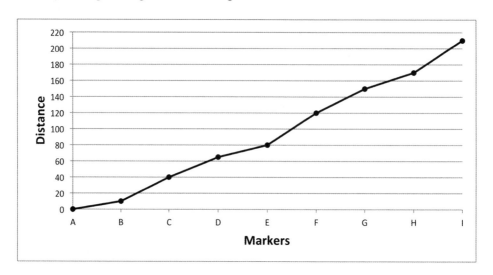

Each stage is referred to by the two letters that mark the beginning and end of the stage e.g. AB or GH. During which two stages did the skier travel the same distance?

A   BC and CD ×

B   AB and DE ×

C   CD and FG

D   BC and FG

E   CD and GH

Handwritten annotations:

BC : 40-10: 28 30

CD: 68-40 : 28·

AB = 10.

DE = 18

FG ≈ 30

8   Mobile phone technology is improving at an incredible rate. In the last twenty years we have developed mobile phones that are capable of taking photographs, connecting to the internet and being very small and sleek. But it is not clear how the future of this technology will develop and scientists even argue that we have reached our peak in terms of mobile phones. However, there is certainly more scope for developing this technology and research should be conducted into nanotechnology to assess whether mobile phones can be made even smaller. Also, existing data and call handling of mobile phones is not always adequate and much could be done to improve this.

Which of the following best expresses the main conclusion of the argument above?

108

A   Mobile phone technology has grown at an exponential rate.

B   We may not have reached our peak in terms of mobile phone technology.

C   There are still problems with mobile phones that need to be corrected.

D   Nanotechnology is the way forward for mobile phones.

E   There is dispute between scientists as to the current state of mobile phone technology.

9   In order to win the competition, I need good clothing and lots of practice. Despite the fact that I don't have lots of practice, I still believe that I will win the competition.

Which of the following most closely parallels the above reasoning?

A   I was told that I would need a 10% deposit and a strong credit rating in order to buy a new car. Despite only having a 5% deposit and a weak credit rating, I was still able to buy the car.   ✗

B   Even though there is a lot of fog, I reckon we will still take-off soon despite the fact that we were told that the flight will not leave until everybody is on board and the weather is clear.   ✓

C   For the party to be re-elected into government, it will need a two-thirds majority victory in the polls and the backing of the President. The party does not currently have the backing of the President and so is unlikely to be re-elected into government.   ✗

D   In order for me to get good exam results, I need a lot of luck and some last-minute revision. I have just heard that my lucky subjects will appear on the exam and I have done plenty of revision for tomorrow's exam, therefore I feel confident of getting good exam results.   ✗

E   Even though we were docked points and lost key players, I still believe that my football team will win promotion this season despite the fact that we were told that we wouldn't after these two blows.   ✗

10 Lee and Katie have both arranged to see a show tonight, but Katie wants to watch Dogs and Lee does not. Here are the details for tonight's shows with the title, the start time and the duration of each.

New York 7.30 pm 1 hour 25 minutes
Clarinettist on the Ceiling 8.30 pm 1 hour 30 minutes
Dogs 6.45 pm 2 hours 20 minutes
East Angle Opera 7.15 pm 2 hours
Ghost of the Cinema 8.00 pm 1 hour 20 minutes
The Tiger Queen 7.45 pm 1 hour 25 minutes

8:55

10:00

9:05

9.15

9.20

9.10

If Katie watches Dogs and Lee another show, what is the earliest possible time at which they can meet after their respective shows?

A   10.00 pm

B   9.15 pm

C   9.10 pm

D   8.55 pm

E   9.05 pm

11 Oxbridge United FC have two different ticket prices to come and see their games. It is £5 per ticket for a seat in the family area and £8 for a ticket anywhere else. If the total revenue from last Saturday's game was £21,000 and the total attendance was 3,000, how many people bought a ticket to sit in the family area?

A 2,000

B 1,500

C 750

D 1,750

E 1,000

$$5x + 8y = 21000$$

$$x + y = 3000$$

$$y = 3000 - x$$

$$5x + 8(3000 - x) = 21000$$

$$5x + 24000 - 8x = 21000$$

$$-3x = -3000 \qquad x = 1000$$

12 Person A: 'I would never get in an aeroplane since it essentially involves being propelled across the sky in a tin can.'

Person B: 'But aeronautical technology is superb these days and there is very little risk of anything going wrong.'

Person A: 'But it could still go wrong and the consequences are very often disastrous.'

Person B: 'There are thousands of planes in the sky at any given time and there are very few air crashes in spite of this.'

Which of the following is a conclusion that can reliably be drawn from the above argument?

A Aeronautical technology prevents any air crashes.

B Air crashes are always fatal when they occur.

C It is safer to fly at night than in the day time.

D More crashes occur than are actually reported in the press.

E Air travel seems to be a safe method of travel.

13 Santa needs to arrange his eight reindeer in the following structure:

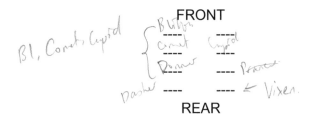

FRONT

REAR

However, Santa needs to observe the following rules about the reindeer:

- Blitzen must always be on the left hand side but not in the rear row.
- Comet and Cupid must be in either of the first two rows, but not necessarily in the same row.
- Dancer must always be directly behind Donner.
- Prancer must always be ahead of Dasher but never on the same side, and never next to Comet or Cupid.
- Vixen must be as far away from Blitzen as possible and not on the same side.

From left to right, which two reindeer make up the rear row?

A Prancer and Vixen

B Dasher and Vixen

C Dancer and Vixen

D Dancer and Dasher

E Vixen and Dasher

14 Bollywood is a huge industry, both in Indian terms and on a worldwide scale, and produces three times as many films as Hollywood. It is not a surprise therefore that the overall quality of the films it produces is lower than that of Hollywood films, which is a shame since the individual actors themselves are as good as those in Hollywood. Bollywood should strive to produce fewer films in order that these actors are given the credit they deserve in higher quality films.

Which of the following is an assumption of the argument above?

A The quantity of films produced affects their quality.

B Bollywood actors are better than those in Hollywood.

C Producing a third more films decreases the quality of each of those films by a third.

D Bollywood is not capable of producing higher quality films.

E Bollywood actors actually deserve credit for these films.

15 Previous governments in the UK have always made it a priority to bring down the amount of knife crime in the country to a low level that is more on a par with other European countries. Until then, there must be resources allocated to this important objective. Over the last five years there has been a significant drop in the level of knife crime in the UK for which these governments, both past and present, should be applauded. Perhaps now is the time to start allocating more resources towards gun crime which is currently at a high level and rising?

Which of the following is the best statement of the flaw in the above argument?

A It only looks at data from the past five years.

B Other European countries may have extremely high levels of other types of crime.

C We shouldn't applaud these governments for just succeeding in one area.

D It fails to explain why the UK needs to be more on a par with other European countries.

E The level of knife crime may still be high despite a significant drop.

16 I have two boxes each with four sides, a lid and a base and which are both capable of being collapsed. One of the boxes is a cube with a volume of 125,000 cm³ and the other is a cuboid with a length of 60 cm, a height of 50 cm and a depth of 40 cm. The cuboid looks approximately like this before and after collapsing (not to scale):

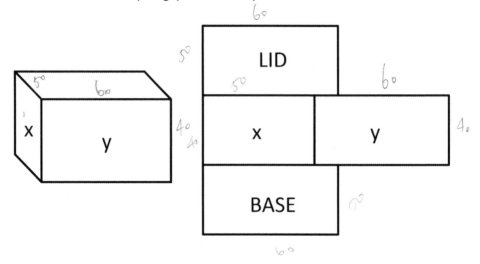

How much surface area will both the collapsed boxes take up when I put them under my bed (assuming that the cube is collapsed in the same way as the cuboid and that they are not stacked on top of each other)?

A 19,800 cm²

B 18,800 cm²

C 20,800 cm²

D 21,000 cm²

E 22,000 cm²

17 An economic argument is sometimes levelled at climate change, based on how the free market deals with renewable and non-renewable fuel prices. Essentially, the model suggests that, at some point, the shrinking supply of non-renewable fuels will push up the prices of these fuels to such an extent that it will be economically viable to start investing in renewable fuels. However, we should resist giving this argument much credit since we don't know when this point will arise and it may only become more economically viable to invest in renewable fuels long after the damage from non-renewable fuels has been done.

Which of the following is a conclusion that can reliably be drawn from the above argument?

A The government should intervene prior to this point to encourage investment in renewable fuels.

B The damage from non-renewable fuels has already occurred.

C The future of non-renewable fuel prices is uncertain.

D The free market will push the prices of renewable fuels down.

E Economic models relating to climate change are unreliable.

18 A stamp factory creates stamps by taking a large piece of paper measuring 100 cm x 120 cm and then cutting five hundred 6 cm x 3 cm rectangles out of it. Of the remaining paper, 80% is reused in another large piece of paper and 20% is discarded. The five hundred rectangles are then turned into stamps and are placed in books containing 20 stamps each.

For each book of stamps made, how many cm² of paper is discarded?

A 30

B 120

C 24

D 750

E 25

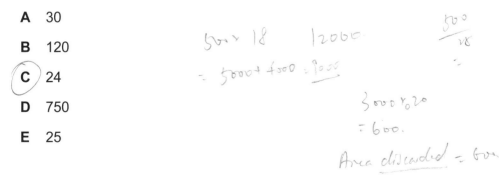

19 Today's generation do not give classical music its full worth. Much of what they listen to comes from artificially created pop groups that do not write their own music and do not, objectively speaking, have as much talent as artists from earlier decades. Classical music is a different kettle of fish altogether – it requires incredible talent, years of hard work and the financial reward is much lower. For these reasons, youngsters today should start to listen more to classical music.

Which of the following, if true, would most strengthen the argument?

A   Listening to classical music would bring generations closer together.

B   A lot of today's music is based on classical music.

C   Youngsters would like classical music a lot more than other genres of music if they listened to it more.

D   Classical music on the radio is now being targeted at younger generations.

E   Composers of classical music wanted their music to appeal to people of all ages.

20 The following shape may only be rotated clockwise:

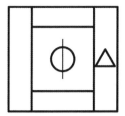

Which of the following could the shape look like after it is rotated?

A

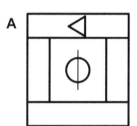

B

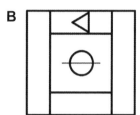

C

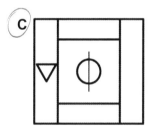

D

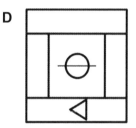

E

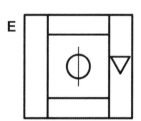

21 Before the trend of super-rich business folk investing in football clubs, at least we couldn't blame anybody but ourselves for the exorbitant sums of money involved in the sport. We, the people, are responsible for creating the demand for tickets, merchandise and television revenue and the free market responds accordingly, allowing huge sums of money to be paid as transfer fees and wages. However, with the intervention of rich investors, the figures are skewed upwards so that transfer fees and wages are set artificially high in order that investors can enjoy the success of their investments.

Which of the following is a conclusion that can reliably be drawn from the above argument?

A   Transfer fees and wages can be affected by forces outside the free market.

B   We, the people, are not free of responsibility, even for artificially high transfer fees and wages.

C   Transfer fees and wages are affected by more than just demand for tickets, merchandise, television revenue and the intervention of investors.

D   There is a decreasing number of football clubs being taken over by rich investors due to a recent economic downturn.

E   Transfer fees and wages actually decrease with the intervention of rich investors.

22 A dodgeball season lasts from May to April. The following table shows that the Harley Dodgeball team has been doing well over the last few seasons and, at the end of each season, they have always achieved more points than the previous season.

Date	Number of Points	Cumulative Expenditure on New Players (£)
30th April 2005	1,380	1.2 million
30th April 2006	1,500	2.5 million
30th April 2007	1,670	4.4 million
30th April 2008	1,850	6.3 million
30th April 2009	2,040	6.7 million
30th April 2010	2,220	7.1 million

In the season that the Harley Dodgeball team achieved the greatest increase in points from the previous season, how much had they spent on new players?

A   4 million

B   6.7 million

C   1.9 million

D   0.4 million

E   6.3 million

23   Jonny is flying from London to City C via City A and City B. City A is five and a half hours ahead of London time, City B is six hours ahead of London time and City C is seven hours ahead of London time. Here is the flight information with all times in local time:

- Depart London at 06:45
- Depart City A at 23:00
- Depart City B at 06:45 (+1 day)
- Arrive City C at 13:45 (+1 day)

How long did Jonny spend in total waiting for his flight at City A and City B if his total flying time was 14 hours and 35 minutes?

A   Three hours and 15 minutes

B   10 hours and 45 minutes

C   Nine hours and 25 minutes

D   19 hours

E   10 hours and 25 minutes

24 A new species of mistletoe has recently been discovered by scientists. The fact that most people's first reaction will be along the lines of 'will I still be able to kiss somebody under this new species?' reveals a lot about the extent to which people still believe in and embrace traditions such as this. However, most superstitions are irrational and may sometimes lead to odd behaviour such as looking for four-leaf clovers or throwing salt over one's shoulder. Despite the fact that it is often said that humans are inherently irrational, if we can easily discourage irrational behaviour, we should endeavour to do so.

Which of the following best expresses the main conclusion of the argument above?

A   Many people believe in and embrace certain superstitions.

B   Irrational behaviour should be discouraged.

C   We should endeavour to discourage irrational behaviour, if it is feasible to do so.

D   Since most superstitions are irrational, if it is easy enough to do so, we should discourage a belief in them.

E   We should discourage irrational behaviour since humans are inherently irrational.

25 Greg receives a royalty fee of 40% on the profit of each textbook sold. In 2010, 1,400 textbooks were sold with total revenue of £56,000 and a profit of half this sum. In 2011, it is expected that 20% more books will be sold and Greg has negotiated a new royalty fee of 50% of the profit plus £5 for each extra book sold compared to 2010.

If the expectations turn out to be true, and, as in 2010, profit is half of revenue, how much money will Greg receive in 2011?

A   £16,800

B   £25,200

C   £35,000

D   £68,600

E   £18,200

26 Over 60% of graduates are unemployed in the first year after leaving university. These are often highly-skilled, highly-able and driven people who would contribute a great deal to any organisation they join. We need to make employers more aware of the wealth of talent available to them and to give practical advice as to how they can go about recruiting these talented youngsters. Hopefully then, we will be able to bring this statistic down.

Which of the following, if true, would most weaken the argument?

A   Organisations are already aware of the talent available to them.

B   Most graduates do not want a job in the first year after leaving university.

C   There is a general lack of jobs in the current economic climate.

D   It is often difficult to give practical advice on how to recruit graduates.

E   Most graduates are not a burden on society when unemployed.

27 Protests against an increase in university fees will prove to be futile at best because of the violence that emerges from them. Governments in the past have responded negatively to violent protests by dismissing their credibility and not changing any policy as a result, whereas it is well known that peaceful protests have tended to affect government policy significantly. The current grievance with university fees should therefore be aired using more peaceful methods in order that the current government responds positively to it.

Which of the following is an assumption of the argument above?

A   The current government will respond in a similar way to previous governments.

B   All of the protesters were violent.

C   The credibility of a protest affects whether the government will change policy.

D   The protesters are justified in protesting against an increase in student fees.

E   Violent protesting should be banned altogether.

28 The diagram shows a piece of paper that has been folded once in half:

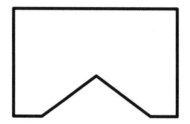

Which of the following diagrams (not to scale) could NOT be the piece of paper unfolded?

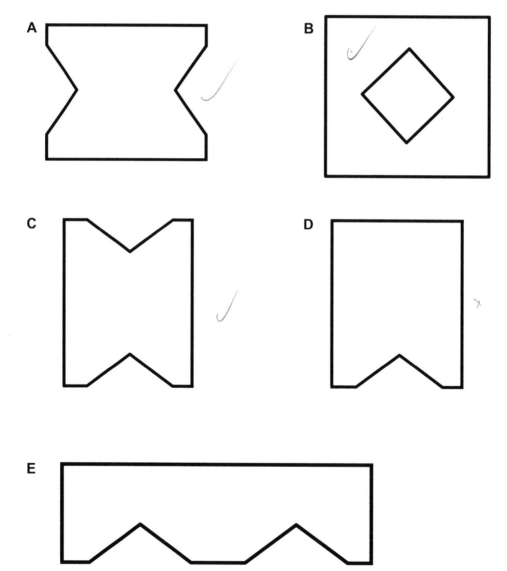

29 It is mostly young adults (aged 18 to 25) that make up the number of fatalities and casualties in car accidents and the majority of these young adults are male. Allowing young adults to drive, instead of waiting until they are a little bit older, is always asking for trouble since they are at that age where they like to impress others. This can be done by driving a car too fast or in a risky manner, which leads to accidents.

Which of the following is a conclusion that can reliably be drawn from the above argument?

A Most young adults have been involved in a car accident.

B Males tend to drive in a more risky manner or faster than females.

C In any given car accident, there is a 50% chance or higher that the driver is a young adult.

D By increasing the legal minimum driving age to 25, the number of car accidents should fall.

E Most young adult males have been involved in a car accident, whether fatal or not.

30 When Caroline's book is released, she will have a surge in profits since she has the only book on that particular subject and there are always people who have pre-ordered them. After a few months, sales will slow down and eventually a new book will be released at which point profits will quickly drop significantly. Caroline is confident that profits will pick back up when people realise that her book is better than the rival book. The following graphs show Caroline's profit level on a month-by-month basis (as opposed to a cumulative level).

Which graph shows this information?

A

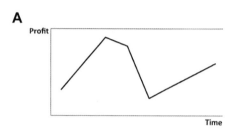

B

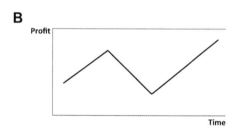

C

D

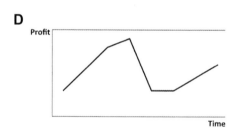

E

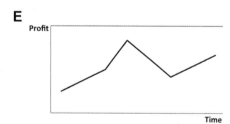

31 Stephen and James both leave Point A at the same time. James travels 6 km north then 4 km east. He then travels 5 km north and 2 km west. At the same time, Stephen travels 8 km south and then travels east the same distance as James' total distance covered. If Stephen then travels 19 km north, how far will he be from James?

    A   13 km

    B   17 km

    C   15 km

    D   12 km

    E   11 km

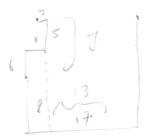

32 Between 6.30pm today and 8.30pm eight days from now, through how many degrees in total will the hour hand of a clock have moved?

    A   2,880

    B   2,940

    C   5,820

    D   5,100

    E   5,760

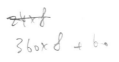

33 You can only become good at computer games if you have good hand-eye coordination. My brother does not have good hand-eye coordination, so he is not good at computer games.

Which of the following has the same structure as the above argument?

    A   You can only become a good musician if you have an ability to distinguish different tones. You have an ability to distinguish different tones, so you can become a good musician.

    B   You can become good at computer games if you have good hand-eye coordination. My brother is not good at computer games so he must not have good hand-eye coordination.

    C   Rihanna can only go out in the rain if she has an umbrella. She doesn't have an umbrella and therefore she cannot go out in the rain.

    D   Eric can be a good football player if he has good football boots. Eric has good football boots, so Eric must be a good football player.

    E   You can become a good musician if you have an ability to recognise different pitches of sound. You don't have this ability, so you can't become a good musician.

34 What is the point of space travel? We hardly ever discover anything significant that furthers us as a species and it costs a ridiculous amount of money that could be used better helping people in need on this planet. We should start lobbying for countries to stop pumping so much money into their space programmes and focus on more important objectives.

Which of the following best illustrates the principle underlying the argument above?

A No one should pay the part of their tax liability that contributes to their country's space programme.

B Despite its obvious benefits, we should encourage countries to stop investing in green technology as it is currently very expensive.

C The EU should scrap its farming subsidies policy and, instead, focus on encouraging farming using a more efficient set of incentives.

D No one should buy shares in any energy companies since they are expensive, they are often unsuccessful in their projects and renewable fuels are clearly the way forward for humankind.

E We should start investing more money into foreign aid since it clearly helps those most in need.

35 The chart below shows the sales distribution of Mr Spedding's pie shop in a given day. There were 128 pies sold on this particular day.

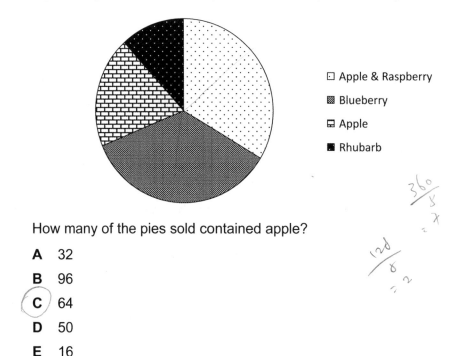

☐ Apple & Raspberry

▒ Blueberry

▣ Apple

▓ Rhubarb

How many of the pies sold contained apple?

A 32

B 96

C 64

D 50

E 16

36 London Underground had an equal number of trains running on the Victoria Line and the Piccadilly Line until recently when it invested in new trains on the Victoria Line. If the total number of trains (taking into account both lines) is now 60 and the ratio of trains between the Victoria Line and the Piccadilly Line is now 3:2, how many new trains were bought as part of the investment?

36:24.

A 12

B 8

C 10

D 5

E 6

37 Predicting the weather is still a tricky business despite the exponential rate of technological development during the last century, and society often criticises those responsible for inaccurate forecasts. However, we shouldn't be too harsh on these meteorologists and expect them to be able to utilise this apparently high level technology flawlessly. Firstly, we don't have technology sophisticated enough to be able to predict accurately the state of the weather in advance and secondly, more importantly, these predictions are wrought with uncertain variables that are constantly changing and which make it extremely difficult to predict the weather accurately.

Which of the following is a conclusion that can reliably be drawn from the above argument?

A We will have technology sophisticated enough to be able to predict the weather accurately in the future.

B Technological development has not occurred in the area of weather prediction.

C Uncertain variables will always make it impossible to predict the weather accurately.

D Sophisticated technology, if it existed, would enable meteorologists to control these uncertain variables.

E Meteorologists are the people that predict the weather.

38 Tessa sets off from Point A on her bicycle travelling at 20 miles per hour. Matt sets off from the same point at the same time following the same route in his car, travelling at 40 miles per hour. After 30 minutes of travelling Matt realises that he has forgotten something behind at Point A and turns back to go and get it, travelling at the same speed. Matt takes 15 minutes to gather his belongings and then sets off again on the route, this time travelling at 50 miles per hour. At the same time as Matt sets off again, Tessa stops to take a long rest.

How long after Matt sets off again will he pass Tessa?

A   30 minutes

B   15 minutes

C   60 minutes

D   20 minutes

E   45 minutes

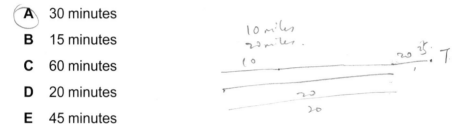

39 People who work regular night shifts tend to be less productive overall at work. Research has shown that people who work regular night shifts are more productive when they are asked to perform the same duties during the day. This same research also found that those on regular night shifts tended to get less sleep during the day than their day shift worker counterparts got at night. This makes sense because it is unnatural for the body to sleep when there is daylight and there are many distractions during the day. Employers need to address this sleep issue if they want to have more efficient workers at night.

Which of the following is the best statement of the flaw in the above argument?

A   It assumes that night shift workers are affected by artificial distractions during the day.

B   It fails to explain how night shift workers are less efficient.

C   It doesn't explain how 'regular' these night shifts are.

D   It creates a causal link between sleep and productivity without explaining why.

E   It fails to provide any credible source for its evidence.

40 Chantel and Sarah live and work together. Every day they leave the house and walk towards a hill, at the top of which is their office. They walk at 3 miles per hour towards the hill and 2 miles per hour up the hill. Then, at the end of their day, they walk down the hill at 6 miles per hour and walk back home at 3 miles per hour.

What is their average speed whilst travelling (in miles per hour) each day?

A 3

B 3.5

C 4

D 5

E 4.5

41 Keeping up with the news is essential to everybody with an upcoming interview, whether that be for a job, a university place or for any other reason. It allows that person to show an interest in the society in which they live and to show that they are aware of any developments that are relevant for the job or university place. Additionally, it enables them to experience and analyse arguments, which is an essential skill that everybody should have. Due to this final reason, I would recommend everybody to read the news as opposed to listening to it on the television or radio.

Which of the following is the main assumption of the argument above?

A People can better experience and analyse arguments if they read them rather than listen to them.

B You can demonstrate that you are aware of developments in society better if you read the news as opposed to listen to it.

C Experiencing and analysing arguments is an important skill in general.

D People will perform better at interviews if they read the news as opposed to listen to it.

E Experiencing and analysing arguments is an important skill to demonstrate in an interview.

42 Satish's black bin is emptied on Thursday each week except when his green bin is also emptied. This occurs once every three weeks and in this case, both bins are emptied on a Tuesday. Satish is going on holiday and wants to let the council know for how many days they can leave his bin out of their rounds. If the green bin was emptied three days ago, how many times are any of his bins, both black and green, scheduled to be emptied in the next 40 days?

A 7

B 8

C 10

D 9

E 6

43 It is only fair that Russia be allowed to host the football World Cup in 2018 since the tournament will provide much-needed help to Russian infrastructure and because the other bidding countries have already hosted it at least once, whereas Russia has not.

Which of the following most closely parallels the above reasoning?

A England should be chosen to host the Olympics in 2020 since it will further improve its already impressive stadia and we have experience of hosting large sporting events.

B Resources should be reallocated to the public transport system since it is in dire need of updating and has been ignored in terms of investment since its creation.

C More money needs to be invested in universities since they are currently underfunded.

D The government needs to allocate welfare benefits on a fairer basis, including giving more money to those on disability benefits.

E Everyone should support the use of ID cards since they will improve national security and many other European countries have adopted the idea.

44 It is far better to buy a mobile phone these days on a fixed-term contract rather than buying a 'pay-as-you-go' package. Fixed-term contracts are generally reasonably priced and are available in many different combinations to suit the consumer. Furthermore, the fact that the consumer does not have to worry about the amount of 'credit' left on the phone is an attractive quality. Therefore, everyone should choose a fixed-term contract deal instead of the obsolete 'pay-as-you-go' system when buying their next mobile phone.

Which of the following is the best statement of the flaw in the above argument?

A   It assumes that the advantages of a fixed-term contract will suit every consumer.

B   It fails to acknowledge the flaws of a fixed-term contract.

C   It assumes that all mobile phones are available on a fixed-term contract.

D   It assumes that the 'pay-as-you-go' system is out-dated.

E   It fails to justify why a fixed-term contract is better than the 'pay-as-you-go' system.

45 Emma is worried about the nutritional benefit of the food that she gives to her baby. She wants to find the baby food that gives her baby the most vitamins, the least calories and which is available at the cheapest price.

Below is a table showing the nutritional information and cost of the various baby food products on offer:

Product	Vitamin content (per jar)	Calories (per jar)	Price (per jar)
Babies Foodies (100 g jar)	28 g	180	£1.82
Baby Food plc (200 g jar)	60 g	240	£3.60
Food for Young 'Uns (150 g jar)	60 g	135	£2.46
Healthy Babies (100 g jar)	36 g	200	£1.84
Health Kids (200 g jar)	80 g	200	£3.30

Which of the products should Emma choose?

A   Babies Foodies

B   Baby Food plc

C   Food for Young 'Uns

D   Healthy Babies

E   Health Kids

46 Lie detector tests are a waste of time and not at all suitable for any major evaluation of whether or not a person is telling the truth. These tests measure a variety of factors including heart rate, blood pressure, respiration and skin conductivity, all of which contribute to the assessment of whether a person is lying or not. Those conducting the test must therefore rely on a large range of physiological responses which can vary hugely in a test subject. If any of this data is inaccurate, in the sense that it suggests that a person is lying when they are in fact telling the truth, then major decisions based on the test could prove to be wrong.

Which of the following is the best statement of the flaw in the above argument?

A   Just because there is a large range of physiological responses, this does not mean that there may necessarily be any inaccuracy.

B   Just because there is some inaccuracy, this does not suggest that a person is lying.

C   Just because there are a variety of factors used, this does not mean that the test is measuring a large range of physiological responses.

D   Just because there is some inaccuracy, this does not mean that lie detectors are a waste of time and unsuitable.

E   Just because major decisions based on the test could prove to be wrong, this does not mean that lie detectors are a waste of time and unsuitable.

47 The following table shows the notice periods required for any employee wishing to terminate their employment with the company. Notice periods vary depending how long employees have worked for the company:

Length of Employment	Notice Period
Less than 6 months	1 week
Between 6 months and 1 year	2 weeks
Between 1 year and 5 years	3 weeks
More than 5 years	4 weeks

The following six employees all handed in their notice to terminate their employment with the company on 1st January 2011 and the table shows the date they joined the company and their weekly wage:

Name of Employee	Joining Date	Weekly Wage (£)
Roberta	8th November 2010	450
Sinclair	1st January 2008	375
Arthur	10th December 2009	410
Moira	21st July 2003	330
Patrick	24th October 2009	290
Suhail	3rd March 2010	515

Which of the six employees will earn the most money between handing in their notice on 1st January 2011 and the date on which they finally leave the company?

A Suhail

B Roberta

C Arthur

D Moira

E Sinclair

133

48 Each time I break in a game of pool there is a chance that a ball will go in a pocket. A ball will go in a pocket once out of every three breaks. If I take three consecutive breaks, what is the probability that I will pot a ball?

A $\frac{1}{27}$

B $\frac{1}{3}$

C $\frac{1}{9}$

D $\frac{8}{27}$

E $\frac{19}{27}$

49 Reasons to buy a stand-alone camera should decrease dramatically since mobile phones are now capable of incorporating a camera. Everybody has and carries around a mobile phone and, with more of them incorporating cameras, it doesn't seem necessary anymore to buy a stand-alone camera as well. In addition, cameras on phones seem to be as good as stand-alone cameras and, with phones being as small as they are, there is the added convenience factor of having a phone with a built-in camera.

Which of the following, if true, would most weaken the argument?

A It is cheaper to buy a phone with a camera than to buy them both separately.

B Phones with cameras do not have a video function on them which many stand-alone cameras have.

C Despite the fact that mobile phones are capable of incorporating a camera, there is still only a tiny proportion of them that have one.

D Cameras are getting smaller as well and thus becoming more convenient.

E You are more likely to get mugged if you have a mobile phone with a camera on it.

50 Any decision at X plc requires at least three quarters of all board members to agree to that decision and board members have three options: they can vote for the decision, vote against the decision or abstain from voting at all. So, if X plc has a number of board members that is wholly divisible by four, then you would need three quarters of this number to vote for a decision. For example, if it has 100 board members, then 75 of them need to vote for a decision in order for it to pass. At the present time, X plc has 15 board members but three quarters of this number would not be a whole number and so X plc would not be able to pass a decision.

Which of the following is the best statement of the flaw in the above argument?

A It applies too rigorous a mathematical analysis to the issue.

B X plc will not always have this number on its board.

C It ignores the fact that voters can abstain.

D You only need a whole number larger than three quarters in order to pass a decision.

E It assumes you do not need a whole number in order to pass a decision.

Cambridge TSA – END OF PAPER

Oxford TSA – TURN OVER FOR SECTION 2

Oxford TSA section 2

You must answer only ONE of the following questions:

1. **What is the difference between fact and opinion?**

2. **Is it more justified to donate money to charities that help less economically developed countries than those that help more economically developed countries?**

3. **Should human rights be universal?**

4. **Is reality television a cause, or an effect, of a desire to observe the lives of other people?**

Thinking Skills Assessment: Practice test 1 commentary

Cambridge TSA paper: commentary
Oxford TSA section 1: commentary

1   The specific argument here is that tigers are dying out, governments are trying to save them but that they need more support from charities and the wider public and therefore that we, the public, should help the government in order to save tigers. **A** is not correct since it is stated that governments need *further* support from charities and the wider public and that we should help *more* which implies that these bodies already give some support (although it is not specified how much support). In addition, the argument does not rely on the fact that charities and the wider public do not currently support governments – irrespective of this, the argument still works and merely states that we should provide more support to save tigers. **B** could be assumed although, again, the argument does not rely on the assumption that governments are the *only* institutions capable of saving tigers. It merely states that governments are doing something and that we should help them, and not that they are the only institutions taking measures. **D** is not correct since the reasons for the decreasing tiger population are not relevant to the conclusion that we should help governments. **E** is incorrect because it is stated in the argument that governments have already been successful in their measures and is therefore not an assumption. **C** is correct because, in arguing that charities and the wider public should do more to help these governments, the argument takes for granted that there is any reason at all to save tigers and this is an assumption of the argument.

2   The first task in finding out the fraction of toiletries needed on this week's list is to convert all fractions into percentages (and not the other way around since dealing with percentages is generally easier than dealing with fractions – even in this case where you have to convert a percentage back into a fraction in order to find the correct answer). Once you convert the fractions, you should find that Fruit & Vegetables amounts to 25%, Frozen Food 10%, Cleaning Products 12.5% and Cereals 10%. Next, you should add up all the percentages together in order to find out what percentage of toiletries is needed to give us a total of 100%. You should calculate this to be 7.5%. Finally, you should convert this percentage into its simplest fraction, which can't be just $\frac{7.5}{100}$ since a fraction should have a whole

137

number as the numerator (or denominator) and furthermore this isn't one of the answers given. $\frac{7.5}{100}$ is the same as $\frac{15}{200}$ which can then be simplified to $\frac{3}{40}$ and therefore **C** is the correct answer.

3   The argument here is essentially that the main problem with buying a brand new car is that its value falls significantly as soon as it is bought and therefore we should buy only second-hand cars, which do not suffer such steep decreases in value immediately following purchase. **A** is incorrect as the argument does not go so far as to compare the similarities between second-hand and brand new cars and indeed, does not even suggest that they are similar. **B** could be loosely inferred from the argument but is incorrect because the argument actually states that we should not buy brand new cars and so, logically, is not stating anything about how you should go about buying a brand new car. **D** is more of an underlying assumption in this argument and the conclusion goes further than just stating the importance of value; it argues that we should change our buying habits based on the issue of value. **E** is incorrect because there is only one reason given in the argument for buying second-hand cars and therefore this statement is too vague. **C** is a concise statement of the argument and is therefore correct.

4   Firstly, find out how many traders it takes to complete 1 deal in 1 day, which is 3 (120 ÷ 40 = 3). Next, find out how many deals there need to be in 1 day if there are to be 735 deals in 7 days, which is 105 (735 ÷ 7 = 105). If it takes 3 traders per deal per day, then you would need 315 traders to complete 105 deals in 1 day (105 x 3). There are currently 120 traders, so I would need 195 *more* traders to complete these extra deals per day and hence 735 deals in 7 days (315 - 120 = 195). Therefore, **B** is the correct answer.

5   The argument here is quite specific, stating that children are spending too much time indoors playing computer games and watching television and are not currently benefiting sufficiently from the advantages of being outdoors, and therefore the government should discourage children from playing computer games and watching television. **A** is too general to be the conclusion of the argument. **B** is incorrect as parents aren't even mentioned or implicated in the argument. **C** is incorrect since it is far too sweeping a statement to suggest that our government should model itself on that of Australia or New Zealand and this is not suggested by the argument, least of all because it would require a strong assumption that it is the government in those countries that has created the beneficial situation there. **D** is a premise for the conclusion and not the conclusion itself. **E** is correct because the argument specifically states that the government

needs to discourage the use of computer games and television.

6   The easiest way of approaching this question is to find a common volume and price that can be used as a standard against which each of the bottles can be measured. 200 ml seems to be appropriate (although you could also use 100 ml) and, from the information given in the question, you know that Lucinda pays £2.60 for every 200 ml of wine she buys. The next task is to apply the fact that 25 ml of wine evaporates overnight to the volumes given in each of the answers. So, if an 875 ml bottle is bought, then, based on the information you are given, Lucinda would get 4 x 200 ml servings from this bottle which she would drink over 4 days. This would also mean that the wine is left open for 3 nights and so 75 ml would evaporate. In other words, she would get 800 ml of wine in total. To compare the value of this bottle, you should simply calculate the rate per 200 ml. For **A** this would be £3.20 and for **D** this would be £2.55. If you started with the 875 ml bottles then you would already have the answer since £2.55 per 200 ml of wine represents better value for Lucinda than her current deal. If you didn't start with these bottles, or if you want to verify the price per 200 ml of the other bottles, you should find that you calculate amounts of £2.60, £3.17 (to the nearest penny) and £3.10 for **B**, **C** and **E** respectively. Therefore, **D** is the correct answer.

7   Despite the fact that you could find out the answer in this question by finding the two stages in which the curve has the same gradient, you will most probably need to work out the distances travelled in each stage in order to be more exact. In order to save some time, you can limit the stages in which you work out the distance to just those stages referred to in the answers. Working out the distance is simply a question of reading values from the graph and subtracting the distance at the start of the stage from the distance at the end of that stage. You should work out the following distances from the relevant stages:

AB = 10
BC = 30
CD = 25
DE = 15
FG = 30
GH = 20

The skier travels 30 in stages BC and FG and therefore **D** is the correct answer.

8 The argument in this question is slightly convoluted. It is stated that mobile phone technology has come a long way since its inception, although this is largely irrelevant for the argument. There is one view, which is that scientists argue we have reached our peak in terms of mobile phone technology, but then the argument goes on to suggest that there is scope for further development in relation to device size and performance. **A** merely reflects the opening assertion of the argument and is not related to the argument about the current state of the technology. **C** is certainly stated as a conclusion but it is too narrow to be the main conclusion in this argument, which also takes into account improvements in nanotechnology. **D** is similar to **C** in that it too is stated but is also too narrow to capture the main conclusion of the argument. **E** is incorrect since it reads too much into the second half of the argument. It is stated that 'scientists even argue that we have reached our peak' which could imply (although not necessarily so) that all scientists argue we have reached our peak. More significantly however, the conclusion that we can do more in terms of mobile phone technology isn't presented as a view put forward by scientists – it could be the author's opinion or anybody else's – and so it is a step too far to state that there is dispute between scientists. **B** is correct and the final two sentences capture this sentiment, stating that more can be done to improve mobile phone technology and therefore we may not have reached our peak.

9 The argument here is that, in order that a certain outcome is achieved, two conditions must be satisfied. However, even though one of the conditions is not satisfied, there is a belief that the outcome will still be achieved. **A** is incorrect since there is no statement of belief and the outcome was still achieved despite the fact that the two conditions were not satisfied. **C** is incorrect since, although one of the conditions is not satisfied, unlike the argument in the question, the outcome will *not* be achieved here. **D**, too, is incorrect since, even though there is a belief that the outcome will be achieved, this is because *both* of the conditions have been satisfied. **E** is incorrect since there is a belief that the outcome will be achieved and this is in spite of the fact that *both* conditions have not been satisfied as opposed to just one not being satisfied. **B** is correct since there is a belief that the outcome will still be achieved (the flight taking-off) despite the fact that out of the two supposed requirements for this outcome (everybody on board and clear weather), one of them is not satisfied (clear weather). Do not be distracted from this answer by the different position of the outcome and the conditions within the structure of the argument as compared with the argument in the question – **B** is the only answer that contains the same number of conditions satisfied and the same outcome as the argument in the question.

10 In order to answer this question, you should first work out the time at which Dogs finishes in order to know the earliest possible time that Katie is able to meet. This, as you should have worked out, is 9.05 pm (2 hours and 20 minutes after 6.45 pm). Then, you need to work out the finishing times of the other shows in order to find out the earliest time that Lee is able to meet with Katie. You should have found that New York finishes the earliest at 8.55 pm and so the earliest possible time that Katie and Lee could meet after watching Dogs and another show respectively is 9.05 pm (if Lee watches New York). In other words, Lee would finish first and wait 10 minutes for Katie and then they would both meet. Therefore, **E** is the correct answer.

11 Approach 1

Setting up two equations will solve this problem.

Firstly, call the number of people in the family area 'x' and the number of people elsewhere 'y'.

You know that x + y = 3,000 because the total attendance was 3,000.

You also know that 5x + 8y = 21,000, because family area tickets cost £5, tickets elsewhere cost £8, and the total revenue was £21,000.

Since you want to find x, the number of people in the family area, use the first equation to eliminate the other unknown, y, from the second equation.

Rearranging the first equation yields y = 3,000 - x.

Using this definition of y in the second equation yields

5x + 8(3,000 - x) = 21,000.

Therefore, 5x + 24,000 - 8x = 21,000, and so - 3x = - 3,000.

Dividing both sides by -3 tells us that x = 1,000, and so **E** is the correct answer.

Now, you can plug this value back into both equations to test its validity. If there were 2,000 people with a ticket for 'elsewhere' paying £8, then you would have £16,000 in revenue so far. There would be 1,000 people in the family area, each paying £5, giving you a total revenue of £21,000 (£16,000 + £5,000), which is the amount stated in the question. Therefore, the equation works, and there were 1,000 people in the family area. In addition, since the rearranged first equation tell us y = 3,000 - x, it is straightforward to deduce y = 2,000.

Plugging these values into the second equation gives

5 x (1,000) + 8 x (2,000) = 5,000 + 16,000 = 21,000, which is indeed correct.

Approach 2

The above equation is not as simple as some others that you have come across in these papers and so you may not be able to set it up. You could go about this question using trial and error i.e. testing out each answer provided. In order to do this you should use each family area attendance figure provided and work out the amount of the revenue it would generate (so each figure x 5). You should then multiply the remaining attendance (which will be the number of people sitting elsewhere) by their ticket price (£8) to see if the total revenue you get is £21,000. You should find that this only works for **E**.

12 The argument structured as a conversation should make it easier to discern any inferences that can be drawn from it. **A** is incorrect since Person B acknowledges that aeronautical technology does not prevent all crashes from occurring. **B** is incorrect as Person A states that crashes are *very often* disastrous so this does not mean that they are *always* disastrous, nor that 'disastrous' should be equated with 'fatal'. You are not given any information as to the differences between flying at night and in the day time, nor about how and when crashes are reported in the news so **C** and **D** cannot be reliably inferred from the argument. **E**, a fairly general statement, can be reliably drawn as a conclusion from the argument since it is stated that there is very little risk of anything going wrong and the proportion of crashes to flights is very low. In addition, the fact that **E** states that air travel *seems* to be safe adds to the reliability of it as a conclusion to be drawn, as it does not state in definitive terms that air travel *is* a safe method of travel, which would be more difficult to infer.

13 This is a tricky question and it is recommended that you draw out the structure in order to help you place the reindeer. Whether you try and solve the problem first and then check that your answer is one of those listed or whether you go through each of the answers and test them according to the rules, you still need to have a good grasp of the rules to begin with. Starting with the first and last rules, you know that Blitzen must be on the left hand side and that Vixen must be on the right hand side. In order to ensure that they are as far apart as possible, they should go on the front and rear rows respectively. But you know that Blitzen cannot be on the rear row, so you know that Blitzen must be at the front left and Vixen at the rear right. Comet and Cupid must be on the first two rows and, here's the tricky part, they must be on the right hand side, one behind the other (it doesn't matter in what order). This is because they can't be diagonally opposite since that would only leave two spaces on each side and, since you know that Dancer must always be directly behind Donner, that would leave Prancer on the

same side as Dasher, which is not allowed. Nor can Cupid and Comet each be on the second row since that would give us the same problem (Prancer and Dasher on the same side). So, there are now three spaces down the left hand side and one space down the right hand side. Dancer must be behind Donner so they must be on the left hand side and since Prancer has to be ahead of Dasher but not next to Cupid or Comet, Prancer must fill that one remaining space on the right hand side (otherwise he would be next to Cupid or Comet, or behind Dasher). Finally, in order that Dasher is behind Prancer, Dasher would be at the rear left leaving Dancer directly behind Donner on the left hand side. The positions of the reindeer would look like this:

FRONT

Blitzen	Comet/Cupid
Donner	Comet/Cupid
Dancer	Prancer
Dasher	Vixen

REAR

Therefore, **B** is the correct answer.

14 The argument here is that Bollywood produces three times as many films as Hollywood and therefore it is no surprise that the overall quality of the films it produces is lower than that of Hollywood films. The argument then goes on to suggest that this is a shame since the skill of the actors is equal to that of their Hollywood counterparts and so Bollywood should produce fewer films in order that these actors may be given the credit they deserve in higher-quality films. The assumption, which is a fundamental one in order for this argument to work, operates twice in the argument. The first instance should be sufficient for you to identify it. A link is made between the fact that there are three times as many films produced as Hollywood and the poorer overall quality of the films and that this is no surprise. This could be a surprise if, in fact, producing more films actually raises the general standard of films. Naturally, the argument doesn't rely on this since this would not support the conclusion. Indeed, it relies on the opposite of this – that there is a causal link between the quantity of films produced and their quality. There is no indication of the proportionality of the relationship between quantity and quality, so **C** is incorrect. **A**, which does capture this causal connection, is the assumption that is made here, and in the final sentence, and so is the correct answer. **B** is incorrect since it is stated that Bollywood actors are as good as those in Hollywood. **E**, too, is stated in the final sentence so is incorrect. **D** is slightly trickier, although, if you have

143

got to grips with the argument, you should realise that this cannot be an assumption since it would lead to the argument breaking down. In fact, the opposite of it is probably assumed – that Bollywood *is* capable of producing higher quality films, which can be achieved by a reduction in the quantity produced.

15 The conclusion that there could perhaps be more focus on decreasing the prevalence of gun crime is premised on the fact that the UK should have a low level of knife crime (more on a par with other European countries) and that over the last five years there has been a significant drop in the level of knife crime. The flaw in this argument is to link the fact that there has been a significant drop and the need for a low level. The argument to divert resources away from knife crime and towards gun crime relies on the fact that there is now a low level of knife crime, but the mistake here is to assume that a significant drop has led to a low level. However, for example, if a low level is considered to be 20% then a drop from 100% to 60% would be considered significant but 60% is not a low level since it is still a long way off 20%. Therefore, **E** is the correct answer. **A** is not a flaw since the argument only relies on the fact that there has been a significant drop in the level of knife crime and it is irrelevant over how long a period this has occurred. **B** is not correct since this would not affect the argument at all. The argument only refers to other European countries as a marker for where the UK wants its level of knife crime to be and it is irrelevant what else is going on in these countries for the sake of this argument. **C** is incorrect since the normative claim to applaud these governments is not integral to the argument and is more of an incidental point. Aside from that, the argument is not claiming that we should applaud the governments in general, only that we should give some credit for this particular policy (which is probably fair). **D** is incorrect since the argument doesn't need to do this. The argument is more concerned with whether a particular target has been met and the consequences of this, rather than with questioning the target itself.

16 Let's start with the easier cube. If its volume is 125,000 cm³ then this must mean that its dimensions (length, height and depth) are 50 cm each. Therefore, the collapsed cube will have four squares, each with 50 cm sides and so the total area of the cube will be 10,000 cm² (4 x 50 cm x 50 cm).

As for the cuboid, both the lid and the base will have surface areas of 2,400 cm² since the relevant dimensions to multiply are the depth and the length (and not the height). As for the two middle pieces, the one on the left ('x') (when collapsed) will be one of the sides of the box and therefore its surface area would be depth multiplied by height = 40 cm x 50 cm = 2,000 cm². The right piece ('y') would be the side of the box you are looking at and its dimensions are the length and the height. So its surface area = 60 cm x 50 cm = 3,000 cm². Adding up all these figures, therefore, the total surface area of both collapsed boxes is 19,800 cm² (10,000 + 2,400 + 2,400 + 2,000 + 3,000). Therefore, **A** is the correct answer.

17 One of the most important things to bear in mind when answering this question is that you must draw a conclusion from the above argument and not from any other knowledge or views that you may have. It must be a *reliable* conclusion in the sense that it is drawn only from the information given to you in the argument. As such, you may be tempted by **A**, but this is going much further, in terms of what you can infer, than any of the information in the argument allows. The argument only deals with discrediting the economic model and does not make any normative claims about the alternatives to this model nor how the government should approach climate change in general. To jump from saying that this model may not be that useful to then concluding that the government should therefore intervene prior to the point in the model is a step too far and, even though this may be a sensible conclusion from your wider experience, this cannot be *reliably* concluded from the above argument. **B**, similarly, may be true according to some people, but this cannot be inferred directly from the argument. It is stated that it *may* only be economically viable long after the damage has been done, but there is no indication or theory in the argument about whether or not this point has actually occurred and so **B** cannot be reliably drawn as a conclusion. **D** is incorrect since the only detail of the model that is stated is that the shrinking supply of non-renewable fuels will push up their prices until a point at which it becomes economically viable to invest in renewable fuels. You are given no indication as to how the free market would affect the price of renewable fuels and so, based on the information given, you cannot draw any reliable conclusion about the price of renewable fuels let alone how the free market would affect it. **E** is incorrect since, although a particular economic model in the argument is discredited, there is no opinion stated about any other specific economic models relating to climate change or any economic models in general. Therefore, you do not have enough information in the argument to conclude anything about the reliability of economic models relating to climate change other than that this one may be unreliable. You can reliably draw **C** as a conclusion based on the workings of the model. It is stated, in relation to the model, that the shrinking supply of non-renewable fuels will increase their prices to a point where it becomes economically viable to invest in renewable fuels but it is not clear when this point will occur. Combining these two pieces of

information, you can reliably conclude that the future of the price of non-renewable fuels is uncertain. There may be other variables in the model that would create uncertainty as to when this point would occur but you are given no information about them, only about the prices of non-renewable fuels, and so you can only reliably conclude **C**.

18 First, you should find out how much paper is discarded overall. To do this, you should work out the total area of paper used to create the stamps, which is 12,000 cm². Next, work out the total area taken up by the five hundred rectangles, which is 6 x 3 x 500 = 9,000 cm². Of the remaining 3,000 cm², 20% is discarded, which amounts to 600 cm². Next, you know that there are 20 stamps per book which means 25 books are made from the 500 stamps (500 ÷ 20 = 25). Therefore, you should divide 600 by 25 to apportion the total discarded paper between each book and you should find that the amount of discarded paper per book is 24 cm². Therefore, **C** is correct.

19 The argument here is that, because classical music requires more talent, more hard work, and does not generally pay much, youngsters should start to listen more to classical music. Assessing each of the options in turn, **A** would strengthen the argument to a certain extent as it would support the notion that youngsters should listen to classical music more. However, this is based on the assumption that bringing generations closer together is a benefit and without this assumption, perhaps it would even weaken the argument. **B** may strengthen the argument since it adds more credibility to classical music, although, you would have to make the link between this fact and the claim that youngsters should, therefore, listen to it more, which may not be the case. **D** does not really affect the argument since, just because classical music is being targeted at youngsters on the radio, does not mean that youngsters *should* listen to it more. **E** may strengthen the argument since you could say that youngsters should at least try and appreciate something that was intended for them in the first place, although it does not add much credibility to the general claim that they should listen more to classical music. **C** strengthens the argument significantly since, although it rests on the assumption that you should listen to the music you like, which is probably a fair assumption, if youngsters would like classical music more than they like the music they currently listen to, then surely they should start listening to it. Essentially, here you have another reason as well as those given in the argument, but this reason appears to be the most compelling as to why youngsters should listen more to classical music.

20 **A** is incorrect because, if the shape was in that position, then the line in the middle would be horizontal and not vertical. **B** is incorrect because the triangle is in the wrong box (it's in the smaller rectangle rather than the larger one). **D** is incorrect since, with the shape in this position, the triangle should be pointing to the right and not to the left. **E** is incorrect because the shape is in the same position and the triangle is pointing the wrong way. **C** is therefore correct and accurately shows the shape when rotated through 180 degrees.

21 Remember that you can only draw a conclusion that is supported from the information given in the argument and not from your own knowledge. There is no information given as to why **B** would be a reliable conclusion to draw from the argument. For example, it doesn't link the idea that rich investors can only set transfer fees and wages artificially high *because* they are already exorbitant after we, the people, have caused them to be such. Perhaps, irrespective of what level we would cause transfer fees and wages to be at in the free market, rich investors would still set them at the same artificially high level. Therefore, you should not link these two concepts, which in the argument appear as independent, and so it is perfectly plausible that we, the people, are free of responsibility even for artificially high transfer fees and wages. If you cannot tell either way, then you cannot reliably conclude anything about responsibility. **C** is incorrect since the only factors which are stated as affecting transfer fees and wages in the argument are demand for tickets, merchandise, television revenue and the intervention of investors. Admittedly, the argument does not explicitly limit the effects to just these but, based on this information, it would be unreliable to conclude that there are more factors than those presented. **D** is incorrect since an economic downturn is not even mentioned and, if anything, it is stated that there is a 'trend' towards rich investors taking over football clubs. **E**, similarly, is incorrect because the opposite seems to be true from the argument. It is stated that, with the intervention of rich investors, transfer fees and wages are 'skewed upwards' and that they are set 'artificially high' and therefore it is not at all reliable to conclude that transfer fees and wages decrease with the intervention of rich investors. **A** can reliably be concluded from the argument since it is the intervention of rich investors which the argument suggests leads to transfer fees and wages being 'set artificially high'. The fact that they are 'set' and the use of the word 'artificial' imply something other than the free market, described earlier in the argument, is responsible for these high figures or, in other words, that a force outside the free market can affect transfer fees and wages.

22 The first task with this question is to understand what it is asking you to find out. You are asked to find out how much money was spent on new players in the season in which the Harley Dodgeball team achieved the greatest increase in points from the previous season. In other words, you need to find out in which season the team increased its points by the largest amount across all the seasons given, and then work out how much it spent on new players in that season. To do this, work out the differences in points to begin with. You should find that between 30th April 2008 and 30th April 2009 i.e. in the 2008/2009 season, the team achieved the greatest increase in points from the previous season. Next, you know that, before the start of this season, the team had spent £6.3 million on new players and by the end of the season it had spent £6.7 million cumulatively. Therefore, in this season, the team spent £0.4 million on new players making **D** the correct answer.

23 The easiest way to approach this question is to convert all the timings into London time. This is a similar technique to finding a common denominator in that you can change the values of certain information given to you in order to make a comparison or calculation easier. In this case, Depart from City A would now be 17:30, Depart from City B would be 00:45 and Arrive City C would be 06:45. Working with these times, you can take two approaches:

Approach 1

You know that there was 6 hours of flying time between Depart City B and Arrive City C (taking into account the time difference) and so there must be 8 hours and 35 minutes of flying time between Depart London and Depart City B (14 hours and 35 minutes minus 6 hours). You then know that there were 18 hours in total between Depart London and Depart City B (from 06:45 to 00:45) therefore there must have been 9 hours and 25 minutes of waiting time in total (18 hours minus 8 hours and 35 minutes) and so **C** is the correct answer.

Approach 2

A slightly quicker way to solve this question, still from the London-adjusted times, is to work out that there are 24 hours between departing London and arriving in City C and therefore, if there are 14 hours and 35 minutes flying time, then there must be 9 hours and 25 minutes of waiting time (24 hours – 14 hours and 35 minutes). Therefore, **C** is the correct answer.

24 This question requires you to identify accurately the main conclusion of the argument. Essentially, it is stated that people still believe in and embrace superstitions but that these are irrational and lead to odd behaviour and so, despite the fact that it is often asserted that humans are inherently irrational, we should endeavour to discourage irrational behaviour if it can be done easily. **A**, as should be evident from the summary above, is a premise in this argument instead of any sort of conclusion. **B** is only half of the conclusion and is too general. It is stated that we should endeavour to discourage irrational behaviour *if it can be done easily* and so there are limits on when we should do this. **D** is too specific since the conclusion in the argument seems to be more general – applying to all irrational behaviour and not just that behaviour concerning superstitions. **D** could certainly be inferred from the argument, but this is because the actual conclusion is more general. **E** is incorrect, firstly, because it doesn't contain the caveat that we should endeavour to discourage irrational behaviour *only* if it is easy to do so and, secondly, because the notion that humans are inherently irrational is not given as the reason for which we should discourage irrational behaviour; rather it is given as a claim that is made in relation to humans that may weaken the conclusion but which the argument claims we should disregard for the purposes of the conclusion. **C** is the best expression of the conclusion of the argument since it captures both elements: firstly, that we should endeavour to discourage irrational behaviour and, secondly, that we should do this only if it can be done easily. **C** is therefore the correct answer.

25 One method of answering this question would be to calculate the profit per book in 2010. This would be (£56,000 ÷ 1,400) ÷ 2 = £20. In 2011, there will be 1,680 books sold (1,400 x 1.2). Therefore, if Greg takes 50% royalties from the new profits, this would be simply 1,680 x £10 (or 1,680 x £20 x 0.5) giving £16,800. £5 for every extra book would be £1,400 ((1,680 – 1,400) x £5). Therefore, Greg would receive £18,200, making the correct answer **E**. If you got one of the other answers, check that you were using the royalty figure and not the profit or revenue figures and that you added £5 for each extra book sold in 2011 and not £5 for all books sold in 2011.

26 The argument here is that more than half of all graduates are unemployed in the first year after university and that these are talented individuals and we should therefore help companies or organisations access them in order to bring the statistic down. **A** would perhaps weaken the conclusion that we should make organisations aware of the talent available to them but, since this is only one aspect of the conclusion, it does not fatally weaken the argument. **C** would weaken the argument but not to a large extent since the argument is a general one and not confined to the current economic climate. **D** may weaken the argument but not greatly since, as with **A**, it is only one aspect of the conclusion and, in addition, despite it being difficult, it does not state that it is impossible. **E** is incorrect as the argument does not suggest that we should get more graduates into work because they are

a burden on society (the argument would not regard this as material), but because they are talented and could contribute much to any organisation. **B** is therefore correct and significantly weakens the argument since we will not be able to bring the unemployment statistic down by making employers aware of the talent and giving them practical recruitment advice if most graduates don't want to work anyway.

27 The argument here is that previous governments responded to violent protests negatively, protests against an increase in student fees were violent and therefore that protesters should turn to more peaceful methods of protest in order to influence current government policy. **B** is incorrect since it does not matter how many of the protesters were violent; the same conclusion – that protesters should be more peaceful – still applies irrespective of how many were violent. **C** is incorrect since it is stated that *as a result* of a lack of credibility, policy was not changed. **D** is incorrect since the argument is not concerned with whether there is any justification for the protest; rather it focuses on the nature of the protest and its effects. **E** is incorrect because the argument is not concerned with the legitimacy of violent protesting. Instead, it is more concerned with the effects on government policy. **A** is correct since there is a link made between the responses of past governments to violent protests and the response of the current government. This link relies on the fact that the current government will respond in a similar way to previous governments and this fact is therefore assumed.

28 This is a fairly straightforward question as long as you can visualise the folded piece of paper being unfolded at all four of its edges or if you can visualise folding each of the shapes provided along an axis. If the shape in the question is folded along either of the two side edges and you unfold it, then you will get a shape that looks like **E**. If it is folded along the top edge then you would see either shape **A** (assuming that the original piece of paper is rotated 90 degrees) or **C**. Shape **B** would be the result of unfolding along the bottom edge. If you fold shape **D** along a horizontal axis halfway up the image, you'll be left with a rectangle, rather than the original image. Therefore, **D** is the correct answer.

29 You need to understand the statistic presented to you in order that you are not tempted to choose one of the statements that sounds like it follows from the statistic even though it is actually very different. The statistic tells you about the age group and gender of those people in car accidents and not anything about people in any age group or gender in general. Therefore, **A** is incorrect since you are not told about how many young adults in the wider population have been involved in car accidents, only that those people who

have been involved in car accidents tend to be young males. Similarly, **E** must also be incorrect for this reason. You may be tempted to infer **B** but what you would be doing is causally connecting two statements given to you without there being any logical reason to do so. It is stated that young adults tend to drive in a more risky manner and that the majority of young adults involved in car accidents are male. You do not have sufficient information to conclude reliably that males therefore drive in a more risky manner than females; there could be a whole host of other reasons as to why the majority of young adults involved in car accidents are male. **C** is incorrect because, firstly, it is sometimes difficult to infer numerical percentages when you are not given any in the argument (although arguably here the words 'mostly' and 'majority' could support the 50% statistic). Secondly, and more importantly, it doesn't state in the argument that it is the *driver* that is the casualty in these accidents, only that these young adult males make up a sizeable proportion of casualties. They may all have been passengers in these recorded accidents. **D** can be inferred since it is stated that at the age that young adults are, they like to impress others and this sometimes leads to risky driving and therefore accidents. You can reliably conclude therefore that when they are over 25 (and so necessarily not 'at that age'), they will tend not to drive in as risky a manner or as fast and therefore there will not be as many accidents. This is supported by the fact that it is mostly young adults (aged 18 to 25) that make up the number of fatalities and casualties in car accidents and so by removing this category from possible drivers, the number of fatalities and casualties should fall. Finally, the statement does not even add that the number of car accidents should fall proportionally to the number of cars on the road and so, on the reasonable assumption that if the legal minimum driving age were raised then the number of cars on the road at any given moment should decrease, then it follows that the number of car accidents should also decrease.

30 The first thing you should understand in this question is the fact that the y-axis represents the profit level and not number of sales or any other value. Therefore, when Caroline's sales surge, the curve will rise, as is depicted on all of the graphs. However, when sales slow down, the curve should now fall since her profit level will decrease. The curve falls (as opposed to rising less steeply) because her profit level is calculated on a month-by-month basis and is not cumulative. Therefore, you can already dismiss graphs **D** and **E** since, in these graphs, the curve rises. When a rival book emerges and her profits quickly drop significantly, this would be shown by the curve continuing to fall but at a now steeper rate since her profits will drop in less time and to a lower level than the previous decrease in profit level. Graph **C** shows the curve fall less steeply and so this can be dismissed. Graph **B** doesn't even show the difference in rate and so it too is incorrect. When Caroline is confident that her profit level will begin to increase again, Graph

A shows the curve rising and therefore accurately depicts information and is the correct answer.

31 The easiest way of approaching this question is to draw out each of James' and Stephen's routes. You should find that James ends up at a point that is 11 km north of Point A and, crucially for this question, 2 km east of Point A. Stephen travels 8 km south and then travels 17 km east (the sum total of James' distances). After travelling 19 km north, Stephen will be at the same latitude as James, the question is just how far east Stephen is from James. If James is 2 km east of Point A and Stephen has travelled a total of 17 km east, then Stephen will be 15 km away from James. Therefore, **C** is correct.

32 Firstly, you need to work out what will happen in the eight days before you can begin calculating. In each 24-hour period, the hour hand will move twice around the clock face (am and pm). In terms of calculating the figure, it may be easier to deal with the eighth day period before adding on the final two hours. Therefore, there will be 8 x 2 x 360 degrees (8 days x 2 cycles x 360 degrees) = 5,760. Then deal with the final two hours. The hour hand moves 30 degrees between each hour (360 ÷ 12) and therefore, since you will be going from 6.30pm to 8.30pm on the 8th day, there will be an extra 60 degrees to add on to your running total. You should have calculated that the total number of degrees is therefore 5,820 and so **C** is the correct answer.

33 This is a tricky question which requires you to understand the above argument and then identify which has the same structure. The argument states that 'you can *only* become good at computer games *if* you have good hand-eye coordination. My brother does not have good hand-eye coordination, so he is not good at computer games' (emphasis added). The fact that the word 'only' is included means that it is a pre-condition that to be good at computer games you have good hand-eye coordination i.e. without this, you cannot be good at computer games. Therefore, if my brother does not have this pre-condition, it logically follows that he cannot be good at computer games. **B** is incorrect as the word 'only' is omitted which already changes the structure significantly – it is no longer a pre-condition that you need good hand-eye coordination i.e. if you have good hand-eye coordination then you can be good at computer games but, crucially, just because you haven't got good hand-eye coordination, it doesn't mean that you can't be good at computer games. Therefore, it doesn't logically follow that just because my brother is not good at computer games, he must not have good hand-eye coordination – there could be a lot of other reasons as to why he is not good at computer games. **D** is incorrect since, again, having good football boots is not a pre-condition for being a good football

player. Also, you know that you *can* be a good football player if you have good football boots, but this doesn't mean that just because you have good football boots, you *must* be a good football player. **E** is similar to **B** and is incorrect since, just because you don't have the ability to recognise different pitches of sound, it doesn't necessarily mean you can't be a good musician. This is because it is not a pre-condition of being a good musician that you have the ability to recognise different pitches of sound – you can still become a good musician without this. **A** and **C** are similar in that they both rely on pre-conditions i.e. they include the word 'only'. In both cases, they are logically sound but **C** is the correct answer because it more accurately reflects the structure of the above argument. This is because it contains a pre-condition and then states that *without* this pre-condition, the result is not possible whereas **A** states that *with* this pre-condition, the result is possible. Therefore, **C** is the correct answer.

34 The essence of the argument is that we should encourage governments to stop allocating resources to something which does not provide human beings with much benefit and costs a lot and, instead, encourage them to concentrate on more important alternatives. **A** is incorrect as it does not reflect the terms of the argument and is more of an inference that could be drawn from the argument as opposed to a similar argument illustrating the principle. **B** is similar to the argument to the extent that it states that we should encourage countries to stop allocating resources to an option that is expensive, however, the fact that it states 'despite its obvious benefits' means that this is incorrect. Part of the reasoning of the argument is that space programmes are not greatly beneficial to human beings. **C** is incorrect since this simply argues for modifying how resources are allocated in relation to a particular area, farming, whereas the argument goes further and argues that the option itself should be abandoned. **E** is incorrect since it is missing information about where this money is coming from. It maps on to the second half of the argument, i.e. we should direct resources into foreign aid as it helps people who are most in need of help but it does not address what we should discard in favour of foreign aid. **D** is correct since it states that we should no longer spend money on a particular option that is expensive (investing in energy companies) and which is not always successful and, instead, it is implied that we should focus more on another option.

35 There are two different pies which contain apple and so this question is testing how well you can judge their proportions merely from the information given in the pie chart and then perform a simple calculation. It seems as if the two relevant segments (Apple and Apple & Raspberry) together make up about half of the pie chart in which case the answer is simply $128 \div 2 = 64$. If you are not sure then you can certainly eliminate three of the other answers, on the basis that they are not even close to this (**A**, **B** and **E**).

153

As for **D**, Apple & Raspberry looks as if it takes up about $\frac{1}{3}$ of the pie chart (which would be about 43). Clearly then, adding the Apple category would add more than just seven so 50 would be an unrealistic answer.

36 Approach 1

As long as ratios don't faze you, these sorts of questions are relatively simple. Take the total number and divide it by the number of 'units' in the ratio i.e. 60 divided by the 5 units in this ratio. 1 unit therefore equals 12. If the ratio now is 3:2, whereas before it was equal (2:2), then you know that there has been an increase of one unit on the Victoria Line and therefore 12 extra trains. You can verify this by checking that a ratio of 2:2, where each of those 'units' is 12, would have led to a total of 48 trains (24 each), and then an extra 'unit' of 12 would give you 60.

Approach 2

An equation here would also give you the answer relatively easily. If you call one unit 'x' and you know that, after the investment, there are 5 units, then you can state that $5x = 60$ and therefore $x = 12$. Since there was one extra unit as part of the investment, there were 12 extra trains. **A** is therefore the correct answer.

37 This question relies on you dismissing some of the options based on the language used and really understanding the relationship between the statements in the argument. Also, as you will see, sometimes the answer is simpler than you may at first think. **A** cannot be reliably concluded since all that is stated is that we do not have the sophisticated technology available to predict the weather accurately. There is no information about the future development of this technology and it would be a step too far to conclude from the fact that we have had exponential technological development during the last century that we *will* have more sophisticated technology in future in this area. **B** is incorrect as there is not really any information that tells us much about the development in this area. It is stated that there has been exponential technological development during the last century and, although it is not clear whether this means generally or specifically in relation to weather prediction, you cannot conclude from this that there hasn't been any technological development in this area. It is stated later that there is no *sophisticated* technology to be able to predict the weather accurately, not that there is no technology at all, and so **B** cannot be concluded from this statement either. **C** is quite a definitive statement which makes it all the less likely that it can be reliably concluded from the argument. Firstly, it is stated that there are uncertain variables (at the moment) and there is no indication that these will always exist. Secondly, it is stated that these variables make it 'extremely difficult' to predict the weather accurately and

so you cannot conclude that it will always be *impossible* to do so – it isn't impossible to do so now, so why should it always be impossible? **D** would require you to infer that the development of sophisticated technology would remove one of the current problems. However, you simply do not have enough information to know or infer how this sophisticated technology would be used or how it would benefit weather prediction. It may be that these variables are impossible to control and that all that technology would bring about is an ability to reduce their uncertainty. So, concluding **D** would not be reliable from the information in the argument. **E**, on the other hand, despite appearing to be very simple and very obvious, is not stated in the argument and you are left to infer that meteorologists are the ones that predict the weather. It is stated that society often criticises 'those responsible' and that we shouldn't be too harsh on 'meteorologists'. There is an implicit link between meteorologists and those responsible for predicting the weather. Therefore, **E** can be reliably concluded.

38 One way of approaching this question is to start by calculating how far Tessa is from Point A when she stops. You know that Matt travels for 30 minutes and then turns around and drives back to Point A at the same speed. Therefore, Matt returns to Point A after one hour. In this time, Tessa reaches 20 miles away from Point A. In the 15 minutes that Matt takes to gather his belongings, Tessa will have travelled another 5 miles (20 ÷ 4). Therefore, Tessa will stop to take a rest 25 miles from Point A. If Matt sets off at 50 miles per hour at the same time as Tessa stops to take a rest, he will pass her after 30 minutes (60 ÷ 2). Therefore, **A** is the correct answer.

39 The argument here is that evidence shows that those who work regular night shifts are less productive, that these people also tend to get less sleep than those who work during the day and therefore that employers need to address this sleep issue if they want more efficient workers at night. The main flaw here is to assume that these two factors are connected when, in fact, no explanation is given as to why the argument concludes that employers need to address one issue to correct the other, i.e. no explanation as to why the argument links these factors together. Therefore, **D** is the correct answer. **A** is incorrect since the argument doesn't need to assume this in order for it to work – there is statistical evidence for less sleep and the explanation is irrelevant. **B** is incorrect as it does state that regular night shift workers are less productive and, more crucially, it doesn't matter *how* they are less efficient; it only matters that they *are* in fact less efficient. **C** is incorrect since, again, it does not matter for the argument how 'regular' these night shift workers are; the argument would still work since there is a statistic referring to a group of night shift workers and the argument does not need to differentiate between different types of night shift worker. **E** may be a criticism for anything you read and it

generally would be a flawed argument if statistics are fabricated. However, sometimes you need to assess the argument, taking for granted the truth of certain evidence. Irrespective of whether the statistics are credible or not, in this case, the flaw of creating a causal connection between two independent statistics is more significant than the credibility of the evidence itself.

40 This is a tricky question and you may feel uncomfortable with the idea of working out an average speed without any times or distances involved. Firstly, the answer is not simply the total speed divided by 4 (the number of stages) since Chantel and Sarah spent different amounts of time going up and down the hill and so **B** is incorrect. You do know that the distance from the house to the hill in both directions is the same as the distance both up and down the hill. Also, since the speed at which they walk to and from the hill is the same, what is relevant is the average speed up and down the hill. To work this out, let's say coming down the hill took time 't'. Going up the hill took time 3t because the speed was three times slower (6 ÷ 2), so the total time up and down was 4t.

Approach 1

The average speed on the hill = total distance ÷ total time

= (distance up + distance down) ÷ total time

= ((speed up × time up) + (speed down × time down)) ÷ total time

= ((2 × 3t) + (6 × t)) ÷ 4t

= (6t + 6t) ÷ 4t

= 12t ÷ 4t

= 12 ÷ 4

= 3

Approach 2

The average speed = (speed up x fraction of total time spent going up) + (speed down x fraction of total time spent going down)

$= (2 \times \frac{3}{4}) + (6 \times \frac{1}{4})$

$= \frac{6}{4} + \frac{6}{4}$

$= \frac{12}{4}$

= 3

So the average speed up and down the hill is 3 miles per hour. Since you know that the speed to and from the hill was also 3 miles per hour, the total average speed must be 3 miles per hour. Therefore, **A** is the correct answer.

41 This is a slightly tricky question and will require you to test out a few of the answers provided in order to verify whether or not they constitute the main assumption of the argument. **B** is incorrect as it is stated that the advantage of reading, as opposed to listening to, the news is for the final reason, which is to experience and analyse arguments and not for either of the first two reasons. Therefore, demonstrating that you are aware of developments in society is not relevant for the reading-listening distinction and so this is not an assumption that is, or needs to be, made in the argument. **C** is incorrect since it is stated that experiencing and analysing arguments 'is an essential skill that everybody should have'. **D** is incorrect since all that is stated is that keeping up with the news is essential to those with an interview and not that you will perform better if you have read the news as opposed to listened to it. This distinction is only relevant to the fact that experiencing and analysing arguments is an essential skill generally, and not to whether you will perform better at interviews or not. You could infer that **D** is true, but the argument does not rely on this as an assumption; the reading-listening distinction only applies as an incidental benefit of keeping up with the news. **E**, again, is not assumed and does not need to be assumed. It is stated that experiencing and analysing arguments is an important skill generally, from which you could infer that it is therefore an important skill in an interview. However, it is only a need to keep up with the news, which is stated to be essential for an interview, in order to demonstrate an interest in society and any developments. The benefit of experiencing and analysing arguments is added on as a general benefit that you would obtain from keeping up with the news, but not one which is stated to be essential in an interview. **A** is the correct answer, since the argument makes the recommendation to read the news as opposed to listening to it, in order to experience and analyse arguments but without explaining this distinction. The assumption behind this implicit link therefore must be that you can better experience (or even experience it at all) and analyse arguments from reading, as opposed to listening to, the news.

42 Firstly, you should work out that today is Friday, since the green bin was emptied three days ago on Tuesday. 40 days from now would therefore take us to a Wednesday in the 6th week from now (with the 1st week ending on the Friday, seven days from now). Both the bins would be emptied in the 3rd week and the 6th week from now (on a Tuesday) and the black bin only would be emptied on Thursday in the 1st, 2nd, 4th and 5th weeks from now. Therefore, there would be eight bins scheduled to be emptied in the 40 days, so **B** is the correct answer.

43 The essence of the argument, in more general terms, is that a decision should be made in favour of one option over other options, because that decision will provide necessary help to that option, and because the other options have already had the benefit of the decision in the past. **A** is therefore incorrect since England already has good stadia which do not *need* improving and because it is implied that England has already had the benefit of hosting the Olympics, which is the antithesis of the second half of the argument. **C** is incorrect because it is incomplete and does not fully parallel the reasoning in the argument since, whilst choosing to invest in universities which need funding, maps onto the first half of the argument, there is no mention of whether universities have had funding before. **D** is incorrect because it does not state that those on disability benefits *need* more money, which is the essence of the first half of the argument. In a similar vein, **E** is incorrect since it is not stated that ID cards are needed to improve national security. **B** is correct since it is stated that British transport is in need of updating in the same way as Russia is in need of better infrastructure, and which, in both cases, the decision will help. Also, in a comparable way to how Russia has not been the host country before, it is stated that public transport has been ignored in terms of investment since its creation.

44 The argument outlines a few advantages to fixed-term contract mobile phone deals and, from this, concludes that *everyone* should choose this over a 'pay-as-you-go' package. The flaw here arises from the conclusion that every consumer should choose a fixed-term contract. Therefore, **A** is correct as it is assumed, from the advantages highlighted, that every consumer will benefit from these. **B** is incorrect since the argument does not need to acknowledge the flaws of a fixed-term contract; it simply states the advantages of this option and uses these to conclude that everyone should choose it. It could be said that, if flaws of the fixed-term contract option were exposed in the argument, then the conclusion that everyone should choose this over the 'pay-as-you-go' package would not appear as valid. However, without acknowledging the flaws of the fixed-term contract option, it is the conclusion itself which is flawed (as in **A**) as opposed to the missing acknowledgement of any flaws of a fixed-term contract. **C** is not a flaw, since it is not a fact that is relied upon in order for the argument to work. In other words, even if all mobile phones were not available on a fixed-term contract, the conclusion that everyone should choose a fixed-term contract still stands, albeit only mobile phones on a fixed-term contract could be chosen. **D** is incorrect as it is stated that the 'pay-as-you-go' system is 'obsolete'. Indeed, you would expect an argument of this sort in order to conclude that everyone should choose a fixed-term contract. **E** is incorrect as there are three reasons provided in the argument as to why a fixed-term contract is better than the 'pay-as-you-go' system and so some justification is presented.

45 The best way of tackling this question is firstly to convert all the values into 100 g values (finding the lowest common denominator). After converting the values, the table will look like this:

Product	Vitamin content (per 100 g)	Calories (per 100 g)	Price (per 100 g)
Babies Foodies (100 g jar)	28 g	180	£1.82
Baby Food plc (200 g jar)	30 g	120	£1.80
Food for Young 'Uns (150 g jar)	40 g	90	£1.64
Healthy Babies (100 g jar)	36 g	200	£1.84
Health Kids (200 g jar)	40 g	100	£1.65

From this, you can conclude that Food for Young 'Uns is the cheapest, has fewest calories and, along with Health Kids, has the highest vitamin content. Therefore, Emma should choose this product and **C** is the correct answer.

46 In order to answer this question, you need to understand the argument fully, especially the conclusion. Essentially, it is argued that there are a large range of physiological responses that are used in a lie detector test. If any of these is inaccurate then decisions based on the test could be wrong, and therefore a lie detector test is unsuitable for its purpose. The key here is the word 'if'. There is no evidence provided as to whether the large range of physiological responses may in fact lead to inaccuracies. Either this is presumed, or the conclusion that a lie detector test is unsuitable for its purpose is still argued, despite there being no link between the large range of physiological responses and a hypothetical situation of inaccuracy. Either way, there is a flaw here and that flaw is to suggest that just because there is a large range of physiological responses there may *necessarily* be some inaccuracy. Since the conclusion seems to rest on the fact that there may be some inaccuracy, if this is not proved or at least argued for, then the conclusion shouldn't flow from this. Therefore, **A** is the correct answer. The other answers are incorrect either because they are stated in the argument, and so the argument is not creating any causal links without saying so (**B** and **C**), or the conclusion can logically flow with them included and so they are not flaws (**D** and **E**).

47 In order to answer this question, you should work out, for each employee, how long they have been employed by the company, how many weeks' notice they therefore need to give the company before they finally leave, and then the amount of money they will earn in this period between handing in their notice and finally leaving. Essentially, you will be multiplying the weekly wage for each employee by 1, 2, 3 or 4. You should find that Suhail requires two weeks' notice thereby earning £1,030 (£515 x 2), Roberta requires one weeks' notice thereby earning £450 (£450 x 1), Arthur requires three weeks' notice thereby earning £1,230 (£410 x 3), Moira requires four weeks' notice thereby earning £1,320 (£330 x 4) and Sinclair requires three weeks' notice thereby earning £1,125 (£375 x 3). Therefore, Moira earns the most and **D** is the correct answer.

48 This question is not as simple as it first seems and the answer is not, as you may first think, $\frac{1}{27}$ since this is the probability of a ball going in a pocket in *all* of the three breaks ($\frac{1}{3}$ x $\frac{1}{3}$ x $\frac{1}{3}$) . The way to solve this question is to ask what the probability is of me *not* pocketing a ball in the three breaks. In each break there is a $\frac{2}{3}$ chance that I will not pocket a ball and therefore in three breaks there is an $\frac{8}{27}$ chance that I will not pocket a ball in any of them ($\frac{2}{3}$ x $\frac{2}{3}$ x $\frac{2}{3}$). Therefore, there is a $\frac{19}{27}$ chance that I will pocket at least one ball in the three breaks.

49 The argument here is that, because mobile phones are capable of incorporating a camera which appears to be as good as a stand-alone camera, and there is added convenience from having a camera on a mobile phone, there should be a dramatic decrease in the reasons to buy a stand-alone camera. **A** is incorrect as it actually strengthens the argument that there should be a decrease in reasons to buy a stand-alone camera. **B** weakens the argument to a certain extent as it implies that stand-alone cameras are better than cameras on phones due to the video function, however this would not dramatically reduce the reasons to buy a stand-alone camera. **D** does weaken the argument, since one of the reasons to buy a mobile phone with a camera – that of convenience of size – may now also be a feature of stand-alone cameras. However, this is only one reason as to why a stand-alone camera is just as good, whereas the argument offers two other reasons as to why there should be a decrease in reasons to buy a stand-alone camera and so it does not significantly weaken the argument. **E** may weaken the argument but it doesn't account for the situation where you have a mobile phone without a camera on it in addition to a stand-alone camera on your possession and this would be the relevant comparison. Also, it is not clear by how much the risk of being mugged increases; it may only be negligible. **C** does significantly weaken

the argument since, if there is still only a tiny proportion of mobile phones which have cameras, despite the fact that they are capable of incorporating one, then there should not be a dramatic decrease in reasons to buy a stand-alone camera. This is because most people would still not have a camera on their mobile phone and so should still have a reason to buy a stand-alone camera, albeit this would be at a slowly decreasing rate.

50 This is a fairly straightforward question and don't be fooled by the numbers at work in the argument. It is stated that X plc decisions need *at least* three quarters of all board members to agree in order that they are passed. It should not matter that the number that is exactly three quarters of the number on the board is not a whole number. It would simply mean that the decision would need the next whole number higher than this number to pass a decision (but it does have to be a whole number because each number represents one person's vote and you can't, for example, have half a vote). Therefore, **D** is the correct answer. **A** is not a flaw since this is a highly subjective statement and also the rigour of the mathematical analysis does not affect the logical flow of the argument. **B** is incorrect, since the conclusion is based on the number of board members at the present time, and the use of the phrase 'at the present time' implies that the argument acknowledges that the number of people on the board will change. **C** is incorrect since the argument does not ignore the fact that voters can abstain; the flaw is based on the connection between a three-quarter majority and this being a whole number, rather than whether voters abstain or not. **E** is incorrect since the argument actually assumes that you *do* need a whole number in order to pass a decision and so the flaw is actually the antithesis of this statement.

Oxford TSA section 2:
Model answer and essay plans

Model answer

What is the difference between fact and opinion?

In this essay, it will be argued that the difference between fact and opinion rests on two factors. These are, firstly, evidence and, secondly, the number of people that accept this evidence as pointing to a certain state of affairs as being the case. This essay will seek to show that, whilst an opinion is a view about a state of affairs that most people consider unsubstantiated by evidence, a fact, on the contrary, is a view considered by most people as being substantiated by the evidence.

It is useful for this essay to refer to a famous opinion which has since become fact in order better to explain the difference between a fact and an opinion. Despite being proposed and rejected on various occasions in history, the statement that 'the world is a sphere' was once criticised as being an opinion rather than anything factual. However, very few people today would categorise this statement as an opinion and most would say that it is a fact. So, what has changed? The answer lies in the amount of evidence, specifically, the number of people that accept that the evidence points to a certain state of affairs being the case. It is submitted that there are two possible reasons for people not accepting a spherical Earth as a fact in the Middle Ages. The first is that there was simply no evidence pointing to this fact. If the statement that 'the world is a sphere' was merely proposed by a member of society one day with no further supporting explanation or evidence, then why would anybody accept this as being a fact? The second explanation is that there could have been evidence for which the person who proposed the statement offered in support of the opinion but which no other person accepted as sufficient, either in terms of amount or quality. In other words, people wanted more or better evidence before they accepted the truth of the statement that 'the world is a sphere'.

Looking at today's society, very few would argue that there is not enough or good enough evidence to support the idea that the Earth is spherical. There is live footage, photographs and eye-witness accounts of this idea, in addition to a plethora of mathematical calculations which support the fact. Most people in society would accept that this evidence points to a state of affairs whereby the Earth is a sphere. This is no longer an opinion therefore; it is a fact, and this transition occurred at some point in history and, most likely, over a number of years.

So, having arrived at the point whereby the difference between a fact and an opinion has been described as a difference in the number of people accepting evidence pointing to a certain state of affairs as being the case, a few questions still need to be answered.

The first is when something becomes a fact. Was it a fact that the world is spherical because one person proposed it as a possibility and, crucially, he or she themselves accepted that there was enough evidence pointing to this as a fact? The answer is no. A 'fact' is inherently something that is *objectively* accepted to be true due to the number of people that accept the evidence pointing towards it.

The next question, inevitably, is how many people are required to accept this in order for opinion to become fact? This is a tricky question. Clearly it is more than just a small percentage, and clearly it doesn't need to be 100% (for there may still be people who don't accept evidence pointing towards a spherical Earth, but this is still regarded as a fact by society). The answer may be specific to each individual state of affairs and is probably found by observing when the state of affairs is regarded by society, in general, as being the case. Usually, however, it will be more than 50% of people.

Finally, it may be asked, what about a situation where evidence seems, in its own right, to point to a state of affairs but where people do not accept that it does? For example, if an experiment was conducted 1,000 times and 999 times yielded the same outcome, would that be intrinsically 'good' enough evidence to point to that outcome as being a fact? If most people accepted that it was, then, as this essay has proposed, it would be a fact. But what if they didn't? Whilst this would be a rare situation, assuming that humans are rational and would interpret such strong results as this in the same, sensible manner, the scenario could still arise. It is submitted, tentatively, that there probably cannot be an intrinsic, objective evaluation as to whether results such as this would point to the outcome being a fact. Otherwise this may undermine the argument here since it would mean that a 'fact' could be something outside the control of people accepting evidence for the truth of something. Therefore, if people did not accept the evidence of an outcome occurring in 99.9% of cases pointing to it being true, then it would not be a fact.

In conclusion, this essay has attempted to argue that the difference between a fact and an opinion lies in the amount and quality of evidence that exists supporting a state of affairs, but more importantly, whether people accept that this evidence does point to the state of affairs as being the case. An opinion becomes a fact when a sufficient number of people accept that the amount and/ or quality of evidence points to the state of affairs as being the case.

<u>Essay plans</u>

Is it more justified to donate money to charities that help less economically developed countries than those that help more economically developed countries?

<u>Definitions</u>

- It may be worth defining 'justified' as meaning justified in some moral sense so that charities that help less economically developed countries are more morally worthy of any money donated than charities that help more economically developed countries.

- 'Charities' don't need defining – this is fairly unambiguous.

- 'Less economically developed countries' and 'more economically developed countries', likewise, are clear, although you may expand on the distinction between these in the main body of your essay.

<u>Possible answers + arguments</u>

Yes, it is more justified to donate money to charities that help less economically developed countries than those that help more economically developed countries:

- The problems that charities help to alleviate in less economically developed countries are more severe than those in more economically developed countries. For example, charities in the latter countries help to improve the quality of life of those who suffered or who experience problems whereas the focus on charities in the former countries is on allowing people to have a life at all. An assumption here is that it is more justified to allow a life at all than to improve the quality of an existing life. Indeed, some may argue that the type of life that people in less economically developed countries is a very poor one. However, this argument rests on the assumption that saving a life is more important than improving the quality of an existing life.

- Less economically developed countries receive little assistance from other sources and are often poor countries generally. This means that state bodies are often powerless to collect and allocate resources to help those most in need whereas in more economically developed countries, there is often an impressive welfare system in order to allocate resources to the most needy. Less economically developed countries therefore need more help from non-governmental bodies such as charities in order that the most needy are given help.

- It is sometimes the case in less economically developed countries that corruption and weak systems of government prevent many resources from being allocated to those most in need. Charities can help in two-ways, therefore. Firstly, they ensure that resources are allocated to those that most need them, but, secondly, they could work on improving structures in less economically developed countries to ensure that in future, resources can be allocated to these people.

- There is a more general argument that it is a question of luck whether one is born into an less economically developed country or a more economically developed country and so those born into the latter should acknowledge this and strive to re-dress the balance by helping those that are more unfortunate than them.

No, it is as justified to donate money to charities that help less economically developed countries as it is to those that help more economically developed countries:

- Helping more economically developed countries is more efficient in terms of how the money is distributed, since charities that help more economically developed countries are less subject to bureaucracy, obstacles and other inefficiencies and so the ratio between money spent and 'good' that results may be higher than if money is donated to less economically developed countries. This would be subject to a counter-argument about the value of a life versus improving the quality of a life (see above).

- Helping more economically developed countries now may benefit less economically developed countries in the long-run. There are two strands to this argument. Firstly, perhaps it could be argued that dealing with problems in more economically developed countries first would allow charities to focus all their efforts on less economically developed countries afterwards (although this assumes that there won't always be on-going problems in more economically developed countries). Secondly, perhaps by improving conditions and problems in more economically developed countries, more can be learnt about how effectively to help those in less economically developed countries. So we could indirectly help people in both less economically developed countries and more economically developed countries by donating money to charities that help the latter countries.

- There is a more general argument that any sort of charity or help given to people is good and there is always a justification in donating money to charities. And, as long as some good is occurring, there is no point in comparing the justification for various charities. This argument would need to address the difference in value of, for example, allowing a child in a less economically developed country to survive versus improving the quality of life of an elderly person in a more economically developed country.

No, it is more justified to donate money to charities that help more economically developed countries than those that help less economically developed countries:

- This would be a difficult position to justify, although similar arguments can be proposed to the position above, that they are equally as justified, but that there are actually more or stronger advantages of contributing money to charities that help more economically developed countries than those that help less economically developed countries.

Should human rights be universal?

Definitions

- It is essential to define the concept of a 'human right' in order to answer this question even if you simply refer to those rights contained in the European Convention on Human Rights. It is also worth citing a few examples, such as the right to life, the right to be free from torture and freedom of expression.

- 'Universal' should be defined too since it could be interpreted in two ways. Firstly, the more conventional understanding, that human rights apply to everybody. Secondly, and perhaps slightly more tenuous, that human rights are absolute so that they cannot be eroded in any way. This second interpretation pushes the semantic boundaries of 'universal' so perhaps it should only be included as an afterthought rather than encompassing the bulk of the essay.

Possible answers + arguments

Yes, human rights should be universal:

- It could be argued that the term 'human rights' speaks for itself so that these rights are labelled as such precisely because they should apply to every human being. It is important that every human being is afforded some basic protection in society, simply as a virtue of being human, since this reflects our moral standards that humans should be treated as equals. Even if you do not adopt a Kantian natural law approach, this proposition can still be accepted. One inherent aspect of this is that these rights are inalienable so that these rights are not contingent on anything (other than being human, of course) and that these rights are always protected in a human.

- If it is argued that these rights are not inalienable and that, in some circumstances, violations of these rights are permitted, then a decision needs to be made, and boundaries demarcated, as to the circumstances in which these violations are justified. This is an extremely problematic situation to face since it essentially results in many people living their life in fear – knowing that they may not always be protected from violations of basic human rights, but not knowing when this may occur – and this is, in addition, a grave violation of the rule of law.

- Finally, if one sacrifice is allowed, so that one circumstance allows for the violation of a human right, then what is to stop more and more of these violations occurring? While one could argue that there would be stringent checks in place to prevent it from occurring, this is a paradigmatic slippery slope argument and, by opening the door, however slightly, to violations of human rights, there is a risk that more and more violations would occur. It also represents an implicit acceptance that the concept of a violation is justified in some circumstances. Instead, to prevent this risk of implicit acceptance, it is better to simply say that there are no circumstances in which a violation is allowed so that every human being is afforded protection.

No, human rights should not be universal:

- The argument here would be that there are situations in which it is possible for a human being not to be afforded the protection of basic human rights and that therefore human rights should not be universal.

- One possible situation could be where the harm that will be caused by not violating a human right would be much greater than where a human right is violated. For example, if a person had planted a bomb which, if it were to explode, would kill thousands of people and torturing this person would reveal the whereabouts of the bomb and save these lives, then it would cause much less harm, to society overall, to torture this person and save these lives. In cases like this, it would be justified in violating this individual's human right (not to be tortured). However, the counter-argument would question how realistic this situation is. Is there a 100% chance you would find out the whereabouts of the bomb from torturing the suspect? If it is only 99% and you would still torture that person, then where is the line drawn in terms of chance of discovering the information?

- A more general argument would be that humans are afforded rights not only as a virtue of being human, but also by virtue of adhering to certain moral standards in society. Hence, if you drop below the level of these moral standards, for example by planting a bomb which could kill thousands, then you sacrifice your protection and human rights may no longer apply to you. The counter-argument to this may be that this is what punishment, such as imprisonment, is designed for – to remove certain rights as a result of behaviour below certain moral standards. 'Human rights', properly called, are in a special category of rights which should not operate in the same way as those that are violated when a person is imprisoned, for example, and which should always be inalienable.

Is reality television a cause, or an effect, of a desire to observe the lives of other people?

Definitions

- It is perhaps worth clarifying the 'desire' (deriving some sort of pleasure from watching others) and maybe giving some examples of reality television, e.g. Big Brother.

Possible answers + arguments

Reality television is a cause of a desire to observe others:

- We have only started to become interested in observing others and their daily lives as a result of reality television. Shows such as Big Brother have led us to realise that we do, as a society, derive some sort of pleasure from observing other people.

- We haven't really had the means to observe others in the past and so television, and reality television in particularly, have showed us that it is possible to delve deeply into the lives of others. Certain reality television programmes, such as Big Brother, have given us the means to do so. It is only after realising that we have the means to observe others so intimately that we have developed a desire to do so.

Reality television is an effect of a desire to observe others:

- People have always expressed an interest in other people and have always had a desire to observe the lives of others. Reality television, despite its relatively recent inception, merely responds to this demand to observe and know about the lives of other people.

- In a similar vein, much of what appears on television is a result of what people want to watch, as opposed to programmes being randomly chosen to be on television and thus fostering an interest in their content. Therefore, the proliferation and increase of reality television programmes is as a result of companies realising that this is what people want to watch and offering it to them.

- People have always had the means to observe and know about the lives of others, for example, a 'café culture' in cities such as Paris is so successful because people enjoy watching the daily lives of others. Since reality television is so recent, it does not follow that it is the cause of a desire to observe others, since this desire existed long before reality television and even television itself.

Reality television is both a cause and an effect of a desire to observe others:

- A combination of the above reasons could lead to this conclusion, but specifically, it could be argued that reality television responded to a desire to observe others so that it was an effect, but it has led to an increase in this desire in society. This could be as a result of more people now expressing a similar desire, based on their enjoyment of reality television, or it could be as a result of each individual now having more of a desire to watch others. So, reality television can be both a cause and an effect of a desire to observe others.

Reality television is neither a cause nor an effect of a desire to observe others:

- This would be a difficult argument to sustain since it would require arguing that reality television, and a desire to observe others, are independent and unrelated. A possible argument could be that the enjoyment that people derive from watching reality television is something unconnected with a desire to observe others; rather they both arise from a common cause, for example, general curiosity.

Thinking Skills Assessment: practice test 1 answers

Cambridge TSA paper: answers
Oxford TSA section 1: answers

1.	C	26.	B
2.	C	27.	A
3.	C	28.	D
4.	B	29.	D
5.	E	30.	A
6.	D	31.	C
7.	D	32.	C
8.	B	33.	C
9.	B	34.	D
10.	E	35.	C
11.	E	36.	A
12.	E	37.	E
13.	B	38.	A
14.	A	39.	D
15.	E	40.	A
16.	A	41.	A
17.	C	42.	B
18.	C	43.	B
19.	C	44.	A
20.	C	45.	C
21.	A	46.	A
22.	D	47.	D
23.	C	48.	E
24.	C	49.	C
25.	E	50.	D

Thinking Skills Assessment: Practice test 2

Cambridge TSA paper
Oxford TSA section 1

Cambridge TSA instructions

There are 50 questions in this paper. For each question there are five possible answers, only one of which is correct. No marks are deducted for wrong answers so you should attempt all 50 questions.

You have 90 minutes to complete this paper. You may NOT use a calculator but you may use a dictionary (book or electronic).

Oxford TSA instructions

Section 1 of this paper contains 50 questions. For each question there are five possible answers, only one of which is correct. No marks are deducted for wrong answers so you should attempt all 50 questions.

You have 90 minutes to complete Section 1. You may NOT use a calculator.

Section 2 of this paper contains four essay questions of which you must choose **one**.

You have 30 minutes to complete Section 2. You may NOT use a dictionary.

1 I have a complicated analogue clock system at work whereby I have two clocks – the first to show me the hour, and the second to show me the minutes past the hour. My first clock looks similar to a conventional clock face except that it displays all 24 hours on it so there are 24 numbers on the clock face. The hand only moves on the stroke of each hour, pointing to the next hour immediately. The second clock face also looks similar to a conventional clock face in that it has 12 numbers on it, except that on this clock face, the numbers represent minutes in intervals of five, such that it shows the numbers 0, 5, 10, 15 and so on to 55. Each clock has only one hand, which points to the hour and the number of minutes past the hour respectively.

How many degrees in total do the hands move through between 23:35 today and 19:25 tomorrow?

A 7485

B 7410

C 7425

D 7440

E 7065

2 People are increasingly illegally downloading music, films and sharing copyrighted files. This does more harm to the relevant industries than most people think. A common argument that people use to assuage their consciences is that they think they are only taking away profits from successful pop stars, who earn an extravagant salary anyway. However, there are many more people behind the scenes involved in these industries who are losing their jobs and struggling to find other employment, such as runners in the film industry and studio workers in music.

Which of the following best summarises the conclusion of the argument above?

A Taking away profits from successful pop stars by illegal downloading and file sharing does more harm than good.

B There is a lack of jobs in the music and film industries.

C Runners and studio workers are most affected by illegal file sharing.

D Illegal file sharing can have a wider effect than most people realise.

E People should start buying music and films legally to save jobs in these industries.

3 Terry is a keen squash player and is trying to find the right type of squash ball to suit his game best. Squash balls vary in terms of speed and cost and Terry is comparing five different balls. He works out their speed by hitting them from the back of the court and timing how long it takes for the ball to return to him. Terry is 12 metres away from the wall against which the balls bounce.

Ball Brand	Cost	Travel Time (seconds)
Whizzball	£1.32 (pack of 3)	0.30
Squashysquash	£1.84 (pack of 4)	0.30
Ballmart	£1.18 (pack of 2)	0.60
Squishsquash	£2.64 (pack of 6)	0.45
Rapidball	£0.44 (per ball)	0.35

Terry wants the fastest balls at the cheapest price (per ball). Which brand of ball should he choose?

A Whizzball

B Squashysquash

C Ballmart

D Squishsquash

E Rapidball

4 Deirdre decides to sell her shares in three companies. She has 15,000 shares split between Company X, Company Y and Company Z in proportions of 25%, 30% and 45% respectively. She first sells her shares in Company X at a rate of £1.50 per share and her shares in Company Y at a rate of £1.60 per share. She then waits a week before selling her shares in Company Z. During that week, the share price of Company Z had a low of £1.10 and a high of £1.50.

If Deirdre had sold her shares in Company Z during that week, what are the minimum and maximum amounts of money that she could have made in total from selling all her shares?

A A minimum of £20,475 and a maximum of £22,950

B A minimum of £22,950 and a maximum of £24,825

C A minimum of £13,050 and a maximum of £17,625

D A minimum of £20,250 and a maximum of £22,950

E A minimum of £20,250 and a maximum of £23,175

5   Binge drinking is becoming a serious problem in society nowadays and has led to an increase in violent behaviour. Alcohol is easy to get hold of, even with an age verification process in place. Further, people have very few other outlets for their stress and the cost of alcohol is still relatively cheap compared to in a lot of other countries. More attention therefore needs to be focused on educating children about the harmful effects of alcohol which will mean that they are less likely to take up the habit.

Which of the following is the main flaw in the above argument?

A   It assumes that education is likely to tackle the problem of underage binge drinking.

B   It fails to acknowledge the benefits of alcohol.

C   It assumes that binge drinking hasn't been a problem until now.

D   It attributes the problem to children, without justifying whether or not they are the problematic group in society.

E   It fails to explain why alcohol is a serious problem in society nowadays.

6   Whilst re-branding their company, Minty and Co solicitors have decided to choose a snappy and unusual mission statement. They have narrowed down their list to the following five words, but they have an added requirement that the word, when stuck onto their transparent glass office doors, must read the same on both sides of the door.

Which word must they choose to fulfil this added requirement?

A   WOOSOOW

B   AMATAMA

C   STOOTS

D   RAAR

E   TANAT

7   Many people campaign against the increase of mobile phone masts on the grounds that they are an eyesore when placed around towns and the countryside. However, firstly, this is not true, as technology has enabled masts to exist discreetly and out of the sight of most people. Secondly, these masts are necessary in order that everybody has adequate mobile phone network coverage across the country. With more and more people relying on mobile phones, not only should we try and silence these campaigners, but we should actively encourage the erection of more mobile phone masts.

Which of the following is the best statement of the flaw in the above argument?

A   It doesn't explain how mobile phone masts have become more discreet.

B   It assumes that we can't use any other technology in order to boost mobile phone network coverage.

C   It fails to demonstrate why we need more mobile phone masts.

D   It doesn't justify why more and more people need to rely on mobile phones.

E   It fails to acknowledge that there may be other reasons as to why the increase of mobile phone masts may be a bad thing.

8   I sometimes go a day or two without eating because it makes me appreciate food a lot more. When I appreciate food a lot more, I tend to cook less food so that there is no chance of any waste. And when I cook less food, I spend less money.

Which of the following most closely parallels the reasoning used in the argument above?

A   During the summer months I stay up later at night in order to make the most out of the warmth. This makes me appreciate the summer a lot more, but often makes me tired.

B   When boxing, I sometimes let myself get hit a few times by the opponent. This makes me realise how much pain I could be in and ensures that I keep up my guard at all times. This generally makes me a better boxer.

C   I make sure that I see my children for at least two hours a day in order that I spend quality time with them. This makes them happy and makes me a better father.

D   I put one sugar in my tea because some sugar is good for the immune system. If my immune system is healthier, then I am less prone to illness in general.

E   Occasionally, I will order a takeaway for dinner. It makes me appreciate home-cooked food and it saves on the washing up but I realise that it is fairly unhealthy.

9 Jim has a new electric car, which is environmentally friendly but needs charging very often. Jim leaves Point A with a fully charged car and travels 4 km south, then 14 km east, then 38 km north. At this point, Jim's car has no power and needs fully charging again, which Jim does. He then travels 4 km east, then 34 km south, then 4 km west and arrives at Point B. There is a straight road between Point A and Point B and Jim leaves Point B on this road towards Point A.

After travelling half the distance between Point A and Point B on this straight road, Jim stops to charge his car. At the point he stops, how much power is left in Jim's car, as a percentage of the total power capacity?

A 17.5%

B 20%

C 12.5%

D 25%

E 10%

10 Research has suggested that children who learn to play a musical instrument from an early age, or at least learn musical notation, tend to perform better across all aspects of the curriculum later on in their education. Studies also find that this correlation is particularly evident in learning languages later on in life. This makes sense because learning a musical instrument or musical notation is similar to learning a language and so trains the brain at an early age to grasp new ideas from scratch.

Which of the following is a conclusion that can reliably be drawn from the above argument?

A Learning a foreign language as a toddler should mean that you will be better able to learn musical notation later on in life than a toddler who didn't learn a foreign language.

B Listening to classical music as a young child should mean that you will be better able to learn a foreign language later on in life.

C Learning to play the recorder in primary school should make you better at learning a foreign language in secondary school.

D Learning a foreign language as a child will mean that you will be able to play an instrument easily later on in life.

E Learning to play the piano as a young child should mean that you will be better able to learn another instrument later on in life.

11 Robert and Jane are having a dinner party. They decide to invite six guests – four men and two women – Bob, Paul, Adam, Ian, Claire and Eve. The narrow table has three chairs on either side of it and one on each end. The seating plan must adhere to the following rules:

- No two women must sit next to or opposite one another.
- Robert must sit at one end of the table with Jane to his immediate right.
- Eve must sit next to Bob, but not opposite Adam.
- No three men may sit next to each other (even if one of them is at an end).
- Claire must sit opposite Ian but not next to Adam.

Who will be seated to the right, left and opposite side of Paul respectively?

A Robert, Bob and Ian

B Claire, Jane and Robert

C Robert, Adam and Jane

D Robert, Claire and Jane

E Robert, Eve and Jane

12 Recent severe wintry weather has exposed weaknesses in Britain's infrastructure. The transport system ground to a halt across the country with many journeys cancelled or significantly delayed. Surprisingly, the majority of airports were closed, often for a number of days. Surely this sort of weather shouldn't cause this much chaos in a well-developed country such as Britain? Other similar countries cope perfectly well with even worse weather. For example, Helsinki airport last closed in 2003, and yet regularly suffers from such extreme weather. Britain should not suffer this badly from this sort of weather.

Which of the following, if true, would most strengthen the argument?

A Many journeys that were cancelled were leisure trips as opposed to business trips.

B The recent severe weather was particularly extreme.

C Helsinki airport has specialist technology to deal with such severe weather.

D Britain has the technology to enable it not to be affected much by this sort of weather.

E Extreme cold weather can render roads, train lines and runways unsafe to use.

13 The 'cut' in a golf tournament refers to the process whereby half the players are eliminated from the tournament after the first round and the other half proceeds to the final round. It is not a random process since it is the players with the lowest scores who are eliminated. The standard of golf during the last few years, however, has declined and special efforts are being made in the forthcoming major tournament to make the golf course a little easier and to attract more players. It is hoped that this will raise the general playing standard as well as the confidence of players. It is also hoped that there will be just as many players in the final round as there are in the first round, with only a few being eliminated.

Which of the following is the main flaw in the above argument?

A   No explanation is given as to why the 'cut' is not random.

B   A causal connection is assumed between making the golf course easier and raising the standard and confidence of players.

C   It doesn't explain why the standard of golf has declined during the last few years.

D   There can never be just as many players in the final round as there are in the first round because of the 'cut'.

E   A causal connection is assumed between attracting more players and raising the standard and confidence of players.

14 There exist a certain number of sports academies around the country to which young sportsmen and women can go; in order to practise their sport to a high level as well as obtaining an academic education at the same time. However, many parents are hesitant about allowing their children to go to these institutions since it is doubtful whether the academic education students receive there is as good as that received at a secondary school.

Which of the following, if true, would most weaken the argument?

A   Most sportsmen and women, who represent their country in a given sport, have attended a sports academy.

B   There is still a considerable emphasis on academic studies at sports academies.

C   90% of the students attending these sports academies obtain higher GCSE and A-Level results than those in most secondary schools.

D   Even though many parents are hesitant, most children who have the chance to attend a sports academy are extremely keen to do so.

E   Sportsmen and women spend three times as much time studying academic subjects as they do playing sports at these sports academies.

15 A recently-opened college is having problems with truancy. This Monday only 16 students came into school. On Tuesday this increased to 20 and on Wednesday this increased again to 24. The following pie charts show which classes those students that did come in attended:

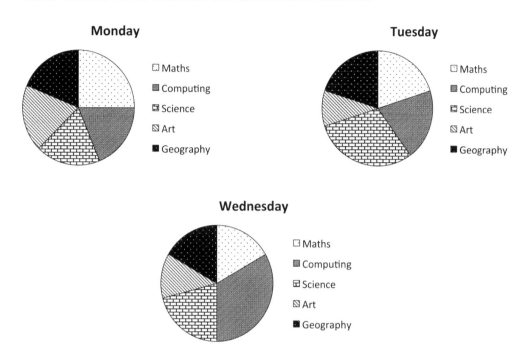

How many students, in total, attended Maths lessons on Monday, Tuesday and Wednesday?

A   8

B   12

C   16

D   20

E   24

16 Competition regulation, which serves to prevent businesses abusing their power, does not do enough to stop large corporations from expanding into small markets and abusing their power. For example, some supermarkets have launched themselves into the mobile phone industry and are able to acquire large market shares by making losses in that industry, more than made up through their other businesses. The law in this area needs to recognise this problem and prevent large corporations from exploiting their power in small markets.

Which of the following best expresses the main conclusion of the argument above?

A   The mobile phone industry is suffering as a result of large corporations.

B   Legal reform needs to address the ability of large corporations to wield power in small markets.

C   Large corporations are able to make losses in some industries in order to acquire large market shares.

D   Competition law needs to change so as to prevent supermarkets from abusing their power in small markets.

E   The law needs to change so as to prevent corporations from abusing smaller ones in the mobile phone market.

17 Paul's driveway is covered in snow to a depth of 15 inches. If Paul clears his driveway so that the depth of the snow is now 9 inches less than the amount cleared, how many inches of snow has Paul cleared?

A   10

B   15

C   11

D   9

E   12

18 Some liberal economists are sceptical of the wide-ranging powers that bodies such as the European Commission can wield over potential merging companies and the mind-boggling sums of money that they can fine companies. One reason is the presence of regulatory bodies such as Ofcom, which can deal with any consumer harm that is caused by these companies. These economists would therefore prefer to allow a merger to go ahead and bring about the potential benefits of a large company and then deal later with any consumer harm through regulatory bodies, instead of assuming that the effects of a merger will harm consumers and prevent this at the outset.

Which of the following conclusions is best supported by the above argument?

A   Ofcom can fine companies after they have merged.

B   The main reason that some liberal economists object to bodies such as the European Commission is because of the large sums of money it can fine companies.

C   All liberal economists would support an increase in regulatory bodies.

D   These liberal economists do not suggest that mergers can never cause harm to consumers.

E   Regulatory bodies are the main reason that some liberal economists would allow more mergers to take place.

19 I fold the following piece of paper along the dotted line:

I then fold the resulting piece of paper again along this dotted line:

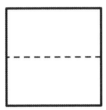

Finally, I cut the folded piece of paper along this dotted line:

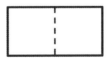

How many pieces of paper am I left with after making this cut?

A 2

B 3

C 4

D 5

E 6

20 Have you ever noticed that after you meet somebody for the first time and they tell you their name, you forget that person's name fairly quickly? This is then followed by often awkward moments in which you try hard to remember but fail to do so and, instead, have to find friends of that person and try and rediscover that person's name subtly. The problem is that people are too busy psycho-analysing first impressions or worrying about etiquette to actually take in and remember the name when told. The solution is simple – next time somebody tells you their name, listen carefully and ensure that you actively and consciously make a mental note of it.

Which of the following, if true, would most weaken the argument?

A   Psycho-analysing people is a valuable tool that most people employ.

B   Many people share the same name.

C   Making a mental note of something doesn't mean that you will necessarily remember it.

D   Part of social etiquette involves remembering somebody's name.

E   It is usually not very awkward to find out a person's name after you have forgotten it.

21 Most people have some sort of commute when they go to and from work every day and over 50% of people that commute complain about the length of their commute. The median length of a commute in the UK is about 45 minutes which isn't that long at all, especially considering that most people will waste the same amount of time, most days, being unproductive in some way or another. In addition, a commute doesn't have to be unproductive time – people can read or listen to music or they can begin their working day, for example, by sending emails.

Which of the following conclusions is best supported by the above argument?

A   Roughly 50% of commuters in the UK have a commute that is 45 minutes or longer.

B   More than half of the population complain about the length of their commute.

C   Those people that do complain about commuting have a commute that is over 45 minutes.

D   Roughly 50% of commuters complain about the distance they have to travel to work.

E   Those people that do complain about commuting have a commute that is under 45 minutes.

182

22 Moira and Mike are antique book valuers. Mike buys the books and Moira values them. Two months ago, Mike bought £12,000 worth of books and Moira valued them at £16,400. Last month, Mike spent a third more on books than the previous month and Moira valued these books as being worth 150% of their price. This month, Mike only spent $\frac{1}{8}$ of the amount he spent on books in the previous month but Moira only valued them at 75% of the amount Mike spent on them.

If Moira and Mike's profit level is the difference between Moira's valuation and the amount Mike spends and they sell all their books, what is their total profit over the three months?

A £11,500

B £11,900

C £9,900

D £13,100

E £12,900

23 Gita is deciding whether or not to buy a pass for her gym which costs £100 and allows her to pay just £12 for each visit to the gym. If it normally costs £15 per gym visit without a pass, what is the minimum number of visits to the gym that Gita must make, in order to make buying a pass the cheaper option?

A 33

B 32

C 34

D 36

E 40

24 Most people do not break the speed limit whilst driving, not because the law would punish them if they did, but because their own moral convictions prevent them from doing something which they believe would cause harm. This applies to a whole host of other crimes as well. Take murder, for example. Most people don't kill others because of the inherent wrong in that conduct and not because they would go to prison for many years. In light of this, lawmakers don't need to punish any immoral conduct since people's moral convictions would prevent them from engaging in such conduct in the first place.

Which of the following is the main assumption of the argument above?

A People have moral convictions to prevent them engaging in every type of immoral conduct.

B Lawmakers are the ones who decide on whether or not people are punished for immoral conduct.

C Moral convictions lead to people not engaging in immoral conduct.

D There is inherent wrong in killing another human being.

E People have any sort of moral convictions.

25 Tom, Paul, Hardeep and Sandra all drive lorries fitted with tachometers that measure average speed. The following graph shows four tachometer readings on a given day, which recorded each lorry's average speed for the previous three hours' driving:

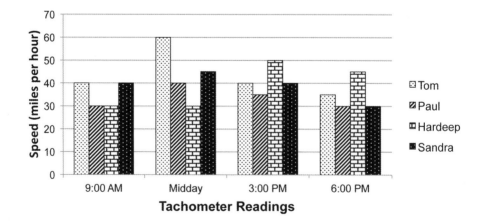

From the four readings for each lorry driver, who covered the most distance during the day?

A   Sandra

B   Tom

C   Paul

D   Hardeep

E   Sandra and Hardeep equally

26   More pubs should start showing sporting events in 3D and fully utilise this fantastic technology. Sports events look a lot clearer when shown in 3D and the detail of the sport truly comes out. People who have watched sports in 3D comment that it feels much more like you are in the sporting venue itself, as opposed to in a pub or wherever else you are watching. As a result, the atmosphere from the sporting venue is contagious and pubs that already have 3D technology have reported that customers seem to enjoy themselves more when watching in 3D.

Which of the following, if true, would most strengthen the argument?

A   Pubs would generate a lot more profit by showing sports in 3D.

B   Many people object to the idea of wearing 3D glasses in social environments.

C   3D technology is becoming cheaper at a significant rate.

D   Customers enjoying sports games more is not necessarily a good thing for pubs.

E   The atmosphere in pubs is one of the most important factors for sports fans.

27   I have a bucket with a volume of 12,000 ml which is 40% full of water. If I buy a new bucket that has a volume that is $\frac{2}{5}$ greater than the volume of the previous bucket and I pour the water from the old bucket into this new bucket, how much more water must I put into this new bucket in order to completely fill it?

A   12,000 ml

B   16,800 ml

C   14,400 ml

D   13,200 ml

E   4,800 ml

28 More and more people are taking up the chance to work part-time (35 hours or less per week) instead of full-time due to an increase in workplace stress and the rising cost of childcare. The government has recently announced that employment protection for temporary workers (those with a fixed length of employment) is to be reduced to discourage their prevalence and so there will be considerable disparity between the law protecting temporary workers and the law protecting permanent workers. Those who switch from full-time to part-time work therefore need to be careful to ensure that they don't lose employment protection when making this switch.

Which of the following is the best statement of the flaw in the above argument?

A It assumes that just because the government has announced something, it will necessarily occur.

B It assumes that temporary workers require protection from employers.

C It doesn't explain why fewer people are working full-time.

D It assumes that people will switch from full-time to part-time work.

E It equates a temporary worker with a part-time worker.

29 Only if I leave school with more than five GCSEs will I go to sixth-form college. If I do well there, then I will go to university. If I perform at an above-average level in sixth-form then I will apply for a place at a top university whereas if I perform at a below-average level, I will apply to a less competitive university. I am aware, however, that if I perform so badly at my sixth-form college that I am in the bottom 10% of students, I may not get a place at any university that I apply to.

Which of the following is a conclusion that can reliably be drawn from the above argument?

A If I perform at a below-average level in my sixth-form college, it must mean that I got five or fewer GCSEs at school.

B Even if my results place in the bottom 10% of students at my sixth-form college, I will still get a place at a university to which I apply.

C If I perform at an above-average level in my sixth-form college, it must mean that I got more than five GCSEs.

D If I obtain five GCSEs, then I will go to a sixth-form college, where, if I perform well, I will apply to a top university.

E The number of GCSEs that I obtain, above the five required to go to sixth-form college, will affect my performance at my sixth-form college.

30 If it takes 50 minutes for three astronauts to replace 12 parts on a satellite, how many astronauts will it take to replace 16 parts on a satellite in 10 minutes?

    A 12

    B 20

    C 16

    D 13

    E 23

31 Three friends and I rented a punt yesterday from 4.15 pm until 5.15 pm from Punts 'R' Us, which has the following price list:

Punting Charges

Before 5 pm: £6.20 per hour

After 5 pm: £7.40 per hour

(The charge for the punt begins when you leave and ends on your return. Charges are not rounded up to the hour.)

One-off fee per punt: £2.50

One-off fee per person: £1.25

What was the total cost of our punting trip?

    A £13.70

    B £14.00

    C £12.75

    D £10.25

    E £14.90

32 My young son wishes to go to the zoo if he can see monkeys, lions and elephants. We found out this morning that only lions and elephants are in the zoo today, but he still wants to go.

Which of the following has the same structure as the above argument?

A The circus will go ahead if all three performers arrive on time. As it stands, one is late and won't make it on time and therefore the circus is unlikely to go ahead.

B The pop group will re-unite if they have the same manager as before, if they have the same name and if all of the members agree to re-unite. All the members do agree but the name and manager must change for various reasons. Despite this, the pop group will re-unite in a month's time.

C I only ever go on holiday if my two brothers and two sisters come with me. This summer, however, my two sisters are ill and so only my two brothers can come with me. Despite hesitating a little to begin with, I will still go on holiday with them.

D The swimmer will be able to cross the Channel if the wind stays calm, the current does not become too strong and there are adequate lifeboats on stand-by. The wind and current are ideal, but there are no adequate lifeboats. The swimmer is still certain that it will be possible to make the crossing.

E The team will win the tournament if they beat their rivals in the final game. As it happens, another team has lost a crucial game and their rivals have been deducted points, so the team will still win the tournament even if they lose to their rivals.

33 If Eva lies about an event 60% of the time and Dawn lies about an event 75% of the time, assuming that they both say the same thing when they lie, what is the chance that they will say different things when asked about the same event?

A 45%

B 35%

C 15%

D 75%

E 85%

34 The following table shows the total GDP of various countries in 2009 and 2010:

Country	GDP - 2009 (£ billion)	GDP - 2010 (£ billion)
UK	1.35	1.16
Spain	0.96	0.45
Greece	0.75	0.14
Portugal	0.64	0.17
France	1.10	1.03
Germany	1.85	1.35

By how much more than the UK was the decrease in GDP of the country with the largest fall in GDP from 2009 to 2010?

A   £0.42 billion

B   £0.32 billion

C   £0.61 billion

D   £0.28 billion

E   £0.19 billion

35 The caste system in India is the main hurdle to any significant social change. This system categorises each individual when born, depending on their parents and the traditional line of work in which the family was once involved. Since it is based on such arbitrary and out-dated factors, the caste system is unfair and illogical in modern-day India. Unfortunately, the link between the caste system and religion has ensured that these arbitrary distinctions remain and this serves to hinder the progress of many Indians.

Which of the following best summarises the conclusion of the argument above?

A   Social reform in India is obstructed by the caste system.

B   The caste system is based on irrational and old-fashioned ideas.

C   The link between religion and the caste system is the main problem.

D   The identity of your parents and the traditional line of work your family is involved in are arbitrary factors.

E   Something should be done to remove these arbitrary distinctions and help social change in India.

36 It is grossly unfair that every tax payer is forced to contribute to the maintenance and construction of new museums and art galleries. There is a significant proportion of society that will never visit either a museum or an art gallery and so will not derive any benefit from their contribution. Surely if museums and art galleries are funded from the public purse then sporting events, too, should receive the same benefit? We shouldn't allow museums and art galleries to be funded from the public purse and instead should charge only those who wish to visit them, in order to create a fairer tax system.

Which of the following best illustrates the principle underlying the argument above?

A I only use a method of public transport once a week and use my own private forms of transport the rest of the time. Therefore, I should only have to pay an amount towards public transport in proportion to the frequency with which I use it.

B A proportion of my tax money goes towards a space programme that this country invests in. However, there is only a small chance that I will ever benefit from this in my lifetime and so I should not have to contribute to this.

C Despite the fact that I sometimes go to the doctors, I am generally very healthy and so, over the course of my lifetime, I don't expect to visit any medical institution very much. In light of the fact that lots of other people often visit a hospital, my contributions to the country's health system should be vastly reduced.

D Art galleries and museums are important cultural institutions that should be encouraged in society. As a result, they should be financed by the public purse in order that everybody has an incentive to derive a benefit from their contributions by using them.

E It is unfair that, despite the fact that I have programmed my television so that I only receive one private news channel, I am still forced to pay a licence fee for public channels that I neither want to watch nor receive on my television. Only those who watch these public channels should be required to contribute towards them.

37 Paris owns a second-hand car dealership. On one day he sells 10% of the cars on the forecourt and on the next day he sells 30% of the remaining cars on the forecourt.

If he started with 2,000 cars and he made £222,000 profit over the two days, what is the average profit per car?

A £411

B £300

C £3,700

D £370

E £3,000

38 We should all be more careful when using social networking sites like Facebook due to the risk of identity theft. Identity thieves operate by getting hold of an individual's home address, which can assist them in perpetrating their fraud. Although the negative consequences of identity theft are often over-stated, it usually leads to a lot of hassle for the victim and sometimes financial consequences.

Which of the following is an assumption of the argument above?

A Identity thieves want to get information about an individual's home address.

B It is possible to obtain home addresses from social networking sites.

C For some individuals, the negative consequences of identity theft outweigh the benefits of showing their address on social networking sites.

D All social networking sites are targeted by identity thieves.

E Fraud based on identity theft necessarily requires an individual's address.

39 I make 18 cardboard cut-outs, each one from a piece of cardboard measuring 12 cm x 10 cm. Each cut-out looks like this:

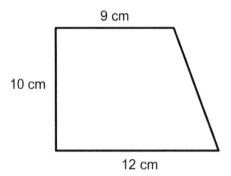

What is the total area of excess cardboard left over?

A   150 cm²

B   270 cm²

C   540 cm²

D   360 cm²

E   225 cm²

40 Restricting immigration seems to be the best strategy in terms of controlling our population and, despite most of the population not having conducted their own cost-benefit analysis of possible alternatives, for example, a one-child policy, we can safely assume that the state has concluded, after careful research, that restricting immigration is the best way of controlling the population. We should therefore encourage some sort of immigration policy as a way of controlling the population.

What of the following is an underlying assumption of the argument above?

A   The state is better informed than the public about immigration.

B   The state is in a position to control immigration.

C   We should control the population at all.

D   It is possible to conduct a cost-benefit analysis of a one-child policy.

E   There are no other possible alternatives to an immigration policy.

41 Every morning on my walk to work, my speed is affected by the various slopes that I encounter, with the result that the steeper the incline the slower the speed and the steeper the descent the quicker the speed. I start off by walking on a flat slope before hitting my first hill, which lasts for about 10 minutes. Fortunately, after this, I hit a constant downward slope on which I walk at a steady speed. I then have one last hill to get into work on which I climb at a steady speed for about 20 minutes.

Which of the following graphs could show this information?

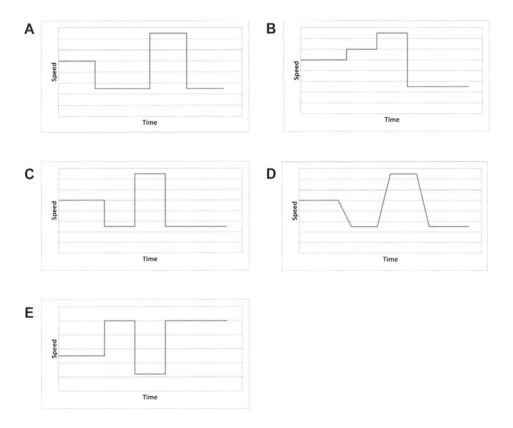

42 The following table shows the distribution of expenditure for Shaw Cross Farm in 2010:

	Jan	Feb	Mar	Apr	May	Jun	Jul	Aug	Sep	Oct	Nov	Dec	TOTAL
Council Tax	35	35			35	35			35	35			*210*
Electricity	12	12	12	12	12	12	12	12	12	12	12	12	*144*
Gas	13	13	13	13	13	13	13	13	13	13	13	13	*156*
Goat Feed	8		19		12		14		16		20		*89*
Horse Feed	12			12			12			12			*48*
Insurance	10		10		10		10		10		10		*60*
Pig Feed		15		17		14		16		19		16	*97*
Rent	50	50	50	50	50	50	50	50	50	50	50	50	*600*
Sheep Feed	9	10	8	6	4	6	7	8	10	8	6	4	*86*
Staff Wages	20	20	20	20	20	20	20	20	20	20	20	20	*240*
Telephone	10		10		10		10		10		10		*60*
Vehicles			5			5			5			5	*20*
Water		7		7		7		7		7		7	*42*
TOTAL	*179*	*162*	*147*	*137*	*166*	*162*	*148*	*126*	*181*	*176*	*141*	*127*	

In which month of 2010 was the cost of animal feed highest?

A   September

B   January

C   April

D   July

E   October

43 Templesan Korfball team plays its matches on Mondays, Thursdays and Sundays. The team may play no more than two games in a seven-day period and no more than one game in a three-day period. If the team plays on Monday, it may not play on Thursday.

What is the maximum number of games it is possible to play in a 31-day month for the team?

A   8

B   7

C   9

D   6

E   10

44 Many people accuse religion of having negative effects globally and cite religious wars as evidence of this. While this is certainly true, and religion has been at the heart of many conflicts, the net gain that we derive from religion supports the existence of it. Many communities, especially in third world countries, derive their moral code from religion. Furthermore, individuals live a 'good' life based on their religious convictions, for example, Christians who believe in heaven and Hindus who believe in karma and reincarnation.

Which of the following summarises the conclusion of the argument above?

A The negative effects of religion outweigh the benefits it brings.

B Many communities depend on religion in order to live 'good' lives.

C There are many benefits that derive from religion.

D Religion does more good than harm.

E Religious wars are a small price to pay for the existence of religion.

45 David sends a telex from Country A to Country C but the telex system means that it has to be delivered via Country B. He sent it at 1.00 am and it arrived the same day in Country C at 1.00 am. If it took 4 hours to travel from Country A to Country B, 3 hours to travel from Country B to Country C, and Country C is 4 hours behind Country B, how many hours behind Country A is Country C? (all times are local times and the telex passed instantly through Country B)

A 6

B 4

C 5

D 3

E 7

46 It is a well-known fact that estate agents affect house prices to a considerable extent. During an economic downturn, estate agents understand that there is more unemployment, a general lack of confidence and therefore a lower demand for houses. As a result, estate agents will place a pessimistic value on a house, thus pushing down the general price level in the housing market. The economy is cyclical, however, and so when there is less unemployment, more confidence and more demand for houses, we would expect that house prices would increase since estate agents will also be responsible for valuing houses during an economic upturn.

Which of the following is the main assumption of the argument above?

A   Estate agents are influential enough to affect house prices.

B   Demand for houses affects their price.

C   That there is still the concept of a cyclical economy.

D   Varying demand for houses will affect the way estate agents value a house.

E   Estate agents will place an optimistic value on house prices during an economic upturn.

47 Matt is technically better than Paul at playing squash and Minty is technically better than Matt at playing squash. However, Matt is the fittest out of all three of them and so, if the three play squash for more than an hour, then Matt usually wins. Paul usually prefers to play squash with Emma, his wife, but unfortunately she is very talented and usually beats him, although she has never beaten Minty.

Which of the following has the same structure as the above argument?

A   Grace has more fashion sense than Kate who has more fashion sense than Suzy. However, out of the circle of four friends, it is Anjali that was chosen to be a super-model. Kate has more fashion sense than Olly, her boyfriend, although he was also selected to be a super-model along with Anjali.

B   Horace has better running shoes than Doris and Boris has better running shoes than Norris. However, Boris is the better runner out of all of them and so would win a race should they all compete. Norris usually runs with Doris, his sister, but she is fitter than him and always wins, although she has never won a race against Horace.

C Craig is a better DJ than Darren but Sanjay is a better DJ than Craig. However, Darren attracts the biggest crowds to his DJ events. Craig usually prefers to DJ with Emily, his girlfriend, but she is a better DJ than him, and in fact she is a better DJ than Sanjay.

D Justine is a better debater than Carina and Sophie is a better debater than Justine. But Justine is more determined and so usually wins an argument. Carina usually prefers to debate with Hermes, her boyfriend, but he is an expert debater and argues better than Carina, although he has never won an argument with Sophie.

E Chris is a better footballer than Tom and Dylan is a better footballer than Chris. However, Chris has been voted player of the season every season since they all started playing. Chris also plays football in another team with Diego, his father, who is a better footballer than Dylan but who has still always lost out to Chris in the player of the season award in this team.

48 Kate and Dylan both set off on their bicycles from Point A, but Kate sets off 2 hours and 15 minutes later than Dylan. If Dylan travels at 20 miles per hour, how fast will Kate have to travel in order that they arrive at the same time at Point B, 120 miles away?

A 30 miles per hour

B 25 miles per hour

C 28 miles per hour

D 35 miles per hour

E 32 miles per hour

49 It is not clear whether a person's taste in music arises as a result of some genetic make-up that means that they inherently prefer a certain type of music or whether it is simply as a result of what they are used to listening to from an early age. On the one hand, evidence shows that musicical taste in identical twins, separated at birth, tends to be similar. However, on the other hand and more convincingly, evidence shows that a person will begin to like a song if it is played to them over and over again. Furthermore, the 'nurture' argument receives more support in relevant scientific literature.

Which of the following best summarises the conclusion of the argument above?

A It seems more likely that a person's music taste stems from 'nature' as opposed to 'nurture'.

B There seems to be better evidence supporting the 'nurture' argument.

C Identical twins that are not separated at birth will tend to prefer the same type of music.

D Scientists would tend to support the idea that humans are designed to prefer one type of music over another.

E Scientists in this area are not in agreement about where a person's taste in music comes from.

50 The following shapes can be put together to make various other shapes:

Which of the following is NOT a possible shape that could be made from putting the above shapes together? (not to scale)

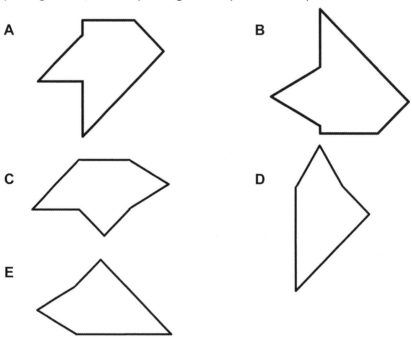

Cambridge TSA – END OF PAPER
Oxford TSA – TURN OVER FOR SECTION 2

Oxford TSA section 2

You must answer only ONE of the following questions:

1. 'Societies should never strive for utopia since the concept is ideological and can never be achieved.' Do you agree?

2. If art galleries and museums are funded by the public purse, shouldn't watching live sport also be funded in this way?

3. 'Any theory based on assumptions is unreliable and not worth using.' Do you agree?

4. Should university tuition fees vary according to subject?

Thinking Skills Assessment: Practice test 2 commentary

Cambridge TSA paper: commentary
Oxford TSA section 1: commentary

1   Approach 1

The first thing to do with this question is work out how many hours and minutes there are between 23:35 today and 19:25 tomorrow: which is 19 hours and 50 minutes. If you struggled on this first calculation, perhaps try simply to add 24 hours onto 23:35 and then work backwards. Next, deal with the first clock which measures hours. Since you know that there have been 20 hours between the times (23:00 to 19:00), the hand on the first clock will not have done an entire revolution and therefore your answer to this enquiry must be less than 360. From pointing to 23, the clock will have moved to point at 19, moving a total of 300 degrees. This is because between each hour there are 15 degrees and you could have worked this out if you know that on a conventional clock face there are 30 degrees between each hour ($360 \div 12$) and therefore, there must be half of this between each of the hours on this clock face. Next, you know that the hand on the second clock will have made 19 revolutions (because there were 19 whole hours) and then would be 10 minutes away from its 20th revolution. Between each 5 minute interval there are 30 degrees on this clock face since it is similar to a conventional clock face and so in 50 minutes the hand would have moved 10 intervals. Therefore, this hand has moved a total of 6840 degrees (360×19) + 300 degrees (30×10) = 7140 degrees. For both hands, the total number of degrees is therefore 7440 (7140 + 300). **D** is, therefore, the correct answer.

Approach 2

With the second clock, you could have worked out slightly quicker that 20 hours would have given you 7200 degrees and so 10 minutes less than this would have been 60 degrees less ($7200 - (30 \times 2)$) giving you 7140.

2   The argument here is that illegal file sharing can have an effect beyond that of just taking away profits from superstars, since other workers behind the scenes are affected too. You may be tempted to choose **A**, however the argument does not go so far as to give a cost/benefit analysis of illegal file sharing and only states that there are negative effects that most people have not thought about. It could be that, despite these job losses, there is

still more good caused than harm. So, this statement is too specific to be the conclusion of the argument. **B** could be inferred to be true but is not really the focus of the argument, which lays the blame at the door of illegal file sharers. **B** does not address the issue of blame. **C** is incorrect since runners and studio workers are merely used as an example and there is no value judgement given as to whether these workers are affected more than others. **E** goes too far in terms of summarising the conclusion since the argument only deals with the effects of illegal file sharing and does not argue that illegal file sharers should now change their behaviour as a result. This could certainly be inferred, but it is not argued in the passage. **D** is a summary of the conclusion since it deals generally with the problem of wider negative consequences in these industries than most people are aware of.

3   This question is a lot simpler than may seem at first sight. Firstly, you should find the cost of each ball from the information given to you for each brand. Once you perform the simple calculations you should find the following:

Ball	Cost (per ball)
Whizzball	44p
Squashysquash	46p
Ballmart	59p
Squishsquash	44p
Rapidball	44p

So you know that there are three brands that are equally as cheap. Next, as long as you know that the quickest ball will be the one that takes the least time to return to Terry after he has hit it, then you know that, out of the three cheapest brands, Whizzball is the quickest. Therefore, **A** is the correct answer.

4   This is quite a time-consuming question and requires you to perform a number of calculations, which you should do carefully. The first task is to work out how many shares Deirdre owns in the three companies. You should find that she owns 3,750, 4,500 and 6,750 shares in Company X, Company Y and Company Z respectively. Next, you know that she sells her shares in Company X at a rate of £1.50 per share and her shares in Company Y at a rate of £1.60 per share so you should find that she receives £5,625 and £7,200 from these shares respectively. In order to find out the minimum and maximum amounts that she could have made overall, you then need to calculate her total revenue if she sold her shares in Company Z for £1.10

and then calculate her total revenue if she sold her shares in Company Z for £1.50. You should find that if she sold her shares in Company Z for a low of £1.10 then she would have made £7,425, whereas if she sold them for a high of £1.50 then she would have made £10,125. Adding the relevant figures together then, you should find that the minimum amount she could have made in the week was £20,250 (£5,625 + £7,200 + £7,425) and the maximum was £22,950 (£5,625 + £7,200 + £10,125). Therefore, **D** is the correct answer.

5   The argument here is that binge drinking is a problem for various reasons and that we should, therefore, educate children as to the harmful effects of alcohol and this will decrease the likelihood of them binge drinking. **A** is incorrect as it is stated that education *will* mean that children are less likely to binge drink. **B** is true and, whilst the argument doesn't do this, it can still work without acknowledging the benefits of alcohol, since it is made on the premise that *binge* drinking is a problem (and not just alcohol in general) and addresses this problem in particular. In other words, whether or not any benefits of alcohol are stated, the argument still remains broadly similar. **C** may be true, although perhaps the addition of the word 'serious' negates this, but the argument doesn't rest on this assumption even if it is made. The argument addresses the need and the means to curb binge drinking in today's society, irrespective of what has happened in the past. **E** is incorrect as it is stated that binge drinking has led to more violent behaviour. **D** is the correct answer since the argument focuses on the reasons as to how and why binge drinking is a serious social problem but then concludes that more resources should be allocated in educating children without connecting this conclusion to the preceding argument. In other words, there is no information or justification as to why this specific conclusion flows from the reasons given in the argument.

6   This question should be relatively straightforward, as long as you can appreciate what each of the words would look like when read from the other side of a transparent surface. There are various methods of trying to ascertain what the word would look like when read in this way. You could turn each letter around 180 degrees on an imaginary vertical axis and re-spell the word in this way. You could also simply turn the whole word around in the same way, although this is slightly more ambitious. You could also work out that, in order for the added requirement to work, each letter needs to be vertically symmetrical i.e. if you draw a line from top to bottom down the middle of each letter, each side must look identical. The only word that would look the same from the other side of the transparent door is AMATAMA. The problem with **A** and **B** is the presence of an 'S,'

which is not vertically symmetrical. Similarly, the 'R' and 'N' would prevent **D** and **E** respectively, from looking identical from the other side of the transparent door.

7   The argument here is that we should silence those who campaign against mobile phone masts on aesthetic grounds as well as actively encouraging the erection of more mobile phone masts on the grounds that they aren't actually an eyesore and are necessary for mobile phone network coverage. **A** is incorrect as the argument does not need to explain how mobile phone masts have become more discreet in order to work logically – it is sufficient that they are more discreet. **B** is incorrect as it is stated that 'these masts are necessary in order that everybody has adequate mobile phone coverage'. In other words, if these masts are *necessary*, then there is no other way to boost mobile phone network coverage. **C** is incorrect as it is stated that more and more people are relying on mobile phones and the masts are used to provide adequate mobile phone network coverage. **D** is incorrect since, as with **A**, the argument does not need to justify this – it is simply sufficient that more and more people are relying on mobile phones. It is important that you judge the argument based on its aims. In other words, the argument is not trying to justify the use of mobile phones; rather it is arguing that, based on this need for mobile phones, we should encourage the erection of mobile phone masts. **E** is the correct answer since the argument is aiming to justify more and more mobile phone masts by discrediting one apparent drawback of them and by providing other advantages. However, it fails to consider or even acknowledge that there may be other reasons as to why an increase in mobile phone masts may be a bad idea, which may undermine the conclusion.

8   The argument here is that I sacrifice something or change my behaviour in order to appreciate it more and, when I do this, there is an initial benefit and then a further consequential benefit. **A** is incorrect because it mentions a negative consequence of the behaviour whereas the argument contains two benefits, one contingent on the other. Similarly in **C**, there doesn't seem to be a clear idea of sacrifice and there is no mention of a change in behaviour which may bring about this sacrifice so this, too, is incorrect. **D** is incorrect for the same reason – there is no real idea of a sacrifice or any shift in behaviour in order to bring about the positive effects. **E** does mention a change in behaviour and does say that consequences arise as a result of this, but one of these is a negative consequence, which is not consistent with the argument which contains two benefits. **B** is correct because it states that there is something sacrificed (here, not getting hurt) in order that this quality is appreciated. There are then two benefits mentioned,

one of which is contingent on the other. This does parallel the reasoning in the argument.

9 In this question, you should first work out that a fully charged car takes Jim 56 km before it runs out of power and needs charging again (4 km + 14 km + 38 km). You then need to work out the distance between Point A and Point B in order to find out how far Jim has travelled when he stops on the straight road. By drawing out the route, you should find that Point B is 14 km due east of Point A. Therefore, if Jim travels half the distance along the straight road from Point A to Point B, he will have travelled 7 km on this road. Since the last charge then, Jim will have travelled 49 km (4 km + 34 km + 4 km + 7 km). Or, in other words, Jim has 7 km worth of power left in the car out of the total capacity of 56 km. At this point then, there is 12.5% of power left in Jim's car as a percentage of the total power capacity (100 x $(\frac{7}{56})$). Therefore, **C** is the correct answer.

10 The key to answering this question lies in understanding the relationship between factors presented in the argument. Crucially, research has found that children who learn to play an instrument or learn musical notation not only tend to perform better across the curriculum later but are also better at learning a language later in life. There is a reason given to you as a possible explanation for this but you should be careful that you do not use this reasoning to draw any conclusions of your own, for example, by stating that learning a language earlier on in life may make you better able to learn to play an instrument later on in life. This is because, firstly, research is referred to which supports one correlation but no other research is referenced. Secondly, the reasoning, even though it sounds like it could support another conclusion (such as the one mentioned above), may not apply to any different correlation. So, for example, perhaps, even though learning to play a musical instrument is similar to learning a language, there are still key differences between the two such that there is something specific that makes the person learning to play a musical instrument early on better able to learn a language later on, but not the other way around. These two reasons mean that answers **A** and **D** are not reliable conclusions that can be drawn. **E** is incorrect since the research links learning to play an instrument to learning a language and not to learning another instrument later in life so this, too, cannot reliably be drawn as a conclusion. **B** is incorrect as it is not stated that merely listening to music as a child makes you better at learning a language later on in life; it is actually learning to play an instrument or learning musical notation that the research found to be key in the correlation. **C** is correct since the research supports the contention that playing the recorder at primary school should make you better at learning a foreign language in secondary school since it suggests that learning to play an instrument at an early age tends to lead to better performance across the curriculum later on in education, especially in terms of learning languages.

11 The difficulty in answering this question lies in applying the rules to the table so it is recommended that you draw out the diagram to help you understand the constraints of the seating plan. The second rule tells you that one end of the table must be occupied by Robert and that Jane will be to the right of him. Rule five then tells you that Claire must sit opposite Ian, so she cannot be seated opposite Jane or Robert. Therefore, because of rule five which states that Claire and Ian need to sit opposite each other, the pair must be seated in either of the two pairs of unoccupied opposing seats down the table, but as rule one tells you, Claire cannot sit next to Jane. This leaves three spaces that she may occupy. Rule three tells us that Eve must be seated next to Bob but not opposite Adam, which in turn shows us the positions of Ian and Claire. Ian and Claire must be seated in the central seats opposite one another (with Ian next to Jane), for, if they were not, there would be no way to seat Bob and Eve next to each other without placing Adam in one of the two remaining spots, both of which are next to Claire. With this established it is relatively simple to see that Adam must be seated next to Ian, as he cannot be seated next to Claire or at the end of the table, as this would not allow Eve to sit next to Bob. Eve must therefore be placed at the end of the table opposite Robert with Bob (and Adam) next to her, leaving Paul opposite Jane and with Claire on his left and Robert to his right. Therefore, **D** is the correct answer.

12 The argument here is that, whereas Britain's infrastructure – transport in particular – has been hugely affected by recent severe wintry weather causing delays and cancellations, other countries cope well with even worse weather and, therefore, a well-developed country like Britain should not suffer this badly from this sort of weather. **A** does not really affect the argument to a great extent since it is the fact that journeys were cancelled in the first place, as opposed to what type of journeys they were, that is relevant. Perhaps it could be inferred that leisure trips are less important than business trips (although this is a bare assertion) and, therefore, it does not matter that there were delays and cancellations and so Britain may need not worry about being affected so badly by this weather. **B**, if anything, would weaken the argument since, if the recent weather was particularly extreme, implying that perhaps Britain has not experienced weather this severe many times in the past, then it is probably excusable that it was not prepared for weather of this severity and, therefore, it would

be unfair to criticise Britain too heavily for the recent transport problems. **C** could both strengthen and weaken the argument since, on the one hand, it could mean that such technology exists to ensure that airports such as Helsinki can remain open and perhaps Britain should therefore also have such technology. On the other hand, it could be that only Helsinki has this technology which means that it is bound to cope better with such weather and consequently only needs to close rarely. Therefore, respectively, on the one hand, Britain should have coped with this severe weather better, but, on the other hand, perhaps it may have been excusable for Britain, and Helsinki is not a fair standard against which to judge Britain's airports. Without knowing more, you cannot conclude that this therefore strengthens the argument. **E** does not affect the argument to a considerable extent since it is merely a reason as to why there may be transport problems as opposed to strengthening or weakening the normative claim that there shouldn't be problems. It could perhaps be argued that if roads, train lines and runways are 'unsafe' then Britain could not be criticised too much, but the better interpretation of the argument is that Britain should be better able to make these transport links safe and that the effects of the cold weather should be better dealt with. On this interpretation, **E** doesn't add much to the argument. In addition, **E** only states that extreme cold weather *can* render roads, train lines and runways unsafe to use rather than definitively doing so. **D** is the correct answer as it significantly strengthens the argument that Britain should not suffer this badly from this sort of weather since, if it has the technology to enable it not to be affected much by this sort of weather, then there should not be any reason for it to suffer from this sort of weather and it should be better able to deal with it.

13 If the flaw is not immediately clear, try to eliminate the other answers in order to leave you with the correct answer. **A** is incorrect as you are provided with a suitable explanation as to how the 'cut' system is not random because it is based on the lowest scores. **B** and **E** are incorrect since the argument does not go so far as to produce a conclusion, based on a causal connection between making the golf course easier or attracting new players and raising the standard and confidence of players. All that is said is that 'special efforts are being made' and that 'it is hoped that' the changes will lead to successful results. In other words, the argument only hopes that there is a causal connection, as opposed to definitively arguing this or relying on a connection in order to form a conclusion. **C** is incorrect since the argument does not need to explain why the standard has declined – it is enough that it simply has declined and the argument is formed based on this premise. You should be judging the logic of how the argument flows in this case, as opposed to questioning the facts presented. **D** is correct since it is stated at the outset that between the first and final rounds, half of all the players will be eliminated. It therefore cannot follow that there will be just as many in the final round as in the first round with only a few being eliminated. It is a necessary part of the tournament, according to the argument, that a 'cut' will take place and that half of the players will be eliminated and not compete in the final round.

14 This is a tricky question and you may well eliminate two answers but then be left choosing between the remaining three. The argument, first of all, is that there are certain sports academies which young sportsmen and women can attend to develop their sporting skills and study at the same time but that many parents are hesitant about allowing their children to attend since it is doubtful whether the academic education at these academies is as good as that provided in secondary school. **A** doesn't really affect the argument since the quality of the sporting side of the academies is irrelevant to the terms of the argument. Specifically, whether sportsmen and women who represent their country have attended a sports academy does not tell us much about the quality of the education that they received. Similarly, looking at **D**, in spite of the hesitancy of parents, the fact that most children who have the chance to attend a sports academy are extremely keen to do so does not tell us anything about the quality of the education that they receive (or will receive) and so does not really affect the crux of the argument. From the remaining three answers, **B** and **E** are similar in the sense that they both suggest that an academic education is far from neglected at these sports academies and, in fact, compared with the sport, academia is the focus. However, neither of them specifically addresses the quality of the academic education that is received at these academies and you would be left to infer that a focus on academia should dispel any doubt that the education at sports academies is not as good as that in a conventional secondary school. **C**, on the other hand, goes further in dispelling this doubt since you are given a fact that is more relevant to the quality of education than merely the proportion of time spent on academia and sport at these institutions. Despite valid criticism that examination results may not adequately reflect the quality of an education, in this question, the fact that 90% of these sports academies receive higher GCSE and A level results than most secondary schools, significantly weakens the argument that there is doubt as to the quality of the education at academies compared to secondary schools. **B** and **E** may weaken the argument to a certain extent, but **C** goes much further in weakening any doubt about the quality of the academic education received by students at sports academies and is therefore the correct answer.

15 This question requires you to work out proportions from the pie charts provided in order to find out the total number of students that attended Maths lessons across the three days. Starting with Monday, when there were 16

students in total, you can estimate from the pie chart that a quarter of them attended Maths lessons, making the number of students 4. Tuesday is a little trickier, so let's look at Wednesday and then come back to Tuesday. On Wednesday, when there were 24 students in college in total, it seems, from the pie chart, as if one sixth of them attended Maths lessons. You should be able to see this proportion by working out that half of all students attended Computing or Maths lessons and that a third of this number attended Maths lessons, meaning one sixth overall, or 4. So far therefore, you have 8 Maths students. Looking at Tuesday, there were 20 students overall, and a small proportion of these attended Maths lessons. Clearly therefore, **A** cannot be correct since there must be more than 8 students in total. From Tuesday's pie chart, you know that slightly fewer than a quarter attended Maths lessons. A quarter would be 5 so you know that the total figure must be slightly less than 13 (but more than 8). In fact, on Tuesday, one fifth of students attended Maths lessons, which is 4. Therefore, either by eliminating the other figures, or by finding this one fifth proportion for Tuesday, you should work out the answer to be 12. Therefore, **B** is the correct answer.

16 The key to answering this question is correctly understanding the argument and not allowing the example of supermarkets or the mobile phone industry to cloud the real conclusion. It is stated that competition regulation does not do enough to prevent large corporations from expanding into small markets and abusing their power and therefore the law needs to recognise this and prevent it. The example of supermarkets and the mobile phone industry does not detract from the argument nor does it twist the conclusion towards this type of corporation or market. Therefore, **A**, **D** and **E** are incorrect since they mention either supermarkets or the mobile phone market and are, therefore, too specific to be a statement of the main conclusion of the argument, which is far more general. **C** is a premise leading to the conclusion and an application of the 'therefore' test should allow you to dismiss this answer when compared with **B**, which is the correct answer since it summarises the general conclusion stemming from the argument.

17 Approach 1

The easiest way of answering this question is to set up an equation with the amount cleared being 'x'. Then, you can say that $x + (x - 9) = 15$ which can be simplified to $2x - 9 = 15$ and then $2x = 24$. Therefore, $x = 12$ and Paul has cleared away 12 inches of snow.

Approach 2

If you can't form the equation above when you look at this question, then you could still go about finding the right answer by trial and error i.e. by testing each of the answers given. If you start with **A**, then Paul would have cleared 10 inches with one inch of snow left, but this would mean that there were 11 inches to begin with so this is incorrect. With **B**, if Paul cleared all 15 inches then there would be three inches left but this would mean there were 18 inches to begin with so this too is wrong. If Paul cleared 11 inches then there would be two inches left, but this would mean 13 inches to begin with, so **C** is incorrect. **D** must be incorrect since, if Paul cleared nine inches, he would have cleared all the snow, but this cannot be the case when you are told that there were 15 inches to begin with. If Paul cleared 12 inches of snow then there would be three inches left which does work if you had 15 inches to begin with. Therefore, **E** is the correct answer.

18   Paying close attention to some of the words used in the answers will help you to eliminate them and find the correct conclusion. **A** is incorrect as it is stated only that Ofcom can 'deal' with consumer harm and there is no indication about the means by which it does this and so you cannot say as a conclusion that Ofcom has the power to fine companies after they have merged. **B** is incorrect for a number of reasons. Firstly, it may be a step too far to say that these liberal economists *object* to bodies like the European Commission. It is stated only that they are sceptical of the powers of such bodies and that they would prefer to deal with consumer harm later. Secondly, it is not stated how the fact that the European Commission can fine companies staggering amounts of money relates to why these liberal economists object (if they do at all) to bodies such as this. Specifically, it is not stated whether this is the *main* reason for their scepticism and so **B** is not supported by the argument. **C** is incorrect because, even if you can infer that these liberal economists would support an increase in regulatory bodies (even this is doubtful – perhaps they would just prefer an increase in the powers of existing regulatory bodies), you cannot conclude that *all* liberal economists would prefer this. **E** may be a reason as to why some liberal economists would allow more mergers to take place, but you don't know whether or not it is the *main* reason – it is stated only that it is 'one' reason in the argument. **D** is best supported by the argument since these liberal economists are merely objecting to the means of dealing with consumer harm as opposed to suggesting that there isn't any consumer harm at all. It is stated that these economists would prefer to 'deal later with any consumer harm' which clearly indicates that they don't believe that there is never any consumer harm.

19 In order to answer this question, you should try to visualise the folds and the cut on a piece of paper as you work through each stage. After the first fold (assuming you put the left hand side on top of the right hand side), the piece of paper will have a sort of 'hinge' on the left hand edge as you look at it and will be 'open' on the right hand side (or vice versa if you folded the right hand side onto the left hand side) and on the top and bottom. Or, in other words, the shape will now open like a book. After the second fold, there will now be a 'hinge' on the top edge of the piece of paper, the bottom will be 'open' and the right hand side will be 'open' with seemingly four layers (assuming you folded the top piece over and onto the bottom piece). The left hand side will have two thicker layers, one on top of the other. If you then cut the piece of paper as shown, then to the left hand side, only one piece of paper will emerge as a result of that top 'hinge' and the fact that the two layers on the left hand side are joined. On the right hand side, the four layers are not joined, but there is still that 'hinge' on the top which joins the inner two layers together and the outer two layers together. Other than that, the layers are not joined and so the cut will produce two pieces of paper, of identical sizes, on the right hand side of the cut. In total, there will be three pieces of paper and, therefore, **B** is the correct answer.

20 The argument here is that when a person meets someone for the first time, he or she tends to forget the name of that other person quickly and that this can often be awkward. This is usually because he or she is too busy psycho-analysing that other person or worrying about etiquette and so, to solve the problem, he or she should actively and consciously make a mental note of that other person's name. **A** could weaken the argument since it gives credibility to the reason for which people don't remember a person's name. However, even if psycho-analysing people is a valuable tool, it does not necessarily have to be utilised when you *first* meet somebody and, in addition, it doesn't necessarily have to detract from making this mental note. Therefore, **A** may only slightly weaken the argument. **B** is incorrect since, even though it could imply that it is difficult to remember somebody's name if lots of people share that name, the argument doesn't rely on people having unusual or different names and still operates, irrespective of how common a person's name is. **B** could actually strengthen the argument since it matters even more, if people have common names, that you remember that person's name to distinguish them from others. **D** could weaken the argument since it could imply that people already do try and remember somebody's name and so perhaps the problem doesn't simply lie in the techniques that people employ. However, more validly, **D** may strengthen the argument in emphasising the importance of remembering the name of a new acquaintance and arguing that current techniques are not good enough, making a new approach necessary. **E** may weaken the argument since it suggests that not remembering a person's name is not so much of a problem. However, it states that it is not *very* awkward, implying that it still may be awkward to a lesser extent, in which case the conclusion may still follow. **C** most weakens the argument since the solution in the conclusion is to make a mental note of the name and it is implied that this will help you to remember. However, if making a mental note doesn't mean that you will necessarily remember it, then the solution doesn't work and, therefore, the argument is significantly weakened.

21 In order to answer this question, it is vital that you understand the statistics provided to you and the denotation of the word 'median'. **B** is incorrect and is not supported by the passage since it is not more than half of the *population* that complain about their commute; rather it is more than half of *commuters* that complain about their commute – there are, of course, people who don't commute at all to work who still make up the wider population. **C** and **E** are incorrect as they would require some link to be made between the two statistics for which you have no evidence. In other words, you have no information on the length of the commutes for those people that complain about their commutes. **D** is incorrect as commuters do not complain about the *distance* that they travel to work, only the *time* that it takes. **A** is correct since, as a matter of logic, if the median commute time is 45 minutes, then this means that there are roughly 50% of people in the UK either side of this figure with a commute of 45 minutes or more and 50% of people with a commute of 45 minutes or less and so the statement must be true.

22 You could either work out the total amount spent on books, their total value and then work out the overall profit or you could work out the profit on a monthly basis. On either approach, the figures would be as follows:

	Mike's Spending	Moira's Valuation	Profit
Two months ago	£12,000	£16,400	£4,400
Last month	£16,000 ($\frac{1}{3}$ more)	£24,000 (150% of price)	£8,000
This month	£2,000 ($\frac{1}{8}$ of previous month)	£1,500 (75% valuation)	£-500
TOTAL	£30,000	£41,900	£11,900

Therefore, **B** is the correct answer.

23 Approach 1

Setting up an equation is the easiest way to go about answering this question. If you call the number of visits to the gym 'x' then you can work out after how many visits it would cost the same amount regardless of whether she had a pass or not. The equation would be $12x + 100 = 15x$. Therefore, $100 = 3x$ and therefore $x = 33.33....$ So, Gita would have to go more than this number of times in order to make a pass worthwhile, so the minimum she would have to go the gym would be 34 times.

Approach 2

Trial and error i.e. testing each figure provided would also give you the right answer but would probably take longer than using an equation. In order to test each figure you would have to calculate the price based on her having a pass i.e. 100 + (the number of visits x 12) and then you would have to calculate how much it would be for her without a pass i.e. the number of visits x 15. You should find that at 33 visits, not having a pass would be cheaper, but at 34 visits, having the pass would be the cheaper option. Therefore, **C** is the correct answer.

24 The argument gives two examples of crimes that people do not commit, not because of the punishment if they did, but because of their own moral convictions that engaging in that conduct would be inherently wrong. It also states that this applies to a 'whole host' of other crimes too. The argument then concludes that, due to this, lawmakers don't need to punish any immoral conduct since people's moral convictions prevent them from engaging in that conduct in the first place. You should immediately be aware that the argument is concluding generally across all immoral conduct based on two examples and a vague statement that the principle applies to a 'whole host' of other crimes in addition. In order for the conclusion to follow logically from the preceding information, there needs to be some information about whether or not people would not engage in immoral conduct because of their own moral convictions for all immoral conduct. It could be that there are a 'whole host' of crimes for which this principle applies but that there are certain crimes which people refrain from committing simply because of the punishment and not because of any inherent moral conviction against that conduct. Therefore, for the conclusion to state that lawmakers don't need to punish *any* immoral conduct, and without any further information, the argument must assume that people have moral convictions to prevent them engaging in *every* type of immoral conduct. Therefore, **A** is the correct answer. **C**, **D** and **E** seem to be stated in the argument rather than assumed. **B** is trickier since it may be an assumption that 'lawmakers are the ones who decide on whether or not people are punished for immoral conduct' since this is not explicitly stated in the argument. However, even if this is assumed, it is not the *main* assumption and is therefore incorrect.

25 Approach 1

When faced with this question you may be tempted to work out, stage by stage, each person's distance covered using the time and speeds given to you. This is absolutely fine and will give you the answer, but it may take longer than following the easier approach below.

Approach 2

Since you are dealing with the same number of stages, each with the same amount of time for each driver, you should realise that the driver with the highest average speed total during the day will have covered the most distance. So you could simply add up their respective average speeds at each of the four stages in order to find out who covered the greatest distance.

The average speed totals are:
- Tom = 40 + 60 + 40 + 35 = 175
- Paul = 30 + 40 + 35 + 30 = 135
- Hardeep = 30 + 30 + 50 + 45 = 155
- Sandra = 40 + 45 + 40 + 30 = 155

Therefore, Tom has covered the greatest distance and **B** is the correct answer.

26 It is important that you remember the conclusion of this argument in order to find the answer. The argument states that 3D technology has benefits, including a clearer picture and a greater degree of spectator enjoyment and, therefore, that more pubs should start showing sporting events in 3D. **B** would weaken the argument since, if people don't want to wear 3D glasses (on the assumption that they would need to in order to watch 3D sporting events), then it wouldn't make sense for pubs to start showing sports events in 3D since it may not create much extra demand. **C** may strengthen the argument but don't fall into the trap of confusing a rate of decrease with the actual price level. It could be that prices have decreased exponentially but that they are still at an extremely high level, in which case it may not make sense for pubs to invest in the technology. Since you don't know the price level, it is difficult to assess how much, if at all, this fact would strengthen the argument. **D**, if anything, weakens the argument since it implies that it is not certain that pubs would benefit from 3D technology (and, as a

213

consequence, people enjoying sports games more). In fact, it implies that it may not be a benefit for pubs at all. **E** may strengthen the argument to a certain extent since, if the atmosphere is better, then you could conclude that more pubs should, therefore, invest in 3D technology. However, this is not necessarily the case and you would be assuming that pubs want to show sports events or that they want a better atmosphere. In addition, the conclusion is stated from the point of view of pubs whereas this fact is from a sports fan's perspective and you would be implicitly linking an increase in benefit for the latter to an increase in benefit for the former, which may not be the case and, so, would not actually strengthen the argument. **A**, even though it does rest on the assumption that pubs want to make more profit, would strengthen the argument since, if the conclusion is that pubs should start showing sporting events in 3D for a variety of benefits, then you are essentially adding on a huge extra benefit here which would significantly strengthen the argument.

27 This question may sound daunting but is, in fact, not so difficult. Firstly, find out how much water there is in the original bucket: 40% of 12,000 ml = 4,800 ml. Then, calculate the capacity of the new bucket. To do this, simply find $\frac{1}{5}$ of the capacity which is 2,400 ml, then multiply this by 2 and add it to 12,000 ml. You should find that the capacity of the new bucket is 16,800 ml. Finally, simply take 4,800 ml away from 16,800 ml to find how much more water you would have to put into the new bucket in order to fill it up. You should find that the answer is 12,000 ml. Therefore, **A** is the correct answer.

28 This should be a relatively straightforward question, although your mind may not be directed to the significant flaw in the argument until you read one of the answers. **A** could be true to a certain extent, although the fact that the argument states that protection 'is to be' reduced implies that it will occur, rather than it being a proposal or in the pipeline. **B** is incorrect and is not a flaw since the eventual argument is not based on temporary workers but on part-time workers and so the assumption in relation to temporary workers does not bear any relevance to the conclusion about those making the switch from full-time to part-time work. The reason that **B** is wrong is the answer to this question and, if you have not yet worked this out, your reasoning for dismissing **B** should lead you to it. The flaw is that the argument seems to suggest that a temporary worker is the same as a part-time worker. Hence, the argument concludes, those switching to part-time work need to be careful about protection because protection for temporary workers is being reduced. However, they are not the same thing as the information in brackets tells you; the argument only treats them as

the same. It may be perfectly plausible (and common) to have a full-time temporary worker and a permanent part-time worker. **E** is therefore the correct answer and the conclusion doesn't flow unless a temporary worker and a part-time worker mean the same thing, which they may not. **C** and **D** are incorrect because they are not assumed and, instead, are stated since two reasons are provided as to why fewer people are working.

29 This is quite a tricky question that requires you to understand the relationships presented to you in the argument in order that you can logically and reliably conclude one of the answers given. **A** is incorrect since it is stated that *only* if I achieve more than five GCSEs will I go to sixth-form college. Therefore, it must follow that if I am at a sixth-form college, irrespective of how I perform there, I *must* have achieved more than five GCSEs at school. The corollary of this is that, if I got five or less GCSEs at school, I won't go to a sixth-form college and therefore **A** is incorrect. **B** is incorrect since it is stated that I *may not* get a place at a university to which I apply if I am in the bottom 10% of students at my sixth-form college and, therefore, you cannot reliably conclude that I will still receive a place at a university to which I apply, if my results place me in the bottom 10% of students at my sixth-form college. **D** is incorrect for two reasons. Firstly, as noted above, I need *more than* five GCSEs to go to a sixth-form college and, secondly, the word 'well' is too subjective or uncertain to tell us whether it means above or below average and, so, an outcome contingent upon this distinction cannot be reliably concluded if you don't know for sure on which side of the distinction I fall. **E** is incorrect since nothing is stated in relation to the link between the number of GCSEs I obtain above five and how I perform at a sixth-form college. To infer any sort of relationship between these factors would not be a reliable conclusion. **C** is correct since, following the logic described above, if I perform at an above-average level in my sixth-form college, that means that I attend a sixth-form college and I must have obtained more than five GCSEs to attend a sixth-form college.

30 To work out this question, you should firstly calculate how long it takes 1 astronaut to replace 1 part. In order to do so, you should spot that if it takes 50 minutes for 3 astronauts to replace 12 parts on a satellite, then, in the same time, 1 astronaut would replace 4 parts (12 ÷ 3). If it takes 50 minutes for 1 astronaut to replace 4 parts then 1 astronaut can replace 1 part every 12.5 minutes (50 ÷ 4). Next, if you need to replace 16 parts on a satellite, this would take 1 astronaut 200 minutes (16 x 12.5), but since you need to do it in 10 minutes, you would need 20 astronauts (200 ÷ 10). Therefore, **B** is the correct answer.

31 This question requires some simple calculations in order to find the total price. Firstly, you should work out the hire charge for the actual punt based on the timings provided. You are told that the prices are based on when the punt is being used and not the time at which it is initially hired. Therefore, I have the punt for 45 minutes at the cheaper rate and for 15 minutes at the more expensive rate. This works out as £4.65 and £1.85 respectively $((6.20 \times \frac{3}{4}) + (7.40 \times \frac{1}{4}))$. Next you need to add the one-off fee for the punt of £2.50 and, since there are 4 of us (3 friends *and* I), you need to add the one-off fee per person which amounts to £5.00 in total. After adding up these values, you should have calculated the total cost of the punting trip to be £14.00. Therefore, **B** is the correct answer.

32 The argument here is that there are three conditions required for an outcome, but, despite only two of these being satisfied in a certain situation, it seems like the outcome will still come about. Therefore, you are looking for an argument which parallels this reasoning. **A** is incorrect since, despite three conditions required and only two of them being satisfied, the outcome is not likely as a result. **B** is incorrect since there are three conditions and the outcome will still go ahead but this is as a result of only one, and not two, of the conditions being satisfied. **C** is incorrect, although there could be a difference in interpretation as to why. The fact that I will only ever go on holiday if my two brothers and two sisters come with me can be interpreted as being two conditions or four conditions but, importantly, not three conditions and, therefore, this argument does not have a similar structure to the argument in the question. **E** is incorrect since there is only one condition required in order for an outcome but two other factors make that one condition redundant. This is very different in terms of structure to the argument in the question. **D** is the correct answer and does contain the same structure as the argument in the question since three conditions are required (calm winds, not a strong current and adequate lifeboats), only two conditions are satisfied (an ideal wind and current) but the outcome (crossing the Channel) is still possible.

33 Start by working out the two situations in which they will say different things. You know that they will say the same thing if they both tell the truth or if they both lie (since you are told that when they lie they say the same thing). So, the first situation in which they will say different things is if Eva lies and Dawn tells the truth. The second is if Eva tells the truth and Dawn lies. Therefore, in the first case, the chance that they will say different things is 0.60 x 0.25 = 0.15. In the second case, it is 0.40 x 0.75 = 0.30. Then, simply add up these decimals to give you 0.45, or 45%. Therefore, **A** is the correct answer.

34 Firstly, you need to understand what the question is asking. It requires the difference between the UK's year-on-year decrease and the decrease of the country in the table whose year-on-year decrease is the largest. You should, therefore, first work out the UK's decrease which is £0.19 billion (£1.35 billion – £1.16 billion). You then need to work out the decreases of the other countries in order to find out which of them had the largest decrease. You should find that Greece had the largest decrease with £0.61 billion. Finally, you just need to work out the difference between these two decreases which is £0.61 billion minus £0.19 billion. Therefore, **A**, £0.42 billion is the correct answer.

35 The conclusion of the argument is neatly, but somewhat counter-intuitively, given to you in the first line of the argument and is reiterated in slightly different terms in the last phrase. The rest of the argument consists of either an explanation as to why the caste system is a problem (because it is based on arbitrary and out-dated factors and is, therefore, unfair) or some information about the caste system (the social categorisations and the link with religion). **B**, **C** and **D** are therefore summaries of the information within the argument and not the conclusion itself. An application of the 'therefore test' should help you to dismiss these as not forming the conclusion of the argument when you compare them to **A**, for example. **E** could be inferred from the argument but there is no mention of the need for positive action to address the caste system, merely the negative effects of it and its role in frustrating significant social change. Therefore, **A**, which summarises the obstructive role of the caste system outlined in the argument, is the correct answer.

36 The argument in this question is that a certain section of society are forced to pay for something that they do not benefit from and, therefore, we should make the system fairer by making those who want to use it pay for it rather than by funding it from the public purse. **A** is incorrect since there is said to be some benefit derived from the transport system as opposed to the argument in the question where no benefit is obtained at all. In addition, the solution proposed is payment in proportion to the frequency of use of public transport whereas the argument in the question proposes no payment at all by those that derive no benefit. **B** is incorrect since there is an acknowledgement that some benefit may be derived. So, despite the fact that the solution of not contributing at all to this particular service is also proposed in the argument, the difference lies in the acknowledgement of some potential benefit whereas there is no such similar acknowledgement in the argument in the question. **C** is incorrect since it seems to be implied that there is still some benefit, just a smaller amount than that which others derive from the service, and so this argument already differs. In addition, the solution is a reduction in contribution to this service as opposed to no contribution at all, as is proposed in the argument in the question. **D**, as you should notice, is the counter-argument to the proposal presented in the question and so does not best illustrate the principle underlying the argument; it would more likely illustrate the principle used to rebut the argument. **E** is correct since it captures the idea that there is no benefit derived from a service (public channels), yet some contribution (licence fee) must still be paid and the solution proposed is that only those who benefit from this service should be required to contribute to it.

37 You first have to find out how many cars Paris sold over the two days. On day one, he sells 10% of his 2,000 cars, meaning that he sold 200 cars. On the next day, he sells 30% of the *remaining* cars, meaning 30% of 1,800 cars, which is 540 cars. So in total, Paris sold 740 cars. If he made £222,000 in total and you want to find out the average profit per car, then you need to divide 222,000 by 740, which, as you should have spotted, gives a round figure of 300. Therefore, **B** is the correct answer. If you got any of the other figures, check that you: added up the total number of cars and didn't just use the number from the second day; or that you took 30% of the remaining cars on the forecourt rather than of the total number; or that you cancelled the correct number of zeros in the final calculation.

38 The argument here is essentially that we should be more careful when using social networking sites because of identity theft, which occurs when thieves use the home address of an individual to assist in the commission of their crimes. There is an implicit link made between social networking sites and an individual's home address and it is therefore assumed that it is possible to obtain home addresses from social networking sites. If this were not true, then the premise (that thieves use the home address of an individual in their crimes) would not logically lead to the conclusion (that we should be more careful when using social networking sites). Therefore, **B** is the correct answer. **A** is incorrect since it does not matter whether identity thieves *want* to get information about an individual's home address; the argument is concerned with *how* identity thieves operate and not their motivation. **C** is incorrect since the argument does not rely on a comparison of the respective weights of the benefits and costs of identity theft; only that there are some negative consequences, which mean that we should be more careful. **D** is incorrect since the argument does not rely on the fact that *all* social networking sites are targeted by identity thieves; it is sufficient, for the argument to work, that some social networking sites are targeted. **E** is incorrect since, again, the argument relies only on the fact that an individual's address *can* assist thieves in perpetrating fraud in order

to conclude that we should be more careful when using social networking sites like Facebook.

39 For this question you should firstly work out the excess cardboard for each cut-out. This is the area of the triangle that is left over from the original piece of cardboard. To calculate this, multiply the base by the perpendicular height and then divide by 2, i.e. $(10 \times (12 - 9)) \div 2 = 15$. Next, in order to get the total excess amount of cardboard, simply multiply $15 \times 18 = 270$ cm^2. Therefore, **B** is the correct answer.

40 The fact that this question asks for the *underlying* assumption should make you question the very basis on which the argument is premised. It is stated that restricting immigration seems to be the best way of controlling the population and that we should encourage some sort of immigration policy. This is based on the reason that, even though most of us have not researched and evaluated all the alternatives, we can assume that the state has done so and has carefully concluded that immigration is the best way of controlling the population. But, ask yourself this: what if we shouldn't be controlling the population at all? If the answer to this is that we shouldn't be controlling the population, then any argument about the means of controlling it is, by necessary implication, redundant. Therefore, the key assumption, underlying this and any other argument relating to how to control the population, is the assumption that we should control the population at all. Therefore, **C** is the correct answer. **A** is incorrect since it is stated that we can assume that the state has conducted careful research and, even though the word 'assume' has been used, this is not technically an assumption since it is stated expressly, albeit in terms that include the use of the word 'assume'. **B** is incorrect since the conclusion does not rely on the state being in a position to control immigration in order to work logically. The conclusion is simply that *we* should encourage some sort of immigration policy as a way to control the population and not that the state should or must. So, irrespective of who is in a position to control immigration, the conclusion that we should encourage some sort of policy still works. **D** is incorrect since the argument, again, is not relying on this assumption to be true. In fact, it states that *despite* 'most of the population not having done their own cost-benefit analysis of possible alternatives, for example, a one-child policy'. Therefore, it doesn't matter whether a cost-benefit analysis is even possible since the argument asks the reader to disregard the fact that most of the population may not have done a cost-benefit analysis, irrespective of the reason for which it has not been done. **E** is incorrect since the argument does not rely on this assumption in order for it to work and, in fact, it explicitly recognises that there are other alternatives but that the state has carefully evaluated that an immigration policy is the best option.

41 The first important point to understand in answering this question is that there are only uniform speeds in any of the stages of the journey. In other words, the speed curve on the graph should only ever be horizontal and not sloped at any point since the speed will never increase or decrease during a stage of the journey, only that as soon as there is a change in slope, the speed will change instantaneously (and hence there will also be vertical lines between each stage). Therefore, **D** can already be eliminated since, for example, it implies that the speed decreases *before* the first slope which is not true – I walk at a constant speed on the flat slope and then at a slower constant speed on the incline. From the information provided, you know that on the first slope my speed will be lower than it was on the flat slope for about 10 minutes. Therefore, **B** and **E** can be eliminated since they both show a higher speed up the first hill which does not follow from the information that my speed is slower on inclines. You know that the walking time on the first slope is 10 minutes and on the second slope is 20 minutes. Therefore, on a graph, the curve showing the first incline should be shorter horizontally than the curve showing the second incline. **C** shows this whereas **A** shows the first incline being twice as long as the second incline and so you can eliminate this graph. Therefore, **C** is the correct answer.

42 Do not be put off by the amount of data provided in this question since it is actually relatively straightforward. You are looking for the month in which the cost of all animal feed (the sum of all types of animal feed) is the highest. Firstly, identify the categories of expenditure which fall under 'animal feed'. You should have four: Goat Feed, Horse Feed, Pig Feed and Sheep Feed. Next, add up the four values for each of these in every month of the year given to you as possible answers. You might be tempted to take a shortcut by dismissing the months where only two types of feed were bought, but you will find that these are not necessarily the months in which the least amounts were spent. It is better to find the total amounts for all the months. You should find that in October, the total amount spent on animal feed was 39 and this was the highest amount. Therefore, **E** is the correct answer.

43 This is a very tricky question and I would recommend that you write out the dates of a month in calendar format so that you can visualise and count the days with greater ease. With questions like this, it is worth trying to make some initial deductions which may help with your analysis later. Firstly, work out the various combinations of possible games in a week. So, Templesan may play on Monday and then Sunday, in which case, it wouldn't be able to play on the Monday immediately after that Sunday and would have to wait until Thursday or the following Sunday. It could also play on Thursday and then Sunday (and then Thursday again). The most efficient combination, in terms of playing as many games as possible, seems to be playing on Thursdays and Sundays. This is because, as described above, playing on a Monday means you can't play on Thursday that week and, if you play on Sunday, then you can't play the following Monday immediately afterwards and so the next earliest game would be Thursday. Therefore, to allow more games to be played, the team should play its first game on the Thursday or the Sunday, thereby allowing it to play on the Sunday or Thursday respectively.

Starting a month on a Thursday or Sunday then, in order to fit as many games in the month as possible, if you count the number of games the team can play following the Thursday - Sunday combination, you should find that the team can play a maximum of nine games in a 31-day month. Therefore, **C** is the correct answer.

44 The argument in this question is that, whilst it is accepted that religion does have negative effects such as religious conflicts, the *net* gain from religion supports its existence and examples of the benefits it brings are also outlined. **A** is incorrect as it is actually the antithesis of the argument here. **B** is more a combination of two premises in the argument – that many communities derive their moral code from religion and that people lead 'good' lives based on religion – that lead to the conclusion in the argument rather than being the conclusion itself. **C** is true but is incorrect as the specific conclusion goes further than this and says that the benefits that religion bring about outweigh the negative aspects of it. **E** could be inferred but actually the argument does not say that religious conflict is a *small* price to pay – it certainly is a price – but the argument doesn't put a value on the negative effects of religious conflict. **D** is therefore correct as the phrase 'net gain' tells us that religion does more good than harm.

45 Approach 1

There is a very easy way of working this out if you can get your head around time differences. You know that the package took a total of 7 hours to travel from Country A to Country C and it was sent and arrived at the same local time for each country. By implication, therefore, Country C must be 7 hours behind Country A. If you didn't realise this straight away, you can still work this out the long way around - see Approach 2 below.

Approach 2

It's easier to work backwards so start with working out when the telex passed through Country B (in local time). You know that it arrived at 1 am in Country C, and since you know that Country C is 4 hours behind Country B, it arrived (in Country C) at 5 am in Country B time. This must mean, since you know that it took 3 hours to travel from Country B to Country C, that the telex passed through Country B at 2 am (local time). Next, you know that the telex was sent at 1 am (Country A local time) and took 4 hours. In Country B local time therefore, it was sent at 10 pm. Therefore, you know that Country B is 3 hours behind Country A, and finally you can conclude that Country C is 7 hours behind Country A.

46 The argument here is essentially that estate agents will value a house pessimistically during an economic downturn, which pushes house prices down and so, when estate agents are valuing houses in an economic upturn, we would expect that house prices will increase. It is not explicitly stated how estate agents will contribute to an increase in house prices during an economic upturn, only that they are still valuing houses and that prices will increase. From the information about economic downturns, it could perhaps be inferred that the opposite effect will occur, such that estate agents will place a more realistic or optimistic value on house prices during an economic upturn. However, if the argument does not state this explicitly, then it is merely assuming this. Perhaps it is the case, for example, that actually estate agents don't place a different value on a house during an economic upturn and it is other factors that lead to an increase in house prices. Therefore, it is assumed, when estate agents value houses during an economic upturn and when house prices are expected to increase, that estate agents will place an optimistic value on house prices during an economic upturn. Therefore, **E** is the correct answer. **D** is perhaps assumed to a certain extent, although it is stated that a lower demand for houses will lead to pessimistic valuations by estate agents. The corollary of this in an economic upturn is then being presumed, but **E** captures this assumption more accurately than **D**. **A** and **B** are stated in the argument as shown, respectively, by the first sentence and by the phrase 'as a result...' implying that the change in demand will ultimately affect the price of a house. **C** is also stated explicitly in the argument. You should be careful here not to allow your own views, for example, should you disagree with the fact that the economy is cyclical, to affect your analysis of the argument.

47 There is a lot of information to digest in this question but you need to break down the argument in order to find out which of the answers has the same

structure as the argument in the question. The easiest way to do this is to label the people A, B, C and D in order to discover a similar pattern in the answers provided. So, in the argument, you have the following statements that you can extract:

i) **A is better than B**

ii) **C is better than A**

iii) **A generally wins/does the best**

iv) **D beats/does better than B, but has not beaten/done better than C**

The only answer which adheres to this structure is **D. A** diverges at statement iii, since it is none of A, B nor C that does the best in this answer. **B** does not adhere to statement ii since this omits to tell us about C and A. **C** diverges at statement iv since D has beaten/done better than C in this answer. **E** also diverges at statement iv since D, in this answer, does better than C but does not do better than A, which does not adhere to the structure in statement iv. **D** is therefore the correct answer.

48 Firstly, find out how long it takes Dylan to reach Point B. This is 6 hours (120 ÷ 20). You know then, if Kate leaves 2 hours and 15 minutes later than Dylan, that Kate has 3 hours and 45 minutes in order to travel 120 miles. To work out her speed therefore, you should divide distance by time. This calculation would be 120 ÷ 3.75 (and not 3.45 since you are dealing with hours and minutes) which comes to 32. If you struggle with this calculation then trial and error should lead you to the same answer. Essentially, you can take each speed given to you and find out how far Kate would travel, based on this speed, in 3 hours and 45 minutes. The correct answer is **E**.

49 The argument may be difficult to discern from the information given in this question but it is essentially that there is some evidence supporting the theory that music taste is a question of genetics (the 'nature' argument) but that there seems to be better, or more, evidence supporting the theory that music taste depends on what type of music a person is exposed to (the 'nurture' argument). **A** is incorrect as it is the opposite of what the argument is saying. **C** could be inferred from the argument but no information is given as to the musical tastes of identical twins and this issue is not the main conclusion since the evidence involving twins is only a part of the reasoning behind the 'nature' theory whereas the main conclusion seeks to compare both the 'nature' and 'nurture' theories. **D** is incorrect since, even if the view of scientists is equated with the view in scientific literature, it is stated that this literature supports the 'nurture' theory and not the 'nature' theory (the

latter would state that we are designed to prefer one type of music over another). **E** is incorrect since, although it is stated at the outset that there are two competing theories, it is not stated that scientists are divided on these theories. If anything, you can conclude that scientists may prefer the 'nurture' theory. **B** is correct since the 'nurture' argument is preceded by the words 'more convincingly' which implies, according to the argument, that this theory has more support. In addition, it is stated that the 'nurture' theory receives more support in relevant scientific literature. Remember, it is not whether *you* think there is better evidence for the 'nurture' argument (which you may dispute); rather it is what the argument is saying that is important in this question.

50 In this question you should look for the individual features of each of the three shapes in the question in order to find out which of the five larger shapes cannot be a combination of them. For example, you know that there is one right-angled triangle and one equilateral triangle and you should be able to discern from each large shape where the two triangles are. In shape **A** you should be able to make out the pentagonal shape within the larger shape and you should have noticed that the two remaining triangles both seem to be right-angled triangles and there does not seem to be an equilateral triangle present. Therefore, **A** cannot be made from the three shapes in the question. If you draw lines onto shape **A** in order to split it up into smaller shapes, then this should also make it clear that **A** cannot be made from the three shapes in the question.

Oxford TSA section 2:
Model answer and essay plans

Model answer

'Societies should never strive for utopia since the concept is ideological and can never be achieved.' Do you agree?

I disagree with this statement and this essay will argue that, even though the concept of utopia is ideological and can never be achieved, societies should *always* strive for it. This will be argued on the grounds that a desire to be happier should be intrinsic to every human and therefore societies should strive for a situation where everyone is as happy as they can be. In addition, even if it is not possible to reach utopia, it is still worth striving for, since this will bring about more positive consequences than striving for any other state. Finally, this essay will refute the contention that striving for utopia may result in less happiness than pursuing other avenues.

The concept of utopia can be traced back to Thomas More's sixteenth-century work concerning this abstract concept. Whilst his book does include some aspects of a utopian society, it is worth clarifying what this means. A utopian state is ideal in terms of the social, political and legal nature of the regime. In addition, it is a state where every individual is the happiest they can be, where each derives the maximum amount of utility he/she can and, in economic terms, where there is Pareto efficiency.

Based on this definition, it seems largely uncontroversial that this is a worthwhile system or regime to aim for. Despite it seeming rather circular, it is almost a truism that people should strive to be happier since being happy is inherently good. If it is good, then a society should strive for a situation which maximizes this 'good'. Since utopia is defined as a state in which this 'good' is maximized, societies should strive for utopia.

Despite this sounding rather neat, this essay recognises that a more practical argument can be levelled against it, which is that if we can never get to this situation, then why bother striving for it? It is argued that societies should still always strive for a utopian society for various reasons. The first is that it seems likely that, even if an ideal state of maximum 'good' or happiness is not reached, getting some way there would still lead to some 'good' or happiness, since there is an increasing amount of 'good' on the way to this maximum

225

'good'. In other words, some good will come about in striving for utopia. Secondly, what else should a society aim, for if not to be the best it can be? This rests on an assumption, which seems valid, that a society requires an aim, otherwise anarchy would be the inevitable consequence. Would it be better for a society to aim for the opposite of utopia? The answer to this is clearly 'no'. Maybe it would be better, opponents of the argument so far may argue, to aim for a more realistic conception of 'good'. Perhaps a society where there is an acknowledgement that perfection is unattainable but where society makes the best of what it has and is capable of. However, whilst this sounds like a realistic compromise, it is submitted that this is just as problematic, since where does this 'realistic compromise' lie? No state is able to realise the exact limit of its potential and it would be an unrealistic and, indeed, far from ideal position when one day a state admits that it has done as much as it can do and declares that the society it rules has reached its potential. Instead, it is preferable for a society to aim constantly to better itself so that it does not stagnate artificially and, even when this betterment can go no further, at least there is still a sentiment or an ambition that it can. Essentially, a society should always strive for utopia.

There are two counter-arguments, which this essay will briefly refute. The first is that some 'bad' may arise from aiming for an ideal state and failing to reach it. In other words, disappointment from failing to achieve a goal. However, it is argued that the happiness that is achievable from striving for utopia should outweigh this disappointment, such that the eventual result is a net gain in 'good' or 'happiness'. The second is that perhaps there isn't a spectrum of increasing 'good' leading to utopia and so striving to get closer to utopia may not necessarily lead to an increase of 'good'. However, to state this is just as much an assertion as it is to say that there is an increase in 'good' the closer a state is to utopia. In addition, without the knowledge of what lies on the way to utopia, and when the counter-factuals, striving for 'bad' or striving for some realistic conception of 'good', are undesirable, striving to utopia seems like the most preferable option, if only to discover the truth of these assertions.

In conclusion, it has been argued that all societies should strive for utopia since it is only natural to want to be happier. Even if this ideal state is unattainable, it seems likely that there will be a net gain in happiness to be achieved by striving for the impossible. Finally, it has been argued that striving for utopia seems to be preferable to striving for any other situation or even striving for nothing and so, all things considered, this essay would refute the contention that societies should never strive for utopia.

Essay plans

If art galleries and museums are funded by the public purse, shouldn't watching live sport also be funded in this way?

Definitions

- It is probably worth clarifying that 'public purse' means taxpayers. In addition, you may wish to define 'live sport' as being at the sporting event itself as opposed to watching it live on television, or you may wish to include both of these situations in the definition, depending on your argument.

Possible answers + arguments

No, watching live sport should not be funded in this way:

- There is a fundamental difference between visiting art galleries and museums, and watching live sport in terms of the benefit that society receives when doing each of these activities. An individual is educated when he/she visits an art gallery or museum and is more culturally enriched. Society benefits from better-educated and more culturally-enriched people and so making society pay for this makes sense. Conversely, society does not benefit much when people watch live sport. Those individuals themselves may benefit in terms of utility gains from watching live sport but society doesn't benefit from these gains.

- Sport already receives a lot of money from outside investment, for example, many Premiership football clubs have been taken over by wealthy investors. Art galleries and museums do not often receive external funding or, if they do, the figures are much less when compared with sport. Therefore, the public needs to be taxed in order that art galleries and museums may exist. This relies on an assumption that they wouldn't otherwise exist, if people were simply charged an entry fee whenever they went (a fact which may not be true). It also assumes that there is some intrinsic benefit to art galleries or museums which the first argument seeks to defend.

Yes, watching live sport should also be funded in this way:

- Visiting art galleries and museums and watching live sport both lead to a benefit for the individual that partakes in both of these activities. Whether that benefit is assessed in terms of culture, education, relieving stress or bonding with friends or family is irrelevant. As long as there is some benefit to that individual then there should not be a difference in terms of funding to those activities.

- Even if the above argument is not sustainable in itself (for example, it could be applied to allowing strip clubs to be free), then it is still arguable that society benefits just as much from people watching live sport as it does from people visiting art galleries and museums. Allowing people to lead stress-free lives and having a close-knit family and a strong friendship group generally allows people to be happier, more productive at work and less likely to express dissatisfaction with society. Watching live sport can bring about all these benefits and their consequential benefits and therefore, if taxation is justified by societal good, then watching live sport should also be funded in this way.

- By taxing everyone to fund some sectors but not doing so for others, the state removes an element of choice from an individual's life. Essentially, the state is taking away an element of freedom of choice from the individual and restricting his/her choices depending on the allocation of resources to particular activities. Hobbes argued that 'a free man is he that... is not hindered to do what he hath the will to do' but this would not fit neatly with an individual that wants to watch a lot of live sport and never wants to visit an art gallery or museum since he/she would be considerably hindered financially and more so than someone who regularly visits an art gallery or museum and never watches live sport.

In conclusion, yes, watching live sport should also be funded in this way, but there should still be a difference in the amount of funding that watching live sport receives:

- Perhaps a compromise can be reached between acknowledging the benefits of both art galleries and museums and watching live sport so that the latter should be funded from the public purse but that there may be a difference in the amount of funding it receives. For example, if it is acknowledged that there may be less benefit to society from people watching live sport (but still some benefit), then it could still be partially funded from the public purse in order to reflect this benefit.

'Any theory based on assumptions is unreliable and not worth using.' Do you agree?

Definitions

- It may be worth giving some examples of theories, such as economic or philosophical theories, especially if you want to refer to them as practical examples in the main body of your essay.

- You could perhaps also define an 'assumption' as something that the theory relies upon that is taken for granted or taken to be true, although this seems fairly obvious.

- You could perhaps also explain what it means for a theory to be considered 'unreliable'. This may be that it is misleading or that it cannot fully be trusted when making decisions or drawing conclusions.

Possible answers + arguments

Yes, I agree that any theory based on assumptions is unreliable and not worth using:

- An assumption is something taken to be true. It is because we do not know whether this something is true or not we deem the theory to be unreliable. A theory is created in order to hypothesize about how something works, so that decisions can be made based on the outcome of the theory. If we do not know whether the factors upon which the theory is based are true or not, then it means that we cannot be sure that the outcome is accurate. If the outcome is not accurate then the theory is unreliable, since it would be misleading to rely on it in order to make decisions and these could prove to be erroneous.

- If decisions based on the theory could prove to be erroneous then the theory is not worth using, on the valid assumption that we do not want erroneous decisions. Even if there is only a 50% chance that a decision will be wrong (depending on whether the initial assumption proved to be true or false), then this is still not a good enough success rate on which to base potentially significant decisions.

No, I don't agree. Any theory based on assumptions is still reliable and still worth using:

- Assumptions are usually made because it is not possible to know for sure whether something is true or not, but that it actually is, in all likelihood, true. So, instead of going through the onerous (and sometimes impossible) task of trying to prove the truth of a certain factor, it is often easier just to provide some evidence as to its general validity and assume that it is true from this. Therefore, the theory that relies on this assumption is still reliable because the assumption will generally be a fairly accurate one.

- Even with the fact that the assumption may or may not be true, the theory can still be reliable since it can provide us with accurate information in situations when the assumption is true.

- It could also be the case that some assumptions are so insignificant to the way the theory operates, so that whether they are true or not will not affect the result or the accuracy of the theory. In this case, the reliability of the theory is hardly affected by the presence of the assumption.

- Following on from these arguments, if it is the case that a theory is reliable, then it is worth using. A theory that points to a certain pattern or outcome, which is accurate due to the reliability of the theory, is then a useful platform on which to base decisions. Just because there are assumptions in the theory, it does not necessarily mean that decisions based on the theory will be erroneous, and, in fact, they will often not be.

I agree that any theory based on assumptions is unreliable, but I do not agree that it is not worth using:

- The first half of this argument would be similar to that in the first possible response – that if something is merely presumed to be true, when, in fact, it could be false, then the theory becomes inaccurate and, hence, unreliable.

- However, just because it is unreliable, this does not necessarily mean that it is not worth using. It could be that it is only slightly unreliable (perhaps there is only a slight chance that the assumption is false) and the pattern or outcome which is hypothesized in the theory may still emerge. In this case the theory may still be worth using since decisions based on it may, in most cases, prove to be correct or that, if erroneous, not significantly so. It could be that, despite the unreliability of the theory due to the assumptions, it is only by using the theory that more can be discovered about the assumptions i.e. whether they are, in fact, true or false. Using the theory therefore may help this, and other theories, in the long-run.

Should university tuition fees vary according to subject?

Definitions

- Everything seems fairly self-explanatory in this question.

Possible answers + arguments

Yes, university tuition fees should vary according to subject:

- On the assumption that the taxpayer would still contribute some money for an individual's university education as well as it being funded from fees, then tuition fees should vary according to the benefit that society receives from an individual having studied a certain subject. Empirical data may show that individuals studying certain subjects tend to work in industries that don't help society much or that individuals studying certain subjects tend to move abroad after graduating. In this case, the contribution from society to that individual's university education should be less than in other subjects where there is a clear benefit to society and so fees should vary according to the benefit to society.

- Despite the fact that, in general terms, education is valuable, some subjects studied at university do not educate and enrich a student studying that subject to a great extent, nor do they benefit society much. If these subjects are still allowed to exist, then the fees to study these subjects should be higher. This will still allow a student to choose to study that subject, thereby preserving the notion that any education still carries some value and the notion of free-will, but it will allow fees to reflect society's view of those subjects.

- If the taxpayer did not contribute at all to an individual's university education, then fees should still vary based on other factors. One factor would be the cost to the university of educating that individual, which may vary between subjects. Another factor could be the benefit that individual will derive in future as a result of studying a certain subject. If it is shown that the average salary for a graduate of a certain subject is ten times higher than the average salary for a graduate of another subject, then it may make sense to charge the first student more for studying that subject since, assessed in monetary terms, that student will gain more than the student studying the second subject.

No, university tuition fees should not vary according to subject:

- The benefit derived from a university education, both for society and the individual, is not always specific to the individual subject a student studies. In other words, there is some general benefit to be derived from the mere fact that a student receives a university education. This benefit could be a general increase in intelligence or simply maturing as an individual as a result of going to university, which often entails moving away from home. This benefit arises irrespective of the subject and so fees should not vary since this benefit is uniform across all subjects.

- It is a fundamental aspect of an individual's university education that he/she should be allowed to choose what they wish to study. This is vital since this choice plays a role in the eventual career of that individual. If an individual is not in his most suited career later in life, then it is likely that his productive efficiency would not be as high as it could be and it also leads to a loss of allocative efficiency for society as a whole. If tuition fees varied according to subject then the freedom to choose any subject is removed as some students may not be able to afford to study the subject they wish to pursue.

- It should be the case that only subjects that carry some benefit to society should be available to be studied at university. Whilst it is difficult to measure this benefit and then to axe courses based on this, there is a net gain overall. It would justify more of an input from the taxpayer into university funding since the taxpayer would benefit more from the money he/she pays and it would remove the need to vary tuition fees based on subject which is unattractive for the two reasons above.

Yes, university fees should vary, but not according to subject:

- This would be an interesting slant on the essay and, should you choose to follow this line of argument, it is recommended that you answer the question in one of the more conventional ways above and then add this argument as an afterthought. It could be argued that tuition fees should vary but based on another factor. This could be an individual's means whilst he/she is studying, an individual's means later on in life if paying the fees retrospectively, or some other factor that you could argue justified varying university fees.

Thinking Skills Assessment:
Practice test 2 answers

Cambridge TSA paper: answers
Oxford TSA section 1: answers

1.	D		26.	A
2.	D		27.	A
3.	A		28.	E
4.	D		29.	C
5.	D		30.	B
6.	B		31.	B
7.	E		32.	D
8.	B		33.	A
9.	C		34.	A
10.	C		35.	A
11.	D		36.	E
12.	D		37.	B
13.	D		38.	B
14.	C		39.	B
15.	B		40.	C
16.	B		41.	C
17.	E		42.	E
18.	D		43.	C
19.	B		44.	D
20.	C		45.	E
21.	A		46.	E
22.	B		47.	D
23.	C		48.	E
24.	A		49.	B
25.	B		50.	A

Thinking Skills Assessment: Practice test 3

Cambridge TSA paper
Oxford TSA section 1

Cambridge TSA instructions

There are 50 questions in this paper. For each question there are five possible answers, only one of which is correct. No marks are deducted for wrong answers so you should attempt all 50 questions.

You have 90 minutes to complete this paper. You may NOT use a calculator but you may use a dictionary (book or electronic).

Oxford TSA instructions

Section 1 of this paper contains 50 questions. For each question there are five possible answers, only one of which is correct. No marks are deducted for wrong answers so you should attempt all 50 questions.

You have 90 minutes to complete Section 1. You may NOT use a calculator.

Section 2 of this paper contains four essay questions of which you must choose **one**.

You have 30 minutes to complete Section 2. You may NOT use a dictionary.

1   The first viewing figures for my new channel 'Minty TV' have just arrived. It seems as if more people than I expected watch the channel in the morning. However, to my surprise, this figure is cut by roughly half for the lunchtime period. My afternoon shows seem to be a lot more popular than I thought and I get viewers to the tune of about three quarters of my morning slot. My early evening slot is, as expected, quite popular and I get double the number of viewers here than for the afternoon shows. Compared to the afternoon slot, viewing figures for my late evening shows are slightly higher. During the night, my viewing figures amount to about half of my early evening slot.

Which of the following graphs shows this information?

A
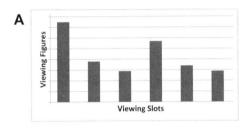

B
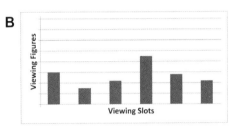

C
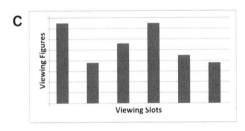

D
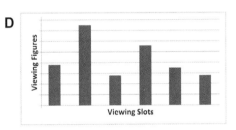

E
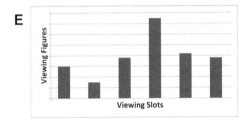

2   The smoking ban in England and Wales will have a twofold positive effect as we approach winter this year. Firstly, as was the initial intention, the effects of passive smoking will be much reduced, which will improve the general health of the non-smoking population. Secondly, more and more smokers will give up their habit as it will involve standing in cold areas which will prove to be too unpleasant for some. However, we should be wary of the disincentives to smoke since smokers constitute an important source of revenue for the government and are crucial in times of austerity.

Which of the following summarises the conclusion of the argument above?

A   We should not force smokers to stand in the cold since they may give up their habit and the government may lose much-needed revenue.

B   Cold winters will disincentivise people to smoke.

C   From the state's point of view, the benefits of smoking outweigh its costs.

D   Smoking contributes a lot of money to the public purse.

E   Society should be cautious before dissuading smokers to give up their habit.

3   The sign of good comedy is that it is timeless. Some older comedy shows, such as Mr Bean and Monty Python, are still enjoyed by many young people today and we would fully expect people to find them funny in decades to come. However, many of these timeless comedies seem to originate from the 1980s and, sadly, today's comedy does not fall under this 'timeless' category where people will find it funny for generations to come.

Which of the following is the main flaw in the above argument?

A   There may be other factors that contribute to a 'good' comedy.

B   Only two examples have been given of 'timeless' comedies.

C   There could have been more comedians in the 1980s then there are today.

D   No evidence has been given to show that some older comedy shows are still enjoyed by many today.

E   We cannot yet know whether today's comedy will be timeless.

4 Creel United has just released updated ticket prices for the upcoming season:

```
┌─────────────────────────────────────────┐
│            Ticket Prices                 │
│                                          │
│  North Stand:      Adult - £18.50        │
│                    Child - £14.00        │
│                                          │
│  South Stand:      Adult - £16.50        │
│                    Child - £12.50        │
│                                          │
│  West Stand:       Adult - £16.00        │
│                                          │
│                    Child - £10.00        │
│                                          │
│   Family Stand (family ticket:           │
│      maximum 2 Adults and                │
│      2 Children): £50.00                 │
└─────────────────────────────────────────┘
```

For a family consisting of 6 adults and 3 children, what is the difference between the most expensive set of tickets and the cheapest set of tickets that the family could buy at any given game, on the assumption that they all sit in the same stand?

A £27.00

B £126.00

C £153.00

D £16.50

E £29.00

5 It is wholly irrational for people to have a phobia of spiders when living in the UK. Unlike spiders in Australia, for example, no spider in the UK is capable of harming a human. Over there, a lot of spiders are venomous and can inflict a fatal bite if necessary. Here, on the other hand, spiders are not venomous nor do they have the capability of inflicting any sort of wound on the victim.

Which of the following is an assumption of the argument above?

A Humans are rational.

B Australia is a reliable counter-factual to use.

C Spiders are not poisonous in the UK.

D There is not another reason for which having a phobia of spiders makes it rational.

E Humans are irrational.

6 Recent immigration proposals aim to cap the number of non-EU skilled workers coming into the country in order to curb a rising number of immigrants. However, there is some disparity between different skilled workers as there is a different cap depending on which industry a skilled worker would be employed in. One such disparity is that there is a stringent cap on the number of non-EU scientists allowed in but a ludicrously high cap on the number of footballers. Taking into account the number of football teams in the country, they could all be filled with non-EU football players. However, this makes sense because people like football in this country a lot more than they do science.

Which of the following best illustrates the principle underlying the argument above?

A People who use a weapon when burgling a house are given a longer custodial sentence than those who don't use a weapon. But this isn't right because we don't believe that it is any worse if you use a weapon when burgling than if you don't.

B Dogs are treated better in this country than cats. But this makes sense because there are more dogs than cats.

C Footballers get paid more than rugby players which doesn't make sense because, as a country, we like rugby more than football.

D People who commit the criminal offence of financial fraud are imprisoned for twice as long as those who assault someone. We think assault is less immoral than financial fraud, so the sentence attached to it is fair.

E There is more of an emphasis on the sciences at school than the arts. But this is completely justified because there are not enough students who go on to study science at higher level establishments.

7 The following table shows the total number of subscribers and a breakdown of their age group for various broadband providers:

Broadband Provider	Percentage of Subscribers to each Provider by Age Group				Total Number of Subscribers
	18 - 24	25 - 39	40 - 64	65+	
Veetee	15	47	29	9	190,000
SpeakSpeak	25	35	21	19	220,000
Yellow	17	25	35	23	205,000
Ground	23	31	28	18	195,000
Quickstyle	34	25	21	20	250,000

Which broadband provider has the highest number of subscribers over the age of 40?

A Veetee

B SpeakSpeak

C Yellow

D Ground

E Quickstyle

8 Travelling to less economically developed countries and being exposed to completely different cultures is something that a lot of British people will experience in their lifetimes, particularly when young. However, many such travellers are distressed by the, often harsh, living conditions and the visible effects of poverty which can discomfort a lot of people and, understandably, make them want to leave. At least though, these people, in the long-run, may be more aware of problems in these countries and encouraged to help more, after seeing first-hand the suffering that a large proportion of the world have to experience. It is therefore, ultimately, not a bad thing for these countries that British people go through this.

Which of the following, if true, would most strengthen the argument?

A British people tend to get involved in charities helping people in Britain after they return from such an experience.

B A lot of Westerners will have the same distressing experience but will also be ultimately encouraged to help.

C British people are much more appreciative of their privileged lives as a result of this experience.

D Travelling foreigners contribute much to the economy of less economically developed countries.

E Many people from more economically developed countries have a similar experience.

9 Angela has just sold all the tickets for her upcoming charity disco. She sold 20 more tickets to under-18s than to parents and she made a total of £380. If under-18s paid £10 per ticket and parents paid £8 per ticket, how many under-18s paid for the disco?

A 10

B 50

C 35

D 40

E 30

10 Marius bought a new flat two years ago for a price of $12,000. Inflation has been steady in the country at a rate of 5%. Marius now wants to sell the flat and he expects to receive 75% of the price he paid two years ago (adjusted for inflation).

What loss will Marius make when he sells the flat?

A $4,200.00

B $2,077.50

C $3,307.50

D $2,076.50

E $3,000.00

11 It often seems to be the case that, after a film has done well at the box office, a sequel is produced that is of such inferior quality to the original film that the original film loses the credibility it gained prior to the release of the sequel. The actors, directors and producers suffer when a poor sequel is released and, despite some short-term extra revenue being generated, the reputation of these people can be detrimentally affected, leading ultimately to long-term financial loss. Therefore, actors, directors and producers should reduce the number of sequels they make.

Which of the following, if true, would most weaken the argument?

A   When a sequel is produced, a third film is usually also subsequently produced which generates even more short-term revenue than the second film.

B   Actors, directors and producers are not able to influence whether a sequel is made or not.

C   Actors, directors and producers are only concerned with their reputation and not the level of profit they make.

D   Whether a sequel is inferior or superior to its prequel is very much a subjective concept.

E   The only concern for actors, directors and producers is the amount of money that they make.

12 Green tea is much healthier for you than ordinary black tea because of the antioxidants it contains, which have been shown to reduce the rate of many illnesses. Green tea is generally grown in China (and other South-East Asian countries) and it is therefore no surprise to hear that Chinese people are generally healthier than Westerners, who drink a lot more black than green tea.

Which of the following is an assumption of the argument above?

A   Chinese people drink green tea.

B   Antioxidants have beneficial health effects.

C   Westerners prefer the taste of black tea.

D   Black tea is not also grown in China.

E   Other South-East Asian populations are also healthy.

13 I place all the books that I own on four shelves. The books are separated according to category and kept in place by book-ends. I have two types of book-end – one for the left hand side of the books and one for the right hand side i.e. the same book-end cannot be used at the right hand side of one category and at the left hand side of another category. The edge of each shelf acts as a barrier so that I don't need (or want) book-ends on the two ends of each shelf.

If I decide to place nine categories of book equally across three shelves and two further categories on the fourth shelf, how many book-ends will I need in total?

A   12

B   10

C   14

D   20

E   18

14 The general standard of mental arithmetic is declining in the UK and more and more people are turning to calculators in order to perform simple calculations. Whilst this is an unattractive prospect and has led to campaigns to ban calculators in schools, working out calculations quickly is an important factor to be considered. The use of calculators should therefore be encouraged.

Which of the following is the main assumption of the argument above?

A   Speed is important in calculations.

B   It is quicker to work out a calculation with a calculator than by using mental arithmetic.

C   Calculators can be used to perform the same calculations that are involved in mental arithmetic.

D   There is widespread use of calculators in schools.

E   Teaching mental arithmetic in schools will make people quicker at performing calculations.

15 A car garage services, on average, 10 cars per day. It is open for 7 days of the week for 40 weeks of the year and has 2 staff, each with an annual income of £11,000. Overheads for the garage are £1,900 per month. How much does the garage need to charge for each service on a car in order to match its expenditure?

   A £16

   B £12

   C £15

   D £26

   E £13

16 Political theorists such as Hobbes, Locke and Rousseau have produced fascinating accounts, both descriptive and normative, about the role of the state in any given society. However, the relevance of their work in contemporary societies is much diminished as a result of the fact that these theorists were writing more than 200 years ago. As a result, we should encourage the reading of their work from a descriptive point of view – to understand the political structures that existed during their lifetimes – but we should not base any thoughts about our own political structures on their writings. For example, Rousseau explains 'democracies', 'aristocracies' and 'monarchies' in terms that are not congruous with the modern conception of these political structures.

Which of the following best expresses the main conclusion of the argument above?

   A We should encourage the reading of political theorists such as Hobbes, Locke and Rousseau since their work is interesting.

   B We should not form opinions on our own political state based on the writings of theorists such as Hobbes, Locke and Rousseau who wrote more than 200 years ago.

   C The writings of political theorists such as Hobbes, Locke and Rousseau are less relevant today than they were during the lifetime of these people.

   D 'Democracies', 'aristocracies' and 'monarchies' denote different things today than they did 200 years ago.

   E We should not judge our own political structures based on the writings of political theorists who wrote in the past.

17 If I start my daily jog by running at 6 miles per hour for 90 minutes but then slow down to a slower rate for 4 hours and 15 minutes, at what speed am I running at this slower rate if the total distance I cover is 26 miles?

A 4 miles per hour

B 4.15 miles per hour

C 5 miles per hour

D 4.25 miles per hour

E 3.75 miles per hour

18 Hypothetically, if sensitive, diplomatic and apparently confidential information was released to the public via some 'underground' means, there would be different reactions worldwide. On the one hand, some of the information should be kept confidential on national security grounds and one reaction would be to deplore the availability of this information. On the other hand however, more information available to the public increases transparency between state institutions and the people and leads to a more democratic process at election time.

Which of the following is a conclusion that can reliably be drawn from the above argument?

A On balance, the benefits of releasing this information would outweigh the costs of doing so.

B Information released via 'underground' means leads to a more democratic process at election time than if the information was released through official channels.

C Some sensitive, diplomatic and apparently confidential information has already been released to the public.

D Information released via 'underground' means is more deplorable than information released through official channels.

E The better the public is informed about its state bodies, the more democratic elections would be.

19 Here is a standard digital clock face showing hours and minutes. It is in 24 hour mode, meaning that the hours continue past 12 onto 13, 14, 15 etc. until 00.

If a line of symmetry is drawn, as shown above, on how many occasions in a 24 hour period (i.e. from 00:00 until 23:59) would the clock face be symmetrical (assume for the purposes of this question that 11:11 is symmetrical)?

A   16

B   13

C   9

D   11

E   20

20 People worry about the effects of coffee on the body when in fact there is no cause for concern and we should not discourage its consumption. This is because the diuretic or dehydrating effects of caffeine are overstated. People regard caffeine as contributing to a significant loss of water from the body and, because of this, are reluctant to drink too much of it. However, when you take into account the fact that you are, by necessary implication, consuming water when drinking coffee, the net effect for the body is an increase in water and not, despite some diuretic effect, a net loss.

Which of the following, if true, would most weaken the argument?

A   A lot of coffee sold in cafes is not from fair trade sources.

B   Coffee is a good stress reliever.

C   Drinking pure water would give you a higher net gain of water than drinking coffee.

D   Small quantities of milk are often added to coffee which can make it quite fatty.

E   Caffeine has other negative effects on the body.

21 The coalition government needs to be careful of increasing student fees to a level whereby less fortunate, but equally aspiring, students in society are dissuaded from going to university. These students could be the future intellectual elite of the country.

Which of the following most closely parallels the above reasoning?

A Taxes on alcohol and cigarettes should be reduced to such a level whereby government revenue is maximised so that those who smoke or drink will be contributing to society more than they do currently.

B The congestion charge should not be so high as to put off skilled overseas workers from coming to London since these people could contribute to important sectors in the economy.

C Income tax should not be too high in the UK since it may lead to a 'brain drain' and we may lose valuable employees from the job market.

D The UK should be wary of increasing tax on tobacco to such an extent that people stop smoking, since we collect a significant amount of revenue from those who smoke.

E The UK should not privatise the health system since many people may be unable to afford basic health care.

22 Anjali has four pets: a dog, a cat, a rabbit and a guinea pig. Each day when she leaves for work, Anjali has to put each pet in either the house or the garden or a combination of the two. She must do so based on the following facts:

- **If it is a cold day, the rabbit cannot be outdoors.**
- **If it is a warm day, the dog cannot be indoors.**
- **The guinea pig cannot be left alone either indoors or outdoors.**
- **The dog cannot be in the same place as the cat or the guinea pig, unless the rabbit is also in that place.**
- **The guinea pig cannot be in the same place as the rabbit.**

On a warm day, which of the following combinations of pets will be found in the garden?

A The dog, the cat and the rabbit.

B The dog and the rabbit.

C Only the dog.

D The dog and the cat.

E All of them.

246

23 Rap music is given a tough time by a large section of society and is accused of degrading women and promoting the use of drugs and guns. Whilst this is certainly true of some rap music, it is important that the whole genre is not tarred with the same brush and so those who criticise rap music should be wary of generalising about the whole genre. Some rappers, such as Tupac, write about poignant issues such as racism, the role of the police and combatting poverty.

Which of the following best expresses the main conclusion of the argument above?

A Tupac did not rap about any issues that give rap music a bad press.

B It is important that people are wary before generalising.

C Rapping about racism, the role of the police and combatting poverty would give rap music a better name.

D Critics of rap music should be cautious not to tar the whole of the genre with the same disapproving brush.

E Rappers can sometimes be accused of degrading women and promoting the use of drugs and guns.

24 In a new game at my local fun fair, contestants are given 20 balls and must attempt to throw as many as they can into a basket. At least five balls need to be successfully thrown in the basket in order for the contestant to win a prize. If five balls are successfully thrown, the contestant receives a £3 prize. The prize money increases incrementally after this so that for every two balls, more than the five that are successfully thrown, the contestant receives £1. If there are more than 11 balls successfully thrown in the basket, then the contestant receives 50 pence for each ball more than 11.

If I received £7.50 in prize money, how many balls did I successfully throw into the basket?

A 14

B 12

C 15

D 17

E 13

25 If my girlfriend gets the overseas job she has applied for then I will leave the country to go and live with her abroad. This isn't something that I had contemplated in my life plan but I am quite an adaptable person so I should be able to settle and find a job abroad. However, I recently discovered from a reliable source that my girlfriend won't be given the job and that it will be given to somebody internally. So, I won't have to change my life plan and move abroad after all.

Which of the following is the best statement of the flaw in the above argument?

A   There may be other reasons as to why I may still move abroad.

B   It assumes that my life plan is definitive.

C   It is not yet certain that my girlfriend will not get the job.

D   It assumes that an overseas job requires a person to move abroad.

E   It doesn't provide evidence as to the reliability of the source.

26 Have you ever tried to guess the number of people in a room and ended up being completely wrong? It is one thing trying to turn a qualitative observation into a quantitative one, it is another trying to conceptualise even larger figures. Most people don't grasp just how many people there are in countries like India and China, for example. One way of conceptualising this is that if you count one number per second, then it would take just under 12 days to count to one million but it would take you almost 32 years to count to one billion. Now try and conceptualise the populations of India and China again.

Which of the following conclusions is best supported by the above argument?

A   China has a larger population than India.

B   It takes a shorter amount of time to count to one billion than one million.

C   Most people count at a rate of one number per second.

D   One billion is more than one million.

E   India and China have equal-sized populations.

27 John, Abraham and Bill are travelling to Saigon to see a play. John catches a bus at 2.30 pm. Abraham leaves at the same time as John but takes a train, which means his journey is 40% longer than John's. Bill also takes the bus which takes the same amount of time as John's bus, but he leaves 45 minutes after John, and is due to arrive in Saigon at 4.30 pm. At what time will Abraham arrive in Saigon?

A   5.15 pm

B   3.45 pm

C   4.00 pm

D   5.00 pm

E   4.15 pm

28 The following map shows the possible destinations and the distances (in km) between them to which I may have to deliver certain parcels on any given day. All my deliveries start from Point A, where I pick up each parcel, and there are no other routes to any points other than via those shown on the map.

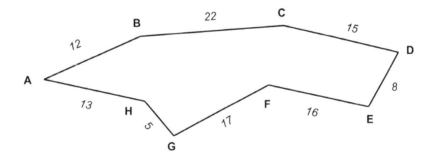

Yesterday, I made five deliveries each starting at Point A and, for each, I travelled 34 km, 51 km, 18 km, 35 km and 13 km respectively (all distances are one-way distances). To which of the Points did I make deliveries yesterday (in no specific order)?

A   B, C, E, G and H

B   B, C, G, F and H

C   C, D, E, G and F

D   D, E, F, G and H

E   C, E, G, F and H

249

29 Cricket, as a sport, is widely criticised for being boring. A lot of people don't find it appealing, arguing that it does not involve much drama or suspense and that a game of cricket lasts too long. However, people need to give the game more of a chance and watch it more often, for it is only really through getting involved with the nuances of the game that one can begin to appreciate it. For example, the micro-tactical battles involving the weather, the positioning of fielders and the coin toss at the start of the game add a whole new fascinating dimension to the game but which can only be appreciated by watching a lot of cricket. People should therefore watch more of the game and give it a chance before dismissing it as a sport which is no fun to watch.

Which of the following, if true, would most weaken the argument?

A Specialist knowledge is required to understand fully the micro-tactical battles.

B Due to time differences, a lot of cricket played overseas takes place during the night over here.

C More forms of cricket are being introduced that make the games a lot shorter.

D Most people are unable to afford to watch cricket, either on television or live.

E A game of cricket can be cancelled or delayed very easily due to bad weather.

30 Assuming that Halley's Comet passes the Earth every 76 years and the last time it did so was in 1986, how many times between the year 3,000 and the year 4,000 (inclusive) will it pass the Earth?

A 12

B 14

C 13

D 11

E 15

31 Simon is three times older than Cheryl. In five years, the sum of their ages will be 74. How old is Simon?

A 64

B 15

C 51

D 48

E 45

32 A goldsmith uses a safe with a rotating reel combination lock, which is programmed with a code, consisting of a sequence of five numbers between 1 and 36 inclusive. To remember the code the goldsmith translates it into an easily memorable sequence of five words, made up of letters from the phrase "A GOLDSMITH". Each letter is given a numerical value, A representing 0 through to H representing 9, and so each word in the phrase represents a single number in the safe's code, which can be found by adding up the values of the letters in that word. For example, the word 'GOLD' would equate to the number 10 (1 + 2 + 3 + 4).

If the goldsmith's safe code is 6, 14, 17, 6, 16, which of the following sequences of words could the goldsmith use to remember the code?

A ALL MATHS IS STILL GOOD

B OLGA HAS TOLD ALL GOATS

C DO MOGS HOLD SOLID LOADS

D SOD OLD SOLID DIM TOADS

E LOG HOLDS SMALL HOT HOST

33 Whenever I work from home I do not get as much work done due to various distractions. However, I'm feeling quite ill and, despite my lower productivity at home, being around home comforts and being more relaxed should actually make me more productive than if I was working whilst ill in the office.

Which of the following has the same structure as the above argument?

A Dockchester Rovers usually win when they play away from home. For their forthcoming away match they are allowed to take twice as many supporters as usual which should mean an even greater chance of winning.

B I regularly buy groceries that are either on offer or reduced because they are close to their sell-by date. During my last grocery shop, I was pleasantly surprised to find groceries that were on offer and near their sell-by date and so I got an even bigger discount.

C I generally prefer to read in a quiet environment, such as a library, rather than somewhere where there is a lot of background noise. I find that I take in a lot more information when reading in a quiet environment.

D Mark generally prefers taking the train, as opposed to the bus, since it is quicker. There are currently strikes affecting all public transport, but which are affecting buses more than tubes, making bus journeys even longer. Therefore, Mark will continue to take the tube.

E I usually train at Tiger's Gym, which is the best-equipped gym in the city, and certainly better than Lion's Gym. Unfortunately, I recently fell out with my training partner, making it difficult to train there. So, even though Lion's Gym is not as well-equipped, I will go there so that at least I can still train.

34 If it is 2 o'clock on a standard analogue clock and, after a power surge, the hour hand turns 4,335 degrees clockwise (with the minute hand also turning accordingly), what time will the clock show?

A 2 o'clock

B Half past 2

C Half past 12

D 12 o'clock

E Quarter past 2

35 The following two tables show the number of hours spent each day on various activities by two sportspeople in a given week:

Stacey

	Mon	Tue	Wed	Thu	Fri	Sat	Sun
Rest	2	5	6	1	4	3	3
Football	4		2	3	2		2
Nutrition Class		3		3		2	1
Rugby		4	1		2	2	

Raj

	Mon	Tue	Wed	Thu	Fri	Sat	Sun
Rest	4	5	3	7	2	1	3
Tennis	1		4		4		3
Travel		4	1	3		3	
Squash	3	2		1	1	4	1

On which day of the week do both Raj and Stacey, combined, spend the most time playing sport?

A Sunday

B Monday

C Wednesday

D Friday

E Tuesday

36 On this standard dartboard, I throw three darts. The first dart lands in 20, the second in 18 and the third in 4.

If the dartboard is turned 270 degrees anti-clockwise and I throw three darts in the same way again, in which number will my second dart land?

A   12

B   9

C   11

D   14

E   8

37 Plagiarism is a notion rife with difficulties once you explore it. Firstly, it is an offence in most, if not all, educational establishments with often grave consequences for the offender. The offence seems to be defined as 'passing off somebody else's work as one's own'. However, in order to escape punishment, this means that you could use somebody else's work constantly and, for example, write an essay solely containing that person's views, as long as you simply cite them as a source in the work. Sometimes, when various sources are used, the writer may forget to cite a source and then get punished. Should the only difference between potentially being expelled from an educational establishment and simply writing a bad essay be just the small matter of referencing a source?

Which of the following is a conclusion that can reliably be drawn from the above argument?

A   Plagiarism is an offence only in educational establishments.

B   Plagiarism leads to the offender being expelled from the educational establishment.

C   You may still be expelled even if you cite somebody else as a source.

D   A bad essay always contains the constant use of somebody else's views.

E   Citing somebody else's work is enough to demonstrate that you are not using it as your own.

38   The following table shows the January booking sheet for a five-bedroom country house in which rooms are available to rent:

Names of Guests	Date of Arrival	Length of Stay
Mr & Mrs Iqbal (+ 1 child)	1st January	8 nights
Mr & Ms Jones	3rd January	6 nights
Mr & Mrs Jingree (+ 2 children)	10th January	2 nights
June & Isabelle	12th January	5 nights
Mr & Ms Grant (+ 2 children)	15th January	9 nights
Peter & Andrew	21st January	6 nights
Ashok & Ghanu (+ 2 children)	23rd January	4 nights

What is the maximum number of people occupying the house in any given night in January?

A   10

B   12

C   5

D   6

E   8

39 If I remove the 16 picture cards (Aces, Kings, Queens and Jacks) from a standard deck of playing cards (containing 52 cards), how many would I have to replace in the deck before the probability of choosing a picture card from the deck was $\frac{1}{7}$?

A 2

B 7

C 6

D 4

E 16

40 The attitude in the UK to owning a house is irrational. There is considerable emphasis in society in the UK on owning a house, and advice and policy are geared towards this fact. In countries such as France and Germany, people are more than happy to rent a house for the whole of their life and there is no disapproving attitude towards this practice. The government in the UK should therefore try to shift the emphasis towards renting, as opposed to owning, a house.

Which of the following is the best statement of the flaw in the above argument?

A The government is not the body that can shift the emphasis towards renting.

B That there should be a shift in emphasis simply based on irrational behaviour.

C No explanation is given as to why France and Germany are valid counter-factuals to use.

D There cannot be a shift in emphasis to renting if advice and policy are geared towards owning a house.

E Irrationality is a difficult concept to understand.

41 Galileo's thermometer consists of a cylinder of water with various different bulbs immersed in the liquid. As the temperature of the water changes, so does its density and so the bulbs will rise or fall, depending on their respective densities. This thermometer is useful in observing the operation of buoyancy, the change in density of water and for practically measuring the temperature of a room.

Which of the following is an assumption of the argument above?

A   The density of water changes with temperature change.

B   The bulbs will rise or fall depending on temperature change.

C   The bulbs have differing densities.

D   The bulbs are contained in the water.

E   The temperature of the water will change according to room temperature.

42 Meat-eaters, who seek to justify their practice, sometimes rely on the argument that man was designed to eat meat, as evidenced by our physiological composition. However, this argument simply doesn't hold weight anymore and the counter-argument is simple: just because we are designed to do something, this doesn't automatically justify it. Also, when you take into account the other costs associated with eating meat – the inhumane treatment of animals, the environmental effects of eating meat and the widespread availability of alternatives – it is clear that the benefit of this practice is minute in comparison.

Which of the following best summarises the conclusion of the argument above?

A   There are considerable benefits to not eating meat.

B   Just because we are designed to do something, this doesn't automatically justify it.

C   Certain features of the human body can help to justify our behaviour.

D   The advantages of eating meat are outweighed by its disadvantages.

E   We should all switch from eating meat to being vegetarians.

43 The following graph shows tachometer readings from my recent commute to work except that, instead of showing my speed as a figure, the readings show my speed as a percentage of the speed limit of the road on which I am travelling at that point:

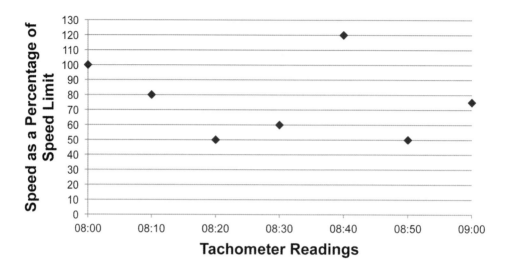

Which of the following can be inferred from the graph above?

A   My speed at 08:20 was less than my speed at 08:00.

B   If the speed limit at 08:40 was 80 miles per hour, then I was travelling at 120 miles per hour.

C   I always travelled at, or below, the speed limit.

D   If the speed limit stayed the same between 08:20 and 08:30, then my speed increased between these times.

E   My slowest speed was 50 miles per hour.

44 More than half of those involved in skiing accidents are male and 60% of these are under the age of 25. But people in this age category are more likely to recover from their injuries than those who are older and so we should not be too worried about this statistic. What is more worrying is the fact that a lot of skiing accidents occur on 'black runs', or, in other words, on the most dangerous ski slopes.

Which of the following is a conclusion that can reliably be drawn from the above argument?

A   More than half of all people involved in skiing accidents are more likely to recover from their injuries than the other proportion.

B   More than half of all people involved in skiing accidents are young males.

C   More than half of all males involved in skiing accidents are more likely to recover from their injuries than the other proportion.

D   More than half of young males have been involved in a skiing accident at some point during their life.

E   More than half of all skiing accidents on a 'black run' will involve a young adult male.

45 The following table shows the world ranking of various countries in terms of their literacy rate in 2010 and the change in ranking from 2009.

Country	World ranking for Literacy Rate (2010)	Ranking change from 2009
Country A	1	(+1)
Country B	3	(+3)
Country C	14	(+14)
Country D	28	(-14)
Country E	5	(-4)
Country F	6	(+2)

Based on this information, which of the following statements is NOT true?

A   Country A was not top of the rankings in 2009.

B   Country E was top of the rankings in 2009.

C   Country C and Country D have swapped places in the rankings from 2009 to 2010.

D   Country E was lower in the rankings than Country F in 2009.

E   Country B was ranked 6th in 2009.

46 The consumption of vitamin supplements has recently been scrutinised and research has suggested that taking vitamin supplements may not benefit the body much. In fact, they may actually harm, us after research found a link between the use of vitamin supplements and the increase in prevalence of various illnesses later in life. However, it is harmful for the body not to have an intake of vitamins and so supplements are beneficial for the functioning of those, who don't otherwise get an adequate vitamin intake. Therefore, the benefits outweigh the costs and so we should not discourage the use of vitamin supplements.

Which of the following is the best statement of the flaw in the above argument?

A   Just because vitamin supplements do not benefit us much, it does not mean that they harm us.

B   No quantitative relationship has been suggested between vitamin supplements and illnesses later in life.

C   No comparison is made between the respective weights of the benefits and the costs.

D   Most people do not get an adequate vitamin intake.

E   The illnesses that could result from the use of vitamin supplements have not been identified.

47 There is too much emphasis put on careers in advice given to undergraduates with the result that many of them feel compelled to jump straight into a job after leaving university which they may not necessarily enjoy. Statistics reveal that out of all people leaving a job, the highest proportion of these are between the ages of 21-25. Therefore, more care should be taken when giving advice to undergraduates to ensure that they don't launch themselves too early into a career which turns out not to suit them.

Which of the following is an assumption on which the argument above depends?

A   People between the ages of 21-25 leaving a job are doing so because they don't enjoy it.

B   Careers information is vital in allowing graduates to find a job.

C   Undergraduates respond to careers advice.

D   People leaving a job will then remain unemployed for a significant period of time.

E   Graduates are in the best position to know whether a job suits them or not.

48 If I throw the brick hard at the window then it will smash the window, whereas if I don't throw it hard, it will still do some damage but will not smash it. Either way, I will be punished with a fine, although this will be higher if the window smashes.

Which of the following most closely parallels the above reasoning?

A If I pedal hard during the first 10 minutes of the race then I will become more tired than if I pedalled at a steady pace. In either case I will lose the race since I am not fit enough to compete.

B Whether or not I work hard towards promotion at my company, I think that I am good enough to be promoted. Due to the strong work ethic at the company, I believe that if I work hard then I will be promoted, whereas if I don't, then I will stay at my current level.

C If I leave for work at 8:00 am then I will encounter some traffic, although it won't be as bad as if I leave at 8.30 am. If I don't leave before 8:00 am then I will be late for work and receive a warning for this, although if I leave at 8:30 am, I will arrive at work later than if I left at 8:00 am and will be sacked from my job.

D I could compete in either the middleweight category or the heavyweight category for my forthcoming boxing match. If it is the latter, then the fight will be tougher than if the former.

E Whether the council sends out 10 ploughs or 20 ploughs, the snow will eventually be cleared. Once this happens, roads in the region can re-open and people can begin to revert back to their usual routines.

49 The following shapes can be put together to make various other shapes:

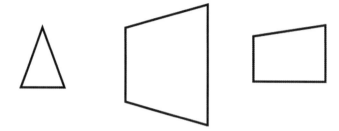

Which of the following is NOT a possible shape that could be made from putting the above shapes together? (not to scale)

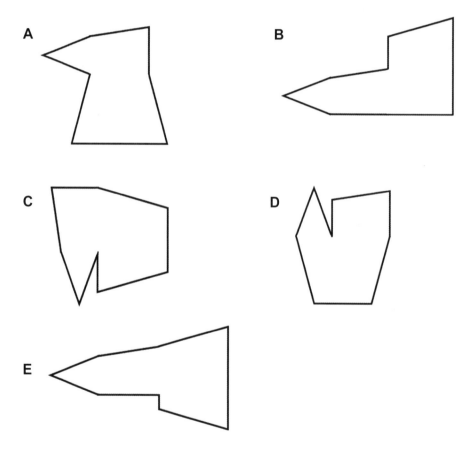

50 Latika has 242 pairs of shoes and is in the process of buying some new shelves in order to fit them all in her bedroom. A large shelf holds 34 pairs of shoes and a small shelf holds 18 pairs. Which of the following combinations of large and small shelves should Latika buy in order to fit all of her shoes exactly?

A 3 large and 8 small

B 4 large and 5 small

C 3 large and 7 small

D 5 large and 4 small

E 6 large and 3 small

Cambridge TSA – END OF PAPER
Oxford TSA – TURN OVER FOR SECTION 2

Oxford TSA section 2

You must answer only ONE of the following questions:

1. Should the minimum legal driving age be raised?

2. Are environmental issues better dealt with by the private or public sector?

3. 'There are no universal characteristics of a democracy.' Do you agree?

4. Can a vacuum be said to 'exist'?

Thinking Skills Assessment: Practice test 3 commentary

Cambridge TSA paper: commentary
Oxford TSA section 1: commentary

1 You should be able to find the correct graph here without eliminating all the others. However, you may still wish to verify this by checking that the others are wrong. You are told that viewing figures for the lunchtime slot are half the morning slot so the bar for the second slot should be half the height of the first bar. You can therefore already eliminate **D**. Next, you know that the third bar (the afternoon slot) should be about three-quarters the height of the first bar (the morning slot), i.e. it should be slightly lower than the first bar. Therefore, you can eliminate **A** because the third bar is around three-quarters of the height of the second bar and not the first bar. By the same process, you can also eliminate **E** because the third bar is higher than the first bar. Next, you know that the early evening viewing figures should be double the afternoon figures and so the fourth bar should be double the height of the third bar. This is clearly not the case with **C** and so you can eliminate it. You are now only left with **B** and this seems to be accurate so far. Checking that it fits the rest of the data, you are told that viewing figures for the late evening shows are slightly higher than afternoon figures, represented on graph **B** by the fifth bar being slightly higher than the third bar. Finally, you can conclude that **B** is the correct graph because the sixth bar (the 'during the night' slot) is about half the height of the fourth bar (the early evening slot).

2 The argument is that, even though more smokers are giving up their habit, we need to be wary about persuading too many smokers to give up since they constitute an important source of government revenue. **A** is too definitive to be a summary of the conclusion since, although you could infer this, the conclusion does not go so far as to suggest ways of ensuring that we do not lose this source of revenue; only that we need to be wary of this fact. **B** is a premise of the argument and not the conclusion of it. **C** is incorrect since it is not suggested that smoking *in general* is beneficial; only that there may be a point at which, from a financial point of view, we should be cautious about persuading smokers to give up. **D** is a premise that leads to the conclusion since it is a fact on which the conclusion is based. **E** is the correct answer because the passage states that smokers contribute to government revenue and so society needs to be wary of dissuading people from smoking.

3   The definition of a 'timeless' comedy in the argument is a comedy, which people in generations after its original time of production and transmission still consider humorous. Thus, in this argument, comedies from the 1980s are stated still to be enjoyed by young people today. The argument then goes on to state that today's comedy cannot be said to be 'timeless', where people will find it funny for generations to come. However, if 'timeless' is a concept that is contingent on the future reception of something, then there is no way of telling yet whether or not today's comedy will be timeless – the "timelessness" of it can only be judged retrospectively. Therefore, **E** is correct. **A** may be true but the argument is concerned with whether today's comedy is 'timeless' and not whether it is 'good' or not. **B** is true but not a flaw, since the argument does not rest on the fact that there are two timeless comedies; in fact it does even not matter if there have been timeless comedies in the past. The argument is that today's comedy is not timeless and, whether there are two or twenty examples given of past timeless comedies, is irrelevant for this argument. **C** could also be true but does not affect the validity of the argument since, for example, even if there is only one comedy show today, the claim that it is not timeless could still apply. **D** is incorrect and it is not a flaw that no evidence has been provided because, firstly, the claim can still stand and must be evaluated, irrespective of whether or not any evidence has been provided for it. Secondly, the conclusion about today's comedy still stands, whether or not there is any evidence provided for older comedy shows being enjoyed by many today.

4   In order to calculate the answer to this question, you should work out the total price for the family based on the four different stands in which they could sit together. For the North, South and West stands, you should calculate that the total price for the family would be £153.00, £136.50 and £126.00 respectively. For the Family Stand, in order that all six adults could sit together, they would need three family tickets (even though they would have three spare child tickets) amounting to £150 in total. The most expensive set of tickets would therefore be in the North Stand and the cheapest set of tickets would be in the West Stand. The difference between them is £27.00 (£153.00 - £126.00). Therefore, **A** is the correct answer.

5   The argument here is that spiders in the UK cannot harm humans and therefore it is irrational to have a phobia of them. **A** and **E** are incorrect because the argument does not rely on, or even address, the rationality or irrationality of humans generally. If anything, the argument may suggest that certain humans living in the UK are irrational, so **A** is definitely not an assumption. **E** is far too general and the argument is that a phobia of spiders is irrational for people in the UK, which does not rely on an assumption that humans are generally irrational. **B** is incorrect since the counter-factual here does not actually add much to the argument, which rests on the premise that spiders in the UK cannot harm humans. It does not matter about the rest of the world, nor whether any counter-factuals are reliable or not, as the passage does not purport to assess the rationality or irrationality of the behaviour of people living outside the UK. **C** is incorrect as it is clearly stated in the argument that, in the UK, spiders are not venomous. **D** is correct since, from the premise that spiders cannot harm humans, the argument concludes that a phobia of spiders is therefore irrational. It may be that there are a whole host of other facts about spiders in the UK which make it wholly rational for people living in the UK to have a phobia of them.

6   This is a tricky question and requires you to understand the principle in the argument, before you begin to assess each of the possible answers provided. The argument, in basic terms, suggests that one group of people is treated more favourably than another group of people but that this makes sense because society has a more favourable view of the action of that group of people in comparison to the other group. So there are three elements involved: firstly, one group being treated more favourably than another; secondly, some acknowledgement that this makes sense, and thirdly, the reason for this difference being that people like what the first group does over the second group. **A** contains the first element, but not the second or the third since it states that the difference isn't right and that there is no difference in attitude between the two groups. **B** contains the first and second elements but not the third because there is no reference to the rationale for the preference. **C** contains the first and third elements but not the second, since it states that the distinction doesn't make sense. **E** contains the first and second elements, but again, like **B**, there is no reference to the rationale for the preference. **D** contains all the elements: there is difference in treatment of two different groups, an acknowledgement that this makes sense and the reason being that we look more favourably at what the better-treated group of people do in comparison to the other group.

7   To answer this question correctly, you need to find out which broadband provider has the greatest number of subscribers over the age of 40. You therefore need to add together the percentages in the '40 - 64' and '65+' categories and then find out how many subscribers this constitutes, as a proportion of the total number of subscribers given to you for each provider. Some of the calculations may seem tricky (especially when you don't have a calculator), but you can approximate to begin with and then accurately

calculate the figures should there be any close results. So, for example, 38% of Veetee's subscribers are over 40, but perhaps you can take 40% as a ballpark and work this out so that Veetee has approximately 76,000 subscribers over the age of 40 (with the actual figure being slightly lower). If you take ballpark figures like this for all of the providers, you should find that only Yellow and Quickstyle have more than 100,000 subscribers over 40, so you can dismiss the others (as long as your ballparks are not too inexact!). From here, you can calculate the number of subscribers for these two providers exactly (if you don't trust your approximate calculations or want to be sure). Yellow has 118,900 subscribers over the age of 40 (58% of 205,000) and Quickstyle 102,500 (41% of 250,000). Therefore, **C** is the correct answer.

8   It is crucial to understand the exact conclusion of this argument in order to find out which of the answers most strengthens the argument. Essentially, the argument is that a lot of British people who visit less economically-developed countries are distressed by the standard of living, but that ultimately, despite this experience, they are more aware of problems that exist in the countries and are therefore encouraged to help them. Specifically, the conclusion is therefore that, from the point of view of less economically developed countries, the experience of these British people isn't a bad thing. **A** does not strengthen the argument since, if British people get involved in charities that help British people, the less economically developed countries are not benefitting from this experience since resources are allocated to local, British charities. In fact, these resources might otherwise have been allocated to the less economically developed countries, so this fact may actually weaken the argument. **B** and **E** are incorrect because they are not relevant to this specific argument. They refer to 'Westerners' and 'people from more economically developed countries' (respectively) whereas the argument specifically concludes that less economically developed countries benefit from *British* people's experiences. **C** may strengthen the argument if being more appreciative necessarily means helping out in a tangible way to less economically developed countries. However, you don't have enough information to conclude on whether this is the case or not, and, on the face of it, there is no evidence to suggest that **C** would lead to a benefit to these countries and so it may not strengthen the argument at all. **D** is correct since, if the conclusion is that less economically developed countries benefit from the experience of British people because they are encouraged to help in the long-run, then it must be another benefit (a more short-term benefit) if, whilst they are there, British people contribute a lot to the economy. If this happens every time a British person goes through this experience then less economically developed countries will benefit in more

ways than just those outlined in the argument. Therefore **D** significantly strengthens the argument.

9   Approach 1

Let the number of under-18s who have bought tickets equal 'x', and the number of parents who have bought tickets equal 'y'.

You know that 20 more tickets were sold to under-18s than to parents, so x = y + 20.

You also know that under-18s paid £10 each, parents £8 each, and that Angela made a total of £380, so you can state 10x + 8y = 380.

Since you are interested in x, the number of under-18s, you can use the first equation to eliminate y from the second equation.

Rearranging the first equation yields y = x – 20.

Using this definition of y in the second equation, it follows that 10x + 8(x - 20) = 380.

Therefore, 10x + 8x – 160 = 380, so 18x = 540.

If you are unfamiliar with multiples of 18, you could divide both sides by 2 to get 9x = 270.

Now it is straightforward to divide both sides by 9 to get x = 30, i.e. 30 under-18s bought tickets. Therefore, **E** is the correct answer.

Approach 2

If you were unable to set up the above equation, or to verify that your equation gave you the correct answer, you could test each figure provided to see if it is the correct answer. In order to do this, you would take each of the number of under-18s given and multiply this number by £10 to work out the revenue from applicants. Then subtract 20 from the number of under-18s and multiply this figure by £8 to work out the revenue from parents. The two revenue figures should add up to £380. Clearly, **A** must be wrong since there cannot be a negative number of parents attending. From the remaining answers, you should find that 30 under-18s (and therefore 10 parents) would give you a total revenue of £380, making **E** the correct answer.

10 This question requires some tricky calculations and also tests your ability to identify and use compound interest. Since the value of the house will have increased due to inflation, you first need to calculate the current value of the house. To do this, you should add 5% onto $12,000 for the first year. One method of doing this is to find 1%, which is $120, and then to multiply this by 5 to give you $600, so the value of the house after the first year is $12,600. Next, and crucially, you need to find 5% of this new figure which is

269

$630 (1% of 12,600 is 126 and multiply this by 5), making the value of the house after two years $13,230. You should not have simply taken 10% of the initial value to find out this value, since this wouldn't take into account the rise after the first year.

Approach 1

One approach of finding the loss is to work out 25% of this value since Marius expects to sell the flat for 75% of the inflation adjusted price. The easiest way to do this is to divide the value by 4. Therefore, $13,230 ÷ 4 = $3,307.50 and therefore **C** is the correct answer.

Approach 2

A slightly longer, but equally valid, approach is to find 75% of this value and then take this away from the inflation-adjusted value. One method of finding 75% is to find half (50%) and then half again (25%) and add up these values. You should have calculated that 75% of the value after two years is $9,922.50. Finally, subtract this figure from $13,230 (and not $12,000, since you need to use the value adjusted for inflation). The answer you get should be $3,307.50 and therefore **C** is the correct answer.

If you got one of the other answers, check that you adjusted the initial value for inflation correctly, that you found 25% correctly and that you calculated the profit using the inflation-adjusted figure for the initial house price.

11 The argument here is that a sequel to a financially successful film is often inferior to the original and, despite some short-term gain in revenue, the long-term effects are a loss to the credibility and reputation of actors, directors and producers, which subsequently leads to financial loss. Therefore, these people should reduce the number of sequels they make. **A** may weaken the argument to some extent, although there is probably not enough information to conclude this for certain. The increased short-term revenue may not be sufficient to mitigate the possibility of long-term financial loss and so, without further information, it is not clear how this information would affect the argument. **C** may seem to weaken the argument since it removes the importance of financial loss as a premise for the conclusion in the argument. However, the argument still states that the credibility and reputation of actors, directors and producers is detrimentally affected when an inferior sequel is produced. The conclusion that these people should make fewer sequels therefore still stands, if this statement is true, since making more sequels can lead to a loss in reputation. **D** would not really affect the argument because, if true, it does not detract from the fact provided in the argument that 'a sequel is produced that is of such

270

inferior quality to the original film that the original film loses the credibility it gained prior to the release of the sequel'. Whether or not inferiority or superiority is subjective, this fact still applies. **E** is incorrect since it would most likely strengthen the argument. If the only concern for actors, directors and producers is the amount of money that they make, then the assertion that there may be long-term financial loss from making sequels supports the idea that they should reduce the number of sequels they make. It could be argued that the loss of credibility and reputation, as a result of making sequels, is not therefore relevant to the argument if this is true but, since it is stated that a loss in reputation *leads to* financial loss, the fact that profit is the only concern is still affected by reputation and therefore the argument is strengthened by this statement. **B** is the correct answer as, if true, the conclusion could not follow from either the premises or the argument since, if actors, directors and producers are not able to influence whether a sequel is made or not, then how can they reduce the number of sequels that are made? The conclusion that actors, directors and producers should themselves reduce the number of sequels which are made would be fatally undermined if those persons were unable to influence whether or not a sequel is made.

12 The argument states that green tea is healthier than black tea because of evidence linking it to lower rates of illnesses. It also states that green tea is grown in China and therefore it isn't surprising to learn that Chinese people are generally healthier than Westerners (who drink more black than green tea). There is a causal connection created implicitly between the fact that green tea is *grown* in China and that Chinese people are generally healthier than Westerners. What if all the green tea they grow is exported and none of it left for Chinese people to drink? This should point you in the direction of the clear assumption being made that Chinese people actually drink green tea, i.e. the causal connection between growing the tea and being healthier is assumed. Therefore, the correct answer is **A**. **B** is incorrect since it is stated that antioxidants are beneficial to health. **C** is not relevant to the argument and is not an assumption that the argument makes, or needs to make, in order to work. **D** is also irrelevant since the argument is concerned with the prevalence of green tea and a healthier population, rather than the issue of whether or not black tea is also grown in China. **E** is incorrect since the conclusion relates specifically to Chinese people - the health of other South-East Asian populations is irrelevant to the argument.

13 You should try to visualise each shelf, or even draw them out, in order to work out how many book-ends will be needed. On the three shelves, each with three categories on them, two categories will use the edge of the shelf as a barrier thereby only needing one book-end each for the other side of the category. The category in the middle will need a book-end on each side of it (since you are told that the same book-end cannot be used at the right hand side of one category and the left hand side of another category) therefore giving you four book-ends required for each of the three shelves. As for the final shelf, the edge of the shelf will act as a barrier for each of the two categories leaving two book-ends required in the middle to separate them, with the same rule as above. Therefore, two book-ends are required on this shelf and 12 for the other three shelves (four on each). **C**, 14, is therefore the correct answer.

14 The argument here is that, despite the fact that the standard of mental arithmetic is declining in the UK, more and more people are using calculators, which is an unattractive prospect, leading to campaigns to ban calculators in schools. However, since the speed of calculation is an important factor, the use of calculators should therefore be encouraged. An implicit link has been made between the importance of working out calculations quickly and encouraging the use of calculators without any further information. This implicit link is an assumption that calculations can be worked out quicker using a calculator than through mental arithmetic and therefore **B** is the main assumption in this argument. **A** and **C** are stated in the argument and therefore not assumed. **D** is not relevant for the argument, since all that is stated concerning schools is that there have been campaigns to ban calculators in schools which, itself, isn't actually relevant to the conclusion of the argument. **E**, again, is not relevant to the argument and seems antithetical since the implicit premise here is that calculators are quicker than mental arithmetic and that is the key assumption in the argument.

15 When deciding whether to use monthly or annual figures as the basis for your calculations, try to work out quickly which numbers will be easier to work with by testing out one of the calculations. Dividing the annual incomes of the staff by twelve to find out a monthly figure does not give a whole number, whereas multiplying the monthly overheads by twelve does. It is therefore a good idea to use annual figures as the basis for your calculations. The starting point should be to work out how many cars the garage will service when it is open. This would be (number of weeks multiplied by the number of days in a week the garage is open, multiplied by the number of cars serviced each day) or (40 x 7 x 10) which is 2,800. Next, you need to work out the annual expenditure. For the staff incomes, this is simply £22,000 (£11,000 x 2). For the monthly costs, £1,900 x 12 = £22,800. Total annual expenditure is therefore £44,800 (£22,000 + £22,800).

Finally, you need to divide 44,800 by 2,800 to find out how much the garage should charge per car in order to match this expenditure. You can work this out by long division but one other method with these sorts of calculations is to multiply 2,800 by a few easy round numbers to see if any of them produce an answer near 44,800. 2,800 x 15 = 42,000 and then there is just an additional 2,800 to take you to 44,800. 2,800 x 16 = 44,800 so the garage would need to charge £16 per car serviced in order to match its expenditure. Therefore, **A** is the correct answer.

16 The argument here is that the work of political theorists such as Hobbes, Locke and Rousseau, because they were writing more than 200 years ago, should not be used as a basis for any thoughts about our own political structures and, perhaps, that we should only read them to discover more about the political structures that existed during their lifetimes. **A** is part of the conclusion but does not grasp the important cautionary note which is that we should not base any thoughts about our own political structures on their work and **A** is therefore not the *main* conclusion here. **C** is incorrect as the question of relevance is raised, in order to lead to the conclusion that these writings should not be used as a basis for any thoughts about our own political structures but does not itself express the conclusion. An application of the 'therefore' rule should lead you to eliminate this as the main conclusion. **D** is incorrect as this is simply an example of why we shouldn't base our own thoughts on their work and so is more of a premise leading to the conclusion as opposed to the conclusion itself. **E** is incorrect as it is not specific enough to be the conclusion. The specific argument rests on the premise that their work is older than 200 years and *therefore* that we shouldn't base any thoughts about our own political structures on their work. **E** is too general since it states that we shouldn't judge our own political structures based on the work of political theorists that wrote in the *past*. However, the past can mean 10 years ago or 1,000 years ago and the argument does not go so far as to suggest that *anything* written in the past shouldn't be relied upon. Therefore, **B**, which specifically refers to political theorists such as Hobbes, Locke and Rousseau, captures the main conclusion here – that we shouldn't base our thoughts on our own political structures on the work of theorists such as these that wrote more than 200 years ago.

17 The first task with this question is to work out the distance I cover at the slower rate. Since you know that I travel at 6 miles per hour for 90 minutes (or 1 and a half hours), this must mean that I cover 9 miles (6 x 1.5). Next, if the total distance is 26 miles, then I cover 17 miles at the slower rate (26 - 9). If I travel 17 miles in 4 hours and 15 minutes, to find out my speed, you should divide the time by the distance. 17 divided by 4.25 (and not 4.15 since you are dealing with hours and minutes) gives you 4. Or, you could convert the hours and minutes to just minutes and divide by 17, which would be 225 ÷ 17 = 15, which tells you how many minutes it takes me to travel 1 mile. Either way, you should find that I travel at 4 miles per hour at the slower rate. Therefore, **A** is the correct answer.

18 This question requires you to ignore what you know and to use only the information in the passage and to understand the various relationships in the argument. **B** and **D** are incorrect since they both make a comparison between information released via 'underground' means and that released through official channels. However, no evidence is provided concerning information which is released through official channels and so you cannot conclude anything about any consequential effects, beneficial or otherwise, of this counter-factual. If anything, you might have the same effects as if it were released via 'underground' means, since the effects in this argument relate more to the actual information as opposed to the means by which it was released. Either way, no reliable conclusion can be drawn as to the comparative effects of releasing information by different means. **A** is incorrect since, although a positive and a negative effect of the release of information are stated, there is no information as to the respective weights of these effects and therefore you cannot determine whether the positive effect outweighs the negative effect or vice versa. To do so would be to rely on information outside the given argument and in so doing your conclusion would not be reliable. **C** cannot reliably be concluded since, from the information given, you don't know anything about what has happened in reality. Indeed, the first word of this argument is 'hypothetically' and the argument is voiced in the conditional tense. **E** is correct and can reliably be concluded from the final sentence in the argument. It is stated that more information increases transparency between state bodies and the people and that this leads to a more democratic process at election time. Therefore, the better informed the public is about state bodies or otherwise, the greater the transparency and the more democratic elections would be.

19 This is an easier question than may appear at first sight and you may be able simply to think about the various times and count them or, which is perhaps preferable, you could write out each symmetrical time and then count how many of them you have.

274

Approach 1

If you decide to work around the clock, counting the number of times which are symmetrical, then start at a logical time e.g. 00:00. Naturally 00:00 is your first time. You should find that there can only be a maximum of 1 symmetrical time per hour. This is because the digits on the hour side of the clock don't change during that hour. If you follow this approach, you should find that only the following times are symmetrical:

00:00

01:10

02:50

05:20

10:01

11:11

12:51

15:21

20:05

21:15

22:55

There are 11 and so **D** is the correct answer.

Approach 2

You can also work this out without counting the number of times although this may prove to take longer. The first task should be to dismiss those digits that would simply not allow the clock face to be symmetrical. Therefore, any time with any of 3, 4, 6, 7 or 9 in it would not be symmetrical. You can also dismiss 8 since even if it was 8 am or 6 pm i.e. if the hours column had an 8 in it, since the maximum number on the right hand side of the clock is 59, there could not be an 8 in the 'tens of minutes' column i.e. immediately to the right of the 8 in the hours column. The remaining digits, 0, 1, 2 and 5, will reflect symmetrically. You should also realise that there can only be a maximum of one symmetrical time per hour because the digits on the hour side of the clock don't change during that hour. Combining both of these two deductions, there can only be 11 hours during which there is a symmetrical time, and therefore there would be 11 times in total.

20 The argument here is that the diuretic effect of coffee does not lead to a net loss of water in the body and so we should not worry about the diuretic or dehydrating effect of caffeine and consequently not discourage the consumption of coffee. **A** may weaken the argument since the conclusion that we should not discourage the consumption of coffee may not be as valid if coffee from cafes is not from fair trade sources. However, this not only rests on the assumption that the source of coffee should affect whether or not we encourage its consumption, but also, and more importantly, that it is only coffee sold in cafes that this applies to and not coffee in general. So, it may not weaken the conclusion greatly since the argument applies to general consumption. **B** would strengthen the argument since it adds a benefit to drinking coffee which supports the idea that we shouldn't discourage its consumption. **C** is incorrect as it isn't directly relevant to the argument. This isn't an argument about the merits of drinking coffee over other beverages; it is a narrower argument simply about the health effects of coffee. If the conclusion was that we should *encourage* its consumption then perhaps the extra benefits of water may weaken this conclusion but, as it stands, all the conclusion states is that we shouldn't worry about the health effects of coffee and that we shouldn't discourage its consumption. The fact that drinking water may be more beneficial than drinking coffee would not significantly weaken the argument. **D** does weaken the argument to a small extent since it may be that we should discourage coffee consumption if milk is often added and can be quite fatty. However, it could be that these small quantities of fat are not actually that bad for us, but also, more practically, this doesn't weaken the argument greatly. It should be noted also that **D** states that milk "can" make coffee quite fatty, not that it "does" make coffee quite fatty. **E**, on the other hand, significantly weakens the argument since, after discrediting one apparent harmful effect of caffeine, the argument concludes that we therefore shouldn't worry about coffee or discourage its consumption. If caffeine had other negative effects on the body then perhaps we should still be worried and should discourage its consumption.

21 The argument here, in general terms, is that if the cost of something increases, this may dissuade some people from selecting it, which in turn may be detrimental to society in the future. **A** is incorrect as it states that the cost of smoking should *decrease,* whereas the argument warns against an increase in cost. **C**, on the other hand, states that income tax should not be too high; however the consequences are subtly different from the argument. Here, the consequences would be that existing workers would leave, whereas the essence of the argument is that people would be dissuaded from selecting something in the first place. **D**, in a similar vein, warns against allowing people to stop smoking since they are important to society, as opposed to dissuading people from starting in the first place which would be more consistent with the argument. Therefore, **C** and **D** are incorrect. **E** is incorrect because it is missing a second limb. All **E** states is that some people may be unable to afford basic health care and, whilst it may follow that this is detrimental to society, the argument does not state this and so is not consistent. **B** is correct since it warns that the increase of a cost (the congestion charge in London) would dissuade skilled overseas workers from coming to London, who could be important contributors to the economy. The fact that they are dissuaded from selecting something in the first place, and then the fact that this may be detrimental to society, means that **B** most closely parallels the reasoning in the argument.

22 You can either apply the rules and find the correct answer or test each answer against the rules. If you have enough time, verifying your answer using both these methods would be ideal.

Approach 1

If you approach this question by applying the rules, then the first thing you know is that the dog must be outdoors. The other three animals can't remain together inside because the guinea pig can't be in the same place as the rabbit. So you could put the dog, the cat and the rabbit outside, which is allowed because of the presence of the rabbit. However, the guinea pig cannot be left alone so this isn't an option. You can't put the rabbit in the house since this violates two rules and so you must put the cat back inside and leave the rabbit outside with the dog. Therefore, **B** is the correct answer.

Approach 2

Taking each answer in turn and dealing with it should also lead you to eliminate all but one of the answers. Indeed, this method should lead you to the correct answer fairly quickly. **A** is incorrect since it would leave the guinea pig alone which is not allowed. All of **C**, **D** and **E** can be eliminated by the fact that the rabbit and the guinea pig cannot be in the same place together. This only leaves **B,** which is the correct answer.

23 This is not an easy question as all of the answers can arguably be extracted from the argument. However, only one is the main conclusion. The argument is that rap music can be criticised for various reasons but that the whole genre is not necessarily the same (as evidenced by Tupac) and so those who criticise rap music should be wary of generalising about the whole genre. **A** is incorrect, firstly, because it is not known that Tupac didn't write about women, drugs and guns and, secondly, because Tupac is

only used as an example supporting a premise and not as the conclusion of the argument. **B** is too general to be the main conclusion of this argument. It is not argued that people, in general, should be wary of generalising, but only that critics of rap music should be wary of generalising about rap music. **C** is incorrect as the argument does not go so far as to suggest this. It may be true, and so could be inferred, but the argument stops at the point of saying that those who criticise rap music should be wary of generalising about the whole genre and not how the genre could improve its general image. **E** is certainly true from the information given but it is more a premise for the conclusion rather than the main conclusion of the argument. In other words, it is because of this reason that the conclusion is stated. **D** summarises the main conclusion of this argument since it is stated that 'it is important that the whole genre is not tarred with the same brush and so those who criticise rap music should be wary of generalising about the whole genre'. Specifically therefore, the conclusion relates to critics of rap music and cautions that these critics should not assume that the whole of rap music is open to the same criticism that can be applied to a section of it. Therefore, **D** is the correct answer.

24 You should realise that, if there are 11 balls in the basket, then there would be £6 in prize money, since there would be the initial £3 prize for successfully throwing five balls in the basket and then £1 for every two more balls that are thrown in the basket which would occur three times. If £1.50 more is received in addition to the £6 and 50 pence is awarded for each ball on top of the 11 already successfully thrown into the basket, then I must have thrown three additional balls into the basket. Therefore, I would have successfully thrown a total of 14 balls into the basket, and so **A** is the correct answer.

25 The argument, in general terms, is that if my girlfriend gets this job, then I will move overseas, but since she isn't going to get the job then I will not move overseas. This question tests your understanding of the logic behind a cause and effect relationship. Specifically, the flaw is that just because my girlfriend won't get the job, it does not mean that I will not move overseas. This is because the effect that I will move overseas is not contingent on simply this one cause, otherwise the relationship should be phrased as my *only* moving overseas if my girlfriend gets this job. However, there could be other reasons as to why I may move abroad at some point and therefore, just because this one cause is no longer present, you cannot logically conclude that the effect will also no longer be present. Therefore, **A** is the correct answer. **B** is incorrect since the argument doesn't rely on the fact that my life plan is definitive; in fact, it is implied that my life

plan is not definitive if I am willing to change it. **C** and **E** are similar in the sense that they both imply that the flaw arises from the anecdotal evidence that my girlfriend won't be given the job. However, the evidence should be assumed to be true so that the reliability of the discovery that my girlfriend won't get the job is not relevant when assessing the logical flow of the argument. **D** is incorrect since it is stated (or at least strongly implied) in the first sentence.

26 This question is simpler than it may seem, although it will test your understanding of a valid inference. **A** and **E** are incorrect since there is no way of knowing the populations of India and China, comparatively or absolutely, purely from the information in the argument. **B** is incorrect since it is stated that it takes longer to count to one billion than one million. A careful reading of this statement should allow you to eliminate it due to it being the opposite of what is stated in the argument. **C** is also incorrect since, again, you do not have enough information to deduce at what rate most people count. It is only stated that *if* the count rate was at one number per second, those values would emerge. This does not suggest anything about the rate at which, in practice, most people do count. **D**, even though you know it is true and perhaps slightly silly, is not stated explicitly in the argument – you only know that it takes longer to count to one billion than one million – and so this, taking into account the common factor of counting one number per second, is mathematically deducible. It follows therefore, either because you make this deduction or because you have eliminated the other statements, that **D** is the correct answer.

27 The first task in this question is to work out how long John's journey will take. You know that Bill's journey is the same length, but that he left 45 minutes after John and is due to arrive in Saigon at 4.30 pm. It must be the case therefore that John will arrive in Saigon 45 minutes earlier than Bill which means he arrives at 3.45 pm. If he left at 2.30 pm, John's journey is 75 minutes. If Abraham's journey is 40% longer than John's then it must be 105 minutes (75 x 1.4) and if you know that Abraham leaves at the same time as John, then he will arrive in Saigon at 4.15 pm, 105 minutes after 2.30 pm. Therefore, **E** is the correct answer.

28 Approach 1
One way of approaching this question would be to work out the distance of every Point from Point A and then to match up the five deliveries to the distances provided. Naturally, you can get to each point two ways – either starting clockwise or anti-clockwise – but due to the nature of the

distances provided to you in the question, of which the highest is 51 km, a sensible starting point would be to calculate the distances to B, C and D travelling clockwise and to H, G, F and E travelling anti-clockwise. Once you have calculated these distances, you should find that you don't have to go back and calculate the distances if you were travelling the other way around, since the five distances in the question should match up to your calculations. You should have found that Points C, E, G, F and H were visited. Therefore, **E** is the correct answer.

Approach 2

Another way of approaching this question would be to take each of the five distances provided and to start off a hypothetical journey, adding up the distances until you arrive at the distances provided. So, for example, taking the first journey of 34 km and starting from Point A, you should find that if you go via Point B to Point C, that is exactly 34 km and so Point C was one of the destinations (you should also check that no other journey could result in a distance of 34 km, which, in this case, it cannot). Continuing with this technique, you should find that visiting Points E, G, F and H amounts to journeys with distances provided for in the question.

29 The argument here is that, despite cricket being criticised for being boring, lacking suspense and being excessively long, it is only through watching more cricket that people can begin to appreciate the nuances of the game. These nuances make the game fascinating and so people should give the sport a chance and watch more of it. **A** could weaken the argument to a certain extent since, if specialist knowledge is required to understand fully the very elements that the argument relies upon to convince us that cricket is fascinating, it would be difficult to do so. However, the argument doesn't rely on the fact that you need to 'understand fully' these micro-tactical battles; it is only stated that these fascinating micro-tactical battles can be *appreciated* from watching a lot of cricket. If you don't need to understand them fully for the argument to work, then the fact that you need specialist knowledge to understand fully them shouldn't affect the argument that much so **A** does not weaken it to a significant extent. **B** does not weaken the argument significantly for the simple fact that the conclusion is not that cricket should be watched live more frequently – the argument still works if people watch more cricket in a form that allows them to watch it during conventional hours irrespective of whether it is live or not. **C**, if anything, strengthens the argument since, if one of the reasons not to watch cricket is that it is too long, shorter versions of the game would eliminate this reason and thereby encourage people to watch it more often. **E** would perhaps weaken the argument to some extent but not significantly since the fact that cricket can be cancelled or delayed very easily due to bad weather is not given as a reason in the argument to deter people from watching cricket. It can be inferred that if a game can be cancelled or delayed very easily due to bad weather, then this could be irritating and people may not want to watch cricket. It doesn't affect a person's ability to watch cricket and they should, according to the argument and despite this minor inconvenience, still watch it and give it a chance. **D** significantly weakens the argument as it subverts the central contention of the argument. If people cannot afford to watch cricket, either on television or live, then the claim that they should watch more cricket simply cannot work – you cannot claim that somebody should do more of something if they are unable to do it in the first place. **D** fatally undermines the argument and is therefore the correct answer.

30 Approach 1

A long-winded, but valid, approach would be to list all the dates from 1986 until the end of 4,000, adding 76 each time, and then counting them in order to find out how many times between 3,000 and 4,000 the comet will pass the Earth. If you do this, then you should find that it will pass 13 times between 3,000 and 4,000 and therefore **C** is the correct answer.

Approach 2

A quicker way of approaching this question would be, firstly, to find out the first year in the 3,000s when Halley's Comet would pass the Earth. To do this, even if you don't know your 76 times table, you can still skip out each individual addition of 76 by adding 760 to 1986 in order to find out what year you will be in after the Comet has passed for the 10th time after 1986. Then you can add 76 to this figure (2,746) until you get to the first number after 3,000 which should be 3,050. Next, add 760 again as a shortcut to get to 3,810 which is the 11th passing of the comet in this millennium. You should find that you can only add 76 twice more before you would then be in the 4,000s. Therefore, the comet would pass 13 times in the period.

31 Approach 1

The easiest way of solving this problem is to set up a pair of equations. If Cheryl's age is 'x', and Simon's age is 'y', you know that $y = 3x$, since Simon is three times older than Cheryl. You can then state that $(x + 5) + (y + 5) = 74$, since you know the sum of their ages in five years' time will be 74. Using the first equation to eliminate y from the second equation, you have $(x + 5) + (3x + 5) = 74$. Therefore, $4x + 10 = 74$, and so $4x = 64$. Therefore, $x = 16$ and so Simon is 48 (16 x 3).

Approach 2

If you can't form the equation above then you could use trial and error i.e. testing out each answer to see which works within the parameters of the question. Essentially, take each number as Simon's age, divide it by 3 to find out Cheryl's age, then add 5 to each of these ages and add them up. So, with **A** you would get Simon's age in five years as 69 but Cheryl's age in five years wouldn't be a whole number ((64 ÷ 3) + 5 = 26.333...) so this can't be the answer. With **B**, this should seem intuitively wrong because 15 is considerably lower than 74, and if you work it out then, if Simon was 15, then Cheryl would be 5 and in five years' time the sum of their ages would be 30. Looking at **C**, if Simon's age was 51, then Cheryl would be 17 and in five years' time the sum of their ages would be 78 (56 + 22) which is incorrect. If Simon was 45, then Cheryl would be 15 and in five years' time the sum of their ages would be 70 (50 + 20) which means that **E** is incorrect. **D** is correct since in five years' time, Simon would be 53 and Cheryl 21 ((48 ÷ 3) + 5) which makes 74.

32 This question requires some lateral thought and some simple arithmetic. I would recommend writing out the letters with their corresponding values underneath, in order to work out each word easily. Also, why not start with the first word in each answer rather than going through them all word by word, just in case one or more of them doesn't start with a word that adds up to 6. If you do this, you should be able to eliminate **D** since 'SOD' represents 11. Next, follow the same approach with the second words in order to see if any of them do not equate to 14. You should be able to eliminate **A** and **E** on this basis. So you are only left with **B** and **C** and you can continue with the third word. You should find that 'HOLD' represents 18 whereas 'TOLD' represents 17 and therefore **B** must be the correct answer. If you wish to verify this, then perhaps adding up the values of the last two words in **B** would help and, indeed, these do represent 6 and 16 respectively. **B** is the correct answer.

33 The argument, in general terms, is that I usually perform better from choosing one option over another. However, in a particular situation, certain factors mean that I will actually perform better from the seemingly worse option. **A** is incorrect since, firstly, there isn't really an idea of choice in the facts presented and, secondly, and more importantly, even though there is the idea of one situation being better than the other, the extra factor (taking more fans) actually improves the better option rather than serving to improve the less preferable option. **B** is incorrect since the two

options don't appear to be mutually exclusive in the sense that one has to be chosen over the other. In addition, the outcome is that both options are combined in the end for overall gain. The argument in **B** has a very different structure to that in the question. **C** is incorrect since it only contains the idea of one option being better than the other option, but does not address the second half of the argument concerning a particular factor, which means that the seemingly worse option becomes more beneficial. **D** is incorrect since, although it does contain the idea of one option being better than the other (tube quicker than bus), the extra factor (public transport strikes) actually makes the worse option even worse rather than making it better. **E** is correct since it contains the idea of one option being better than another (Tiger's Gym being better equipped than Lion's Gym), an extra factor (falling out with my training partner) and therefore the seemingly worse option (training at Lion's Gym) becoming beneficial (allowing me to train whereas training at Tiger's gym would be difficult). This therefore has the same structure as the argument in the question.

34 You should not be put off by the daunting figure in this question and actually it is simpler than may, at first sight, seem. You need to find out how many revolutions the hour hand makes when rotating round 4,335 degrees in order to find out where it ends up pointing. You therefore need to divide 4,335 by 360. This is not an easy calculation however, nor does it result in a whole number. To make it easier, find out the nearest whole number to 4335 which is divisible by 360. If you tried this calculation using long division then you should have an answer close to 12. If not, you should be able to work out, perhaps by trial and error, that 12 x 360 is near enough 4,335. So, start with this. 360 x 12 = 4,320. You then still have 15 degrees left for the hour hand to turn. If there are 30 degrees between each number on a standard analogue clock (360 ÷ 12), then you know that after 12 complete revolutions the hour hand, having arrived back at 2, will rotate through a further 15 degrees. This means that the hour hand will end up exactly half-way between 2 and 3. If the minute hand moves accordingly, then when the hour hand is between 2 and 3, the minute hand will be pointing at 6, since it will be half past 2. After rotating through 4,335 degrees therefore, it will be half past 2, making **B** is the correct answer.

35 The first task in answering this question is to identify the sports from the various activities shown. You should find that there are four activities that are relevant: Football, Rugby, Tennis and Squash. Next, in order to find the day in which the most time was spent playing sport by both Stacey and Raj combined, you should add up the hours for each day spent on the

four activities. You should find that 9 hours were spent on these activities on Friday, which is the most of any of the days. Therefore, **D** is the correct answer.

36 Approach 1

One way of tackling this question is, firstly, to realise that turning the dartboard 270 degrees anti-clockwise is the same as turning it 90 degrees clockwise. This makes the analysis slightly easier. If it is turned 90 degrees clockwise, the number 11 would now be where the 20 currently is. The second dart would land two numbers to the right of number 11, which is number 9.

Approach 2

You could also work this out by calculating that if the dartboard turns 90 degrees clockwise (which is the same as turning it 270 degrees anti-clockwise), your dart would land in the 5th number to the left. This is because 90 degrees is a quarter turn of the dartboard (90 degrees is one quarter of 360 degrees) and, since there are 20 numbers on the dartboard, if you were to count around the numbers, then for every 5th number you would have covered 90 degrees.

37 You can eliminate a few of the incorrect answers in this question by paying attention to the use (or lack) of certain words which subtly change whether or not you can reliably draw the conclusion in the answer. **A** is incorrect as, even though an educational establishment is the context of this question, there is no information provided as to whether plagiarism is only an offence in this context. You do not know whether, for example, plagiarism could still be an offence in an office context. So you cannot reliably conclude **A**. **B** is incorrect since it is stated that there are 'often grave consequences' and that the offender could *potentially* be expelled. It is not certain that the offender will be expelled from the educational establishment and therefore you cannot reliably conclude this, as it suggests that expulsion is always the consequence. **C** is incorrect as it is stated that you can cite somebody else as a source throughout your essay and not be punished. **D** is incorrect as it is suggested the constant use of somebody else's views constitutes a bad essay, but it is not suggested that this is the only way of writing a bad essay. An essay can be bad for a whole number of reasons and it is not made clear in the argument that a bad essay *always* contains the constant use of somebody else's views. **E** is correct since, if the offence is 'passing off somebody else's work as one's own' and, to escape punishment, you can merely cite that 'somebody else' as a source, then it follows that citing

somebody else's work is enough to demonstrate that you are not using it as your own. **E** can therefore reliably be concluded from the argument.

38 The best way of approaching this question is to work out the dates in January for which the people in each booking are staying and then use this to work out more easily when there are the most people staying in the house. Essentially, you are looking for overlaps and then, for each overlap, working out how many people will be in the house. You should find that there are a few overlaps, for example, from the nights of 3rd to 8th January, 15th to 16th January and 21st to 26th January. From working out how many people will be staying during each overlap, you should find that for the night of 23rd January, there are three separate bookings (Mr & Ms Grant (+ 2 children), Peter & Andrew and Ashok & Ghanu (+ 2 children)) with a total of 10 people staying in the house. This is the greatest number of people during any overlap of stays at the house and therefore **A** is the correct answer.

39 Approach 1

One way of approaching this question is first to calculate how many cards there would be in the deck without the 16 picture cards. This is 36. Then, find the next highest number that is wholly divisible by 7. This is 42 and therefore I would need to replace six picture cards in order that 6 out of the 42 would be picture cards, or $\frac{1}{7}$.

Approach 2

Another way of attempting this question (although perhaps slightly longer) is to try adding each of the number of picture cards given to you until you get a fraction that is equivalent to $\frac{1}{7}$. You should find that, although adding two, three or four cards would give you a sensible fraction, the only way of reaching $\frac{1}{7}$ would be to add six cards, giving you $\frac{6}{42}$. Therefore, **C** is the correct answer.

40 The argument here, in simple terms, is that the attitude in the UK to owning a house is irrational and therefore the government should try to shift the emphasis towards renting. The other information in the argument is provided to show where the current emphasis lies and to support the idea of renting. However, the fact that the attitude in the UK to owning is irrational is the main premise leading to the conclusion in this argument. The problem in this argument is that the conclusion does not necessarily have to follow logically from the assertion that the attitude is irrational. No reasons are given as to why the attitude to owning a house is irrational, only that it is.

So, from the label of irrationality given to this attitude, the argument simply concludes that there should therefore be a shift in emphasis. However, you have no idea why the attitude is irrational or why, just because something is irrational, there should be some change. Perhaps this irrational attitude is too firmly entrenched and that a shift in emphasis would fail and waste resources. **B** is the correct answer. **A** is incorrect since it is implied in the argument, and you should know that the government is in a position to change people's attitudes and behaviour in society. **C** is incorrect since the argument does not need to rely on these counter-factuals in order to work logically – it is sufficient for the argument that the attitude is irrational and therefore there should be a change in emphasis – it does not matter whether the counter-factuals used are true or not. **D** is incorrect because it is simply wrong and, naturally, advice and policy can change depending on circumstances. Perhaps, also, this fact does not prevent the argument from logically flowing since the conclusion merely states that the government should *try* to shift the emphasis and this can still occur even if advice and policy can't change. **E** is incorrect since, although irrationality is a difficult concept, the argument does not rely on any specific meaning (other than perhaps a vague connotation of some negative attitude here) – it is sufficient for the argument that there is some notion of irrationality and therefore a shift in emphasis.

41 This question requires you to spot the difference between facts that are stated and facts that are assumed, which is sometimes more tricky than it seems. **A** is not an assumption as it is stated in the phrase, 'as the temperature of the water changes, *so* does its density' (emphasis added). **B** is also stated in the phrase 'as the temperature of the water changes… *so* the bulbs will rise or fall depending on their respective densities' (emphasis added), which demonstrates that the bulbs will move depending on the relationship of the density of the water and the density of the bulbs, the former being affected by temperature change. **C** is slightly trickier, but a combination of the fact that it is stated that there are 'various different bulbs' and that they will rise or fall 'depending on their respective densities' does give us enough information to conclude that the bulbs do have differing densities and so this is not assumed. **D** is clearly stated since the bulbs are 'immersed in the liquid' (with 'the liquid' referring to the water). **E** is assumed and is therefore the answer since it is stated initially that various changes occur when the temperature of the water changes and then, later, that the thermometer is practically useful for measuring the temperature of a room. However, this relies on the fact that the temperature of the water will change according to room temperature. The water temperature might change based on some other variable, in which case the thermometer is not practically useful in measuring room temperature.

42 This question requires you to find the most accurate summary of the conclusion of the argument. **A** is certainly true according to the terms of the argument, and the various costs outlined in the argument do indicate that there would be considerable benefits to not eating meat. However, the conclusion actually compares these benefits to the costs and states that the benefit of eating meat is 'minute in comparison'. In other words, the argument goes further than just saying that there are benefits to eating meat but that there are also costs; it states that the benefits outweigh the costs so that there is a net gain from not eating meat. **D** is the only statement which captures this entire sentiment and so **D** is the correct answer. **B** is incorrect as it is part of the reasoning for which one of the apparent justifications for eating meat doesn't work. **C** is actually antithetical to the conclusion and it is the fact that this is disproved which helps the argument to conclude later as it does. **E** goes too far and the argument does not suggest this. It could perhaps be inferred but the argument simply stops at the point of stating that the advantages of eating meat are outweighed by its disadvantages and goes no further in claiming any normative consequences of this.

43 In order to answer this question, you need to be clear about what the graph shows. The graph shows my speed as a percentage of the speed limit of the road on which I am currently travelling rather than my actual speed. Therefore, you don't know what my actual speed is at any point unless you know the speed limit. **A** is incorrect and cannot be inferred, since you don't know my actual speed and so cannot infer that my speed was lower just because, as a percentage of the speed limit, it was lower. It could be that the speed limit was higher and my speed remained the same or that it actually increased. **B** is incorrect as a simple calculation or deduction will tell you. The speed limit was 80 miles per hour at 08:40 and you know that I was travelling at 120% of this. You can either calculate one fifth of 80 and add it on to find out my total speed which would be 80 x 10% = 8, therefore 20% = 16 and my total speed is 80 +16 = 96 miles per hour. Or, you can work out that, if I was travelling at 120 miles per hour, then this would be 150% of 80 miles per hour, not 120%. Either way, you know **B** is incorrect. **C** is incorrect since my speed at 08:40 was 20% more than the speed limit. **E** must be incorrect since you don't know what my speed was without any speed limits – all you know is that the 50 refers to the lowest percentage of the speed limit at which I was travelling. You should realise that this could feasibly be the highest speed at which I was travelling during the commute according to the graph. **D** is the correct answer here since, if the speed limit stayed the same between 08:20 and 08:30 and my speed, as a percentage of the speed limit, increased, then my absolute speed must have increased. To put it another way, 60% of 100 is more than 50% of 100.

44 This is a tricky question and requires you to get your head around the statistics provided in the passage. You will most likely need to test out each of the answers against the information provided in order to find which one can reliably be drawn as a conclusion. **A** cannot reliably be concluded because although you can deduce that 60% of males in the under-25 age category are more likely to recover from their injuries than those who are older, you cannot deduce what proportion of all people involved in skiing accidents this 60% would constitute. It could be the case that so many more males than females make up those involved in skiing accidents that 60% of these males does indeed mean that more than half of all people involved in skiing accidents are under 25 and therefore more likely to recover from their injuries than the other proportion, but, without the exact ratio of men to women, you cannot *reliably* conclude this. The same principle applies to **B** – you don't know whether the 60% of young males (assuming that 'young' applies to those under 25) is high enough to constitute more than half of all people, so, again, you cannot reliably conclude this. **D** is definitely incorrect since the statistics provided are about the age and sex of those people who have been involved in a skiing accident and not about the population in general – many people may never have skied at all. In other words, the fact that more than half of those involved in skiing accidents are male is not equivalent to saying that more than half of males have been involved in a skiing accident. **E** cannot reliably be concluded since you do not have a proportion of accidents that occur on 'black runs' as opposed to other sorts of 'runs' and so you cannot therefore deduce what proportion of accidents on 'black runs' involve young males. Even if 'a lot' refers to a proportion higher than 50%, it could still be the case, based on these statistics, that the 60% of young adult males all had their accidents on different-coloured runs. **C** is correct since you know that 60% of all *males* involved in skiing accidents are under the age of 25 and that this category of people is more likely to recover from their injuries than other age groups.

45 As long as you have got to grips with the ranking system in the table then this question is relatively straightforward. Use the ranking change to calculate where each country was ranked in 2009, then you can make a direct comparison and rule out incorrect answers quickly. **A** is incorrect because it is true that Country A was not top of the rankings in 2009; it was ranked 2nd. **B** is incorrect because Country E was top of the rankings in 2009 (it slipped 4 places from 1st to 5th). **C** is incorrect since Country C was 28th in 2009 and Country D was 14th in 2009 and they have therefore swapped places. **E** is incorrect because Country B moved up 3 places to 3rd in 2010, so it was ranked 6th in 2009. **D** is correct since, in 2009, Country E was top of the rankings and Country F was 8th. It follows therefore that Country E was *higher* in the rankings than Country F in 2009.

46 The argument first presents evidence that vitamin supplements may harm our bodies but then suggests that it is also harmful not to have an intake of vitamins at all. It then concludes that the benefits of taking supplements therefore outweigh the costs and so we should not discourage the use of vitamin supplements. However, no assessment is made of the relative merits of the benefits and costs i.e. there is no indication in the argument as to whether it is just as harmful, more harmful or equally as harmful not to take vitamins as it is to take them. Therefore, you have no way of working out which of the outcomes is worse than the other, since there is no comparison of the respective weights of the benefits and costs. **C** is therefore the correct answer. **A** is true as a stand-alone statement and it is certainly stated that vitamin supplements do not benefit the body much. However, it is then stated that research suggests that they do cause us harm, meaning that **A** is not really a flaw. **B** is incorrect because a link has been found between the use of vitamin supplements and an increase in the prevalence of various illnesses later on in life. Even though no figures have been provided, the argument does still suggest a quantitative relationship. **D** is incorrect because you don't know whether this is true or not and, even if it is true, it actually supports the conclusion of the argument. **E** is incorrect because it is irrelevant whether you have the names of the illnesses or not – the key word is 'illnesses' itself and, since it denotes some harmful effect without any further information, this is sufficient for the argument to work.

47 The statistical evidence given here is used to support the argument that graduates take jobs too early after university and these turn out to be unenjoyable. However, it is not stated why these people in the statistic leave their jobs; there could be a number of reasons as to why they leave, not necessarily just because they don't enjoy them. Therefore, there is an implicit link made between the statistic and the idea that graduates take jobs that they don't enjoy soon after graduating. The assumption is that these people leave their jobs because they don't enjoy them. Therefore, **A** is correct. **B** is incorrect since the argument is concerned with the reasons for which graduates leave a job rather than how they initially find a job. **C** is incorrect since it is stated that advice is given to undergraduates 'with the result that many of them feel compelled to jump straight into a job after leaving university which they may not necessarily enjoy' and so it is explicit that undergraduates do respond to careers advice. **D** is incorrect since the argument is not concerned with for how long people, in general, remain unemployed after they leave a job. **E** is incorrect since it is not relevant who is in the best position to know whether a job suits a graduate or not.

48 The argument here is that there are two possible actions (throwing hard or soft), one with slightly less damaging effects than the other (throwing soft). The same consequence (punishment by fine) arises from both of these actions and effects, with a slightly more severe consequence (higher fine) from the action that caused the more damaging effects. **A** is incorrect since, even though there are two possible actions (pedalling hard or pedalling at a steady pace), and one with slightly less damaging effects (being less tired if pedalling at a steady pace), there is no idea of a worse consequence for one of the possible courses of action. In fact, the same consequence is stated to arise as a result of both possible actions which means that this argument does not reflect the reasoning of the argument in the question. **B** is incorrect since, although there seems to be the idea of two possible actions (working hard or not working hard towards promotion), the statement 'I think that I am good enough to be promoted' is not really congruous with the reasoning in the question since it is an opinion rather than a statement of the possible effects. There are two consequences stated (being promoted or not), but the fact that an intermediate stage concerning the immediate effects is not evident means that the reasoning here does not accurately parallel the reasoning in the question. **D** is incorrect since there is only the idea of two possible actions and two possible consequences (albeit with a more severe consequence from one action), however there is no idea of an intermediate effect as with the argument in the question. **D** is therefore missing a stage in the reasoning. **E** is incorrect since, although there are two possible actions presented (10 or 20 ploughs deployed), there seems to be only one effect (the snow being cleared) and no idea of more or less damaging effects depending on the action chosen. There is also only one consequence as a result of this effect (people getting back to their usual routines), as opposed to differing consequences based on the initial chosen action and its effect and therefore this argument differs from the argument in the question in its reasoning. **C** is correct since there are two possible actions (leaving for work at 8:00 am or 8:30 am), with slightly less damaging effects as a result of one action over the other (less traffic at 8:00 am) and with consequences from both of these actions (being punished for arriving late at work), albeit with a more severe consequence (being sacked) from the action with the more damaging effects (leaving at 8:30 am).

49 In this question you should look for the individual features of each of the three shapes in the question in order to find out which of the five larger shapes cannot be a combination of them. For example, the rectangle with one sloping side should have just one sloping side and the trapezium should have two parallel sloping sides. Based on this information, shape **B** is incongruous since the trapezium within it only has one sloping side and so **B** is the correct answer. Another way of approaching a question like this is to draw lines onto the larger shape in order to split it up into smaller shapes and seeing if these match up to the three shapes in the question. For example, you could draw lines onto shape **E** like so:

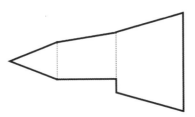

From these dotted lines, the three shapes in the question are clearly visible. Drawing similar lines onto shape **B** should reveal that it is not made up of all three of the shapes in the question and is therefore the correct answer:

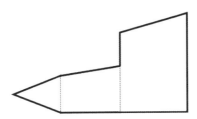

50 This is a relatively straight-forward question and requires you to perform some simple arithmetic in order to find the total capacity of each combination of shelves. Remember that the question is slightly easier in that the shoes need to fit exactly and so one of the combinations will amount to exactly 242. After your calculations, you should find that five large shelves and four small shelves will allow all 242 shoes to fit exactly ((5 x 34) + (4 x 18)) and so **D** is the correct answer.

Oxford TSA section 2:
Model answer and essay plans

Model answer

Should the minimum legal driving age be raised?

In this essay, it will be argued that the minimum legal driving age (in the UK) should be raised from its current age of 17. Various reasons will be offered in support of this conclusion. Firstly, from a statistical point of view, a significant proportion of those involved in car accidents are young people. Secondly, there does not seem to be a pressing need for people to drive at this age and, thirdly, that there will be some environmental benefits from having less drivers on the road. For the sake of clarity, the minimum legal driving age is the youngest age at which someone in the UK is eligible to hold a full driving license and this essay will argue that it is currently too low, although what the new minimum age should be is outside the scope of this essay.

Statistics for those involved in road accidents reveal that a significant proportion of these are young men. Crucially, this proportion is far higher than the proportion of young men in terms of the total population. There are various explanations for this, the most common being that teenagers and young men, still not fully mature, enjoy the ability to show-off their cars and driving skills. This often leads to reckless and dangerous driving and therefore this statistic is not a surprise. Another reason is that teenagers and young men are at a stage in life where drinking alcohol is often a common pastime. Naturally, drink-driving can ensue, which is another significant cause of road accidents. Whilst the argument here relates mainly to the male population and it is acknowledged that this may not necessarily lead to a conclusion of raising the minimum legal driving age in general, it is submitted that this move would be beneficial compared with either not increasing it at all or having two different minimum legal driving ages for men and women respectively, which may lead to a public backlash.

One significant issue which should be addressed is the reason for which young people need to drive. It is argued here that the minimum legal driving age, in light of the alarming statistic above, should be raised since there is very little reason that teenagers and young people have for driving. What reasons are there in general to have a car? Work is probably the best reason that pertains to a 'need' rather than simply convenience and is most people's reason for driving a car. Since it is unlikely that people will work, let alone in a job that requires a car, before the age of 20, then there is no reason for young people to have a car and so there is no major loss, other than that of convenience, in raising the minimum legal driving age. One possible counter-argument could be that public transport is not an adequate enough substitute to make up for this loss in convenience and this essay also acknowledges that there may be a net loss in revenue for the state with less people owning cars. However, it is submitted that the number of lives saved as a result far outweighs this cost.

Finally, despite revenue decreasing for the state due to less people driving, one major benefit, in addition to many more lives being saved, is to the environment. Such a pressing issue in today's society stands to benefit greatly from fewer carbon emissions. When policies such as higher fuel and road tax, which aim to cut down on the number of drivers, only serve to irritate people and reduce their disposable income, surely a policy that does not do this, has a greater effect in terms of reducing carbon emissions and, significantly, that saves people's lives, is a much wiser policy?

In conclusion, it has been shown that young males make up a significant proportion of those involved in road accidents and that young people in general do not have a pressing need to drive a car and so not allowing these people to drive so young will reduce this death toll. In addition, added benefits to the environment from such a policy, more so than policies which have similar aims currently, all point to a conclusion, which this essay proposes, that the minimum legal driving age should be increased.

Essay plans

Are environmental issues better dealt with by the private or public sector?

Definitions

- 'Environmental issues' are probably quite straightforward and do not require further explanation although you could cite climate change as an example. Equally, the 'private sector' and 'public sector' are known terms but, if you wish, you could clarify that the distinction is between private corporations or individuals on the one hand and the government or state bodies on the other.

Possible answers + arguments

Environmental issues are better dealt with by the private sector:

- Private companies and individuals are driven by a profit motive. Environmental issues now affect private firms' profits since their clients and customers judge them on their attitude to the environment. Corporate Social Responsibility has become a huge priority for private firms recently and this includes dealing with environmental issues. Therefore, there is an incentive for private firms to become more environmentally friendly and so these issues can be resolved purely by the private sector.

- Leaving environmental issues to be resolved by governments does not result in a uniform, global strategy and, instead, some states will take greater steps than others. Allowing multi-national firms, of which there are many, to deal with environmental issues instead, would allow environmental issues to be combatted on a truly global level since these firms would have a more uniform and effective policy around the world (since clients and customers would not only judge them on their environmental policy in one country) and we would avoid the problem of apathetic or defiant states not taking any steps towards helping the environment.

- Governments and states in general suffer from too many internal conflicts to be able to deal with environmental issues effectively. The biggest priority is that of re-election, which may not necessarily be congruous with making the biggest inroads into solving environmental issues. In addition, governments are subject to pressures from various lobby groups which may not always result in the most environmentally-friendly policy decisions. Finally, as compared to private firms, governments tend to be more inefficient at dealing with problems in general.

Environmental issues are better dealt with by the public sector:

- There is not yet enough incentive in the private sector for firms and individuals to do much about environmental issues. Whilst Corporate Social Responsibility is an important factor for clients and customers when choosing a firm, it is not as important as other factors such as price and quality of service. So, there is not yet enough of an incentive for firms to combat environmental issues and so some market intervention is needed. In fact, this is precisely the reason for which the government should intervene – when the free market is not able to allocate resources in the most effective way (this is based on the assumption that a government is better able to judge a more effective allocation).

- There can be more co-operation on a global level between public sectors since every country has some governmental institution that can take responsibility for environmental issues. Not every firm is multi-national and so there may not be a uniform, global approach if these issues were left to the private sector. Instead, governments can meet to discuss global strategies that every country can agree upon. International bodies such as the UN or the OECD can help in this respect, as can frequent meetings such as the Copenhagen Summit (although the counter-argument would be that this did not actually achieve much).

- Governments and state bodies generally have better information than private firms and individuals since specialist departments can be set up for the specific task of resolving environmental issues. Private firms generally don't have specialists to advise them on the most effective and efficient environmental strategies and, although they may outsource this to other private firms that do have some specialist knowledge, the incentive for these firms is still profit-driven whereas for state bodies, it is about the most effective strategy.

Environmental issues are better dealt with by both the private sector and public sector:

- It could be argued that a combination of the two is probably the best strategy. This could mean one of two things. Firstly, it could mean that the public and private sectors deal with environmental issues independently, so that the public sector will have its own policies and leave the free market to act of its own accord (in the ways outlined in the first possible answer). Secondly, however, it could also mean that the private and public sector combine their efforts so as to harness more efficient ways of resolving environmental problems. For example, the public sector could recognise that private firms can help in some ways but that, as it stands, the incentives are not yet strong enough. As a result, the public sector could offer further incentives, for example, tax breaks in order that private firms contribute to the overall effort to resolve environmental issues.

'There are no universal characteristics of a democracy.' Do you agree?

<u>Definitions</u>

- Even though it seems as if 'democracy' must be defined in the introduction, the whole essay is, in fact, a discussion of the meaning

295

of a democracy. Therefore, there is little need to try and explain the complex term in the introduction and, instead, it would be well worth acknowledging the fact that the whole essay will deal with the concept. 'Universal' means characteristics that are present in every type of state we call a 'democracy'. Or, perhaps, in a more normative sense, the characteristics a state must have in order to be a democracy.

Possible answers + arguments

No, there are no universal characteristics of a democracy:

- This argument would essentially be saying that democracies can exist in a variety of situations, that there is no one factor that unites democracies together and, importantly, that a democracy doesn't need to have a certain feature in order to be a democracy i.e. that there is no necessary condition for a democracy, otherwise that would be the universal characteristic of a democracy.

- Following on from this, it could be argued that the concept of a democracy varies so much that there is no universal characteristic or objective notion. In other words, what is considered to be a democracy changes around the world and from time to time and it is susceptible to so much change that there may not be any similar characteristics between two democracies. For example, one could argue that a dictatorship in the Middle-East is an example of a democracy but which does not share any similar characteristics as the political regime in the UK today, for example.

- In a more normative sense, it could be argued that a democracy does not need to have a universal characteristic which acts as a pre-condition for a democracy. However, this is difficult argument to run since if you accept that a political regime, such as that of the UK today, is a democracy and you compare a hypothetical regime that does not have any similar features, for example, a tyrannical dictatorship with no concept of rights, could this reasonably be labelled a 'democracy'?

Yes, there are universal characteristics of a democracy and these are x, y and z:

- This is a much easier position to take for this question, although you will be expected to discuss which characteristics are universal across democracies.

- It could be argued that there is only one universal characteristic of democracy and that is an acceptance by the people of the form of government. Indeed, the word 'democracy' comes from 'demos', the

Greek word for 'people'. Essentially, that irrespective of the form of government, whether it be a tyrannical dictatorship or a communist regime, as long as the people have assented to it, then it is a democracy. Rousseau's notion of a Social Contract could be alluded to since he argues that a government should only exist by virtue of the population allowing it to exist. One important feature also needs to be present in this definition of a democracy which is the ability of the people to withdraw their assent in order that, should there be a tyrannical dictatorship in place, this could be removed should the people so wish.

- It could be argued that that there are more characteristics than simply assent by the people that must be present before a regime can be labelled a 'democracy'. This argument may contend that a regime cannot accurately be called a 'democracy' if it does not afford the population basic rights, even if the population has assented to this. The argument may be that a 'democracy' must include a basic level of rights in order to be labelled as such, for example, fundamental human rights and free elections, and other such similar rights that must be present.

Can a vacuum be said to 'exist'?

Definitions

- Since the whole essay rests on the definition of 'exist', it may be futile to attempt to define this in the introduction. It is probably worth clarifying that a 'vacuum' is an amount of space that contains no particles or, in other words, contains no matter.

Possible answers + arguments

Yes, a vacuum can be said to 'exist':

- This argument depends, crucially, on your definition of exist. The first premise could be that for something to 'exist', it does not depend on it containing particles or matter.

- This argument could then work by contending that something that 'exists' is defined by the boundaries around it and that these boundaries consist of things that do contain particles. So, we know that a vacuum is present because of the fact that the boundaries of a vacuum are made up of matter. For example, a vacuum contained in a laboratory may be inside a piece of apparatus which is made from materials which contain matter and definitely can be said to 'exist'. The word 'exist' merely refers to the fact that it can be defined as being present and the circumstances in which it is present, in this case, the amount of space that a vacuum takes up can be determined. There could be a slight problem in saying that the boundaries of the vacuum that exists in space i.e. in which galaxies are contained, can be determined, since it could be argued that the universe is infinite.

- 'Exist' could also mean that the thing is capable of affecting someone or something. This relies on the premise that you or something cannot be affected by nothing (in the sense that if there was nothing then you wouldn't be affected) and so, if you or the thing is affected, then there must be something, and this something can be said to 'exist' by virtue of the fact that it does have some effect. For example, sound cannot travel through a vacuum and therefore sound is affected by the vacuum. Since it is affected, there is something there that affects sound and so this something can be said to 'exist'.

- As a society, we are happy to say that lots of non-physical things, in the sense that they are not made up of atoms, exist. For example, emotions such as anger and happiness or even more conceptual things such as 'validity'. If we are happy to consider that these things exist, then we should be equally as happy in saying that a vacuum exists.

No, a vacuum cannot be said to 'exist':

- The first argument here could rely on the assumption that existence depends on something physical existing. Hence, a vacuum, which does not contain any particles or matter, is not physical and is not made up of anything and therefore cannot be said to exist. Perhaps there is a counter-argument that emotions or feelings are not made up of anything physical, but that they can be said to 'exist'.

- It could also be argued that a vacuum is merely the absence of something that does exist, for example the material surrounding. This is similar to the idea above that, in order for things to exist, they must be made of something physical and so a vacuum is the absence of something physical and does not therefore exist.

Thinking Skills Assessment:
Practice test 3 answers

Cambridge TSA paper: answers
Oxford TSA section 1: answers

1.	B		26.	D
2.	E		27.	E
3.	E		28.	E
4.	A		29.	D
5.	D		30.	C
6.	D		31.	D
7.	C		32.	B
8.	D		33.	E
9.	E		34.	B
10.	C		35.	D
11.	B		36.	B
12.	A		37.	E
13.	C		38.	A
14.	B		39.	C
15.	A		40.	B
16.	B		41.	E
17.	A		42.	D
18.	E		43.	D
19.	D		44.	C
20.	E		45.	D
21.	B		46.	C
22.	B		47.	A
23.	D		48.	C
24.	A		49.	B
25.	A		50.	D

And finally...

If you have made it this far – well done and thanks. We hope you aren't too exhausted!

This is the start of a challenging and rewarding journey and one that deserves your best shot. It's worth it we think (and we've spoken to thousands of students who will support us on this)!

Thanks to Jane Welsh, Mark Rushworth, Rachel Spedding and the team at Oxbridge Applications. Thanks also to Jane Bennett-Rees, Adrian Charbin, Tom Greene, Woody Lewenstein, Simon Templeman, Daniel Thompson, Tim Watson, David Whiteside, Matthew Elliott, Lucinda Fraser, Paul Humpherson, Anjali Jingree, Carina King, Jonathan Newman, Myrice Palor and Sarah Slater.

Information regarding the Thinking Skills Assessment belongs to Cambridge Assessment and is protected by copyright. Permission has kindly been granted by Cambridge Assessment to include this information in the book.

A note from the author

This book is dedicated to the memory of my grandmother, Shantaben Hindocha, and also to my parents.